Practical Data Science with SAP
Machine Learning Techniques for Enterprise Data

Greg Foss and Paul Modderman

Beijing · Boston · Farnham · Sebastopol · Tokyo

Practical Data Science with SAP

by Greg Foss and Paul Modderman

Published by O'Reilly Media, Inc., 1005 Gravenstein Highway North, Sebastopol, CA 95472.

O'Reilly books may be purchased for educational, business, or sales promotional use. Online editions are also available for most titles (*http://oreilly.com*). For more information, contact our corporate/institutional sales department: 800-998-9938 or *corporate@oreilly.com*.

Editors: Jonathan Hassell and Nicole Tache	**Indexer:** WordCo Indexing Services, Inc.
Production Editor: Nan Barber	**Interior Designer:** David Futato
Copyeditor: Jasmine Kwityn	**Cover Designer:** Karen Montgomery
Proofreader: Charles Roumeliotis	**Illustrator:** Rebecca Demarest

September 2019: First Edition

Revision History for the First Edition

2019-09-17: First Release

See *http://oreilly.com/catalog/errata.csp?isbn=9781492046448* for release details.

978-1-492-04644-8

[LSI]

Table of Contents

Preface

The future of data science and artificial intelligence has never looked brighter. AI now beats humans at games ranging from twitchy, reflexive Pong to deep, contemplative Go. Deep learning models recognize objects nearly as well as humans. Some even say self-driving cars perform better than their distracted human counterparts. The past decade's massive gains in data volume, storage capacity, and computing power have enabled rapid advances in data science.

And of course technology has spread into every facet of your business (from finance and sales to production and logistics). However, is each part of your business turbo-charged by data science and AI? Likely not. As wonderful as they might be, if you are not designing a self-driving car or predicting customer behavior, you are probably not using these technologies.

Many organizations may have access to business data from an enterprise resource planning (ERP) system such as SAP, and yours is likely no different. Data coming from a business system such as SAP is largely perfect as often validations and checks are in place before it is allowed to save to the database (and, one of the most essential and least rewarding tasks of a data scientist is cleaning the data). This means ERP data in SAP is ripe for the picking, and data science is here to do the harvesting!

Let's take a hypothetical scenario. The SAP Team at Big Bonanza Warehouse is in a constant state of process improvement. They know how to configure their SAP system to do the tasks their users want, and they play that system like a fiddle, dutifully taking requests and delivering solutions. However, there is a bit of a problem with reporting and analytics; they have a data warehouse and a business intelligence system, but developing reports is a multimonth process. The team often resorts to using standard ALV (ABAP List Viewer) reports, which are quite limited in power because they require a developer to code; in addition, it is very hard to harness the wealth of public data that could be used in conjunction with SAP. Just like at countless other enterprises, SAP data at Big Bonanza Warehouse is an island, siloed within its own system. Teams that don't work with SAP have no idea what's in there, and the teams that do work with it spend so much time maintaining the systems that they don't get the chance to look outside them.

SAP data shouldn't be an island, though. The team knows their data, how to find it, and what they want to do with it. However, when it comes to analyzing that data, everyone's hands are tied by that multimonth report development process.

Sound familiar? It's the story at nearly every SAP shop with whom we've ever worked. And that's a lot in our combined 30+ years of experience.

We want to give that SAP team (and yours!) some modern insight—tools and techniques they can use without defining data cubes, data warehouse objects, or learning complex frontend reports. In this book, we'll present simple scenarios such as dumping data straight out of SAP into a flat file and into a reporting tool. This is useful for ad-hoc reporting and investigations. We'll also consider more complex scenarios, including using extractor tools and neural network models in the cloud to analyze data in ways not possible within SAP or contemporary data warehouses.

How to Read This Book

You'll need to approach this book from a conceptual point of view. We present alternative techniques for analyzing business data. We ask—nay, we beg—the reader to think about business data (in particular SAP data) in new and interesting ways. This book is designed to awaken ideas around how to bridge the gap between your particular business data and the advances in data science. You need not be an expert in the complex algorithms that calculate gradient descent in a neural network, nor do you need to be an expert in your business data. But you *do* need to have a desire to straddle these two camps and have fun in the process.[1]

From the data scientist's perspective, the data science principles in this book are an introduction. If you can spot a sigmoid, tanh, or relu activation function at fifty paces, you can skip those parts. But we're betting that if your guru level is that high in data science, you're a novice at the SAP stuff. Focus in on the SAP stories, showing you how to pull things out and demonstrating working with the real business data in the system.

From the SAP professional's perspective, you'll break out of traditional reporting and analytics models. You'll learn to think of business applications and reporting in machine and deep learning terms. This may sound mystical, but by the end of the book you will have the tools necessary to take this step. Along the way you'll automatically detect anomalies in sales data, predict the future from past data, process text as

---

1 If you're not the kind of person who has fun with data, how did you find this book?

natural language, segment customers into smart groups, visualize all these things brilliantly, and teach bots to use business data.

In our world of AI and data science, asking the same old questions of your data is stale, naive, and (quite frankly) boring. We want you to ask questions of your data that you didn't even know you could ask. Maybe the price of tea in China really *does* have an outsize effect on your sales.

From the developer's perspective, you'll be inspired to learn wonderful programming languages like Python and R. We don't teach you these languages, but we challenge you to dip your toe into these warm and effervescent waters. If you are already an experienced R or Python developer, you're in good shape for the code sections. For the novice, we will point you to resources to get you started. Don't feel left out if you are inclined to use another language such as Java. The "meta" goal of this book is to get you to think of how to think of business data differently and if that means you want to use Java, by all means do so.

Operationalizing data science is a whole book in itself. We'll frequently touch on how to operationalize ideas we present, but it is beyond the scope of this book to dive deep on creating robust pipelines.

 Data scientists may be able to skip over Chapter 2. SAP professionals, you might be able to skip Chapter 3. The stories we tell later in the book merge these two disciplines, so we want readers who come from one or the other side to get a fair understanding of how we'll be poking around to work our magic.

Conventions Used in This Book

The following typographical conventions are used in this book:

Italic
: Indicates new terms, URLs, email addresses, filenames, and file extensions.

`Constant width`
: Used for program listings, as well as within paragraphs to refer to program elements such as variable or function names, databases, data types, environment variables, statements, and keywords.

`Constant width bold`
: Shows commands or other text that should be typed literally by the user.

`Constant width italic`
: Shows text that should be replaced with user-supplied values or by values determined by context.

This element signifies a tip or suggestion.

 This element signifies a general note.

 This element indicates a warning or caution.

Using Code Examples

This book is here to help you get your job done. In general, if example code is offered with this book, you may use it in your programs and documentation. You do not need to contact us for permission unless you're reproducing a significant portion of the code. For example, writing a program that uses several chunks of code from this book does not require permission. Selling or distributing a CD-ROM of examples from O'Reilly books does require permission. Answering a question by citing this book and quoting example code does not require permission. Incorporating a significant amount of example code from this book into your product's documentation does require permission.

We appreciate, but do not require, attribution. An attribution usually includes the title, author, publisher, and ISBN. For example: "*Practical Data Science with SAP* by Greg Foss and Paul Modderman (O'Reilly). Copyright 2019 Greg Foss and Paul Modderman, 978-1-492-04644-8."

If you feel your use of code examples falls outside fair use or the permission given above, feel free to contact us at *permissions@oreilly.com*.

O'Reilly Online Learning

 For almost 40 years, *O'Reilly Media* has provided technology and business training, knowledge, and insight to help companies succeed.

Our unique network of experts and innovators share their knowledge and expertise through books, articles, conferences, and our online learning platform. O'Reilly's online learning platform gives you on-demand access to live training courses, in-depth learning paths, interactive coding environments, and a vast collection of text and video from O'Reilly and 200+ other publishers. For more information, please visit *http://oreilly.com*.

How to Contact Us

Please address comments and questions concerning this book to the publisher:

O'Reilly Media, Inc.
1005 Gravenstein Highway North
Sebastopol, CA 95472
800-998-9938 (in the United States or Canada)
707-829-0515 (international or local)
707-829-0104 (fax)

We have a web page for this book, where we list errata, examples, and any additional information. You can access this page at *https://oreil.ly/practical-data-sci-sap*.

To comment or ask technical questions about this book, send email to *bookquestions@oreilly.com*.

For more information about our books, courses, conferences, and news, see our website at *http://www.oreilly.com*.

Find us on Facebook: *http://facebook.com/oreilly*

Follow us on Twitter: *http://twitter.com/oreillymedia*

Watch us on YouTube: *http://www.youtube.com/oreillymedia*

Acknowledgments

We would like to thank our technical reviewers Hau Ngo, Jesse Stiff, Franco Rizzo, Brad Barker, and Christoph Wertz for their valuable feedback. Each chapter was made better from their suggestions.

To Nicole, our fearless editor: you helped us stay calm and grounded in the process. Without your editorial guidance, we would have been lost in data scientific meanderings and code ramblings. Thank you for making each thing you touched more readable.

Greg would like to thank his wife Alycia for her patience, support, and insight and his brother Cory for help with the graphics. Of course, a leviathan thanks to Paul Modderman for his vision, ingenuity, and courage to embark on this journey.

Paul would like to thank his partner Christa Modderman for her wisdom and strength, his grandmother Lois Stratmann for the example set by her remarkable life in creative work, and his parents Mark and Linda for...everything. He wishes to acknowledge Tony Vanderpoel, Dean Stoffel, and Gavin Quinn for respectively encouraging, entrusting, and inspiring him to better himself professionally. Largest thanks goes to Greg Foss: a remarkable author who never backed down from a commitment to quality. Eleanor Modderman is and always will be his favorite.

Special thanks to Wade Krzmarzick for help with CRM scenarios.

## CHAPTER 1

Introduction

Telling Better Stories with Data

Not enough gets said about abandoning crap.
—Ira Glass

We've all seen them. The intimidating PowerPoint presentations with the army of bullet points marching down the screen. Often the lecturer will even apologize for the busy slide and then continue to present, reading every word on the slide exactly as printed. You start to wonder if you left the oven on last night. We all like stories. A well-constructed narrative in the form of a movie, book, television show, or podcast wraps around us like a blanket and draws our attention. The bullet-ridden PowerPoint…not so much. With the deluge of data that has come with the advent of the internet and IoT, we are tempted to splash some findings in a presentation, wipe our hands, and say "that is that." However, as data professionals we can't just rain data findings down on our audience. The prevailing advice is that you must tell a story with data—make sure it's a compelling story that people want to hear. Don't deny yourself the joy that storytelling can bring.

To tell a compelling story, you must identify it. What is being asked of my data? What insights are my users looking for? A company that specializes in providing services and equipment might ask, "What equipment needs servicing the most? The least? Is there a correlation between equipment type and parts replacement?" At that same company someone in the finance department might ask, "How can we more accurately predict cash-on-hand?" In sales the question might be, "What kind of customer churn do I have?"

After you've identified your story, you'll need to find your audience. There are many ways to break them down, but generally your audience includes executives, business professionals, and technical professionals. While they might manage or direct many business processes, executives often know little about the daily functioning of such processes. The detail is irrelevant (or possibly confusing) to them—they want to know the story in big bold letters. Business professionals are the daily administrators of a business process, such as super users and business analysts. They know the process in detail and can understand raw tabular data. Technical professionals are the smallest segment of your audience; they usually comprise colleagues in data analytics and data science teams. This group requires less business and process background and more technical details such as the root-mean-squared error of the regression or the architecture of the neural network.

Once you've got your story and audience set, you'll need to move forward with the most difficult and tenuous part of the journey: finding the data. Without the data to support your story, your journey will quickly come to an end. Let's say you wanted to tell the story of how sunspots correlate to sales of hats and mittens in the northern hemisphere. Surprisingly, sunspot data is easy to obtain. You got that. However, you only have details on sales of hats, not mittens. You can't find that data. A cautious step is needed here. Do you alter your story to fit the data or do you cut bait and find another story? Reversing the process can be done but it's a slippery slope. As a general rule, do not change your hypothesis to match your data.

Before you fully trust that data, you'll need to vet it and start asking a lot of questions:

Is the source reputable? Did you scrape the data from a table on a website? What sources did that website use for the data, and how was it obtained? Sources such as Data.gov, ProPublica, the US Census Bureau, and GapMinder are trustworthy, but others might need a dash of caution.

Do you have too much data? Are there easily recognizable, worthless features? Look for features that are obviously precisely correlated. In the sunspot data mentioned earlier, perhaps you have a UTC timestamp feature and two other features for date and time. Either the date and time should be thrown out or the timestamp. You can quickly look at correlations using techniques we will discuss later to help you identify when two features are too closely correlated for both of them to be useful.

Is the data complete? Use some preliminary data tools to make sure your data is not missing too much information. We'll discuss this process in more detail later.

With the story in place, the audience identified, and the data vetted, what's next? You're now ready for the art and fun of the story—identifying what tools to use to either support or reject your null hypothesis. To say you're using "data science" as a tool is a slippery slope. You have advanced reporting, machine learning, and deep learning in your arsenal. Often, just the organization of the data into an easy-to-use dashboard tells the whole story. Nothing more needs to be done. As deflating as that has been in our careers, it has happened more times than any other scenario. We start the journey thinking that we have a case for a recursive neural network with either a gated recurrent unit or a long short-term memory module. And the excitement builds while we're gathering the data. Then we realize a support vector machine or a simple regression would do just as well. Later, with not a little disappointment, we realize that a dashboard for users to explore the data is more than enough to tell the story. Not everything requires deep or even machine learning. Although it can often be entertaining, shoehorning your story into these paradigms often does not tell the story any better.

Finally, take a little time to learn a bit about the art of storytelling. Even our dry data science stories deserve some love and attention. Ira Glass is a fantastic storyteller. He has a series of four short videos (*https://www.youtube.com/watch?v=f6ezU57J8YI*) on the art of storytelling. Watch them and sprinkle some of his sage advice into your story.

A Quick Look: Data Science for SAP Professionals

SAP professionals are busy every day supporting the business and users, constantly looking for process improvements. They gather requirements, configure or code in the SAP system, and, more often than not, live in the SAP GUI. They have intimate knowledge of the data within SAP as well as the business processes and can summon an army of transaction codes like incantations. When asked for a report with analytics, they really have two options: code the report in SAP or push the data to a data warehouse where someone else will generate the report. Both of these processes are typically long, resource-intensive endeavors that lead to frustration for the end user and the SAP professional. For one particular client, the biggest complaint from the SAP users was that by the time they actually got a requested report, it was no longer relevant.

Reading this book will help you—the SAP professional—build a bridge between the worlds of the business professional and the data scientist. Within these pages you will find ideas for getting out of the typical reporting and/or analytics methodology that has hitherto been so restrictive. As we discussed earlier, one of the first ways to do that is to simply *ask better questions*.

Here's a typical SAP scenario: Cindy works in Accounts Receivable. She needs a 30-60-90 day overdue report listing past due customers and putting them into buckets according to whether they are 30 days, 60 days, or 90 days past due. Sharon in Finance gets the request and knows that she can have a standard ALV (ABAP List Viewer) report created or can extract the data and push it to a business warehouse (BW) where they will generate a report using Microstrategy or whatever tools they have.

What if we shifted Sharon's perspective to that of a data scientist? Sharon gets the report request. She knows she can deliver just what was requested, but then she thinks, "What more can be done?" She opens up a notepad and jots down some ideas.

Are there repeat offenders in late payments?

Are there any interesting correlations in the data? We know the customer name, customer payment history, customer purchases, and dollar amount.

Can we predict when a person will be paying late? How late?

Can we use this data to help *rate* our customers? Lower rated customers may not get an order when inventory is low and a higher rated customer also makes the same request.

What types of visualizations would be helpful?

Sharon sketches out an interactive dashboard report that she thinks would be very useful for her users. Armed with these ideas and sketches, Sharon asks the department data scientist (or SAP developer) about the possibilities.

There is a distinctive difference in approaches here. The first is a typical SAP response, and limits the creative and intellectual capacity of the business analysts. The second leverages their creativity. Sharon won't just provide the requested information. When she sees the data in SAP and asks better questions, she'll be instrumental in substantial process improvements.

This is just one example. Think of the possibilities with all the requests a typical SAP team gets, and hence this book!

Another way to shift the thinking of the SAP team to be more dynamic and data centric is to *use better tools*. This is the responsibility of the SAP developer. Most SAP developers live in the world of its application programming language called ABAP (Advanced Business Application Programming), and when asked to provide reports or process improvements turn instantly to the SAP GUI or Eclipse. This is where they're expected to spend time and deliver value.

 ABAP was originally *Allgemeiner Berichts-Aufbereitungs-Prozessor*. It's a server-side language specially designed to extend the core functionality of SAP. You can create programs that display reports, run business transactions or ingest outside system data and integrate it into SAP. A great deal of SAP ERP transactions run solely on ABAP code.

ABAP developers often specialize in one or more of the business functions that SAP provides. Since ABAP programs often directly enhance standard SAP features, ABAP developers become very familiar with how enterprises design their processes. It's very common for people familiar with ABAP to perform both technical programming roles and business analyst roles.

SAP developers, we implore you: view SAP as a data source. The presentation layer and logic layer of reports should be abstracted away from the database layer (see Figure 1-1). It is worth noting that SAP data is highly structured with strict business rules. One of the most obvious advantages to this approach is the logic layer has access to other sources of data, such as public data. Within an SAP system, if a request was made to view the correlations between sales of galoshes and weather patterns, the weather data from the NOAA would have to be brought into either BI or SAP itself. However, by using a tiered model the data can be accessed by the logic tier and presented in the presentation layer. Often the data may be an API, which allows for access without storage. This model also allows the logic tier to tie into tools like Azure Machine Learning Studio to perform machine or deep learning on the SAP data.

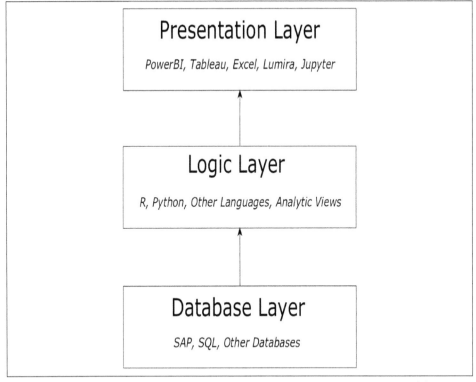

Figure 1-1. A simple, layered approach to databases, logic, and presentation of data science findings

SAP lacks the thousands of libraries in Python or the thousands of packages in R.[1] It also lacks the ability to easily create dynamic/interactive dashboards and visualizations. Don't get us wrong: SAP does have tools to do advanced analytics, dashboards, and visualizations. It's just that they cost a lot of money, effort, and time. Some places have lead times measured in months or quarters before reports can be created, and sometimes the window for a valid business question is measured in hours. With the tools in this book, we intend to close that gap. If you're an SAP developer, we would strongly advise you to learn programming languages like Python and R so that you can use them to do your analytics on SAP data. Firstly, they are not limited to the SAP ecosystem and secondly, they are free.

Outside of SAP, there are numerous other tools to help SAP developers present their SAP data. You can use RMarkdown in R, Shiny in R, Jupyter Notebooks in Python, PowerBI, Tableau, Plotly...the list goes on. In this book we will provide presentation examples using PowerBI, RMarkdown, and Jupyter Notebooks.

A Quick Look: SAP Basics for Data Scientists

The lack of awareness around SAP is often surprising considering its size and ubiquity. Here's an amazing fact: 77% of the world's transaction revenue is involved—in one way or another—with an SAP system. If you spend money, you have more than likely interacted with SAP. And 92% of the Forbes Global 2000 largest companies are SAP customers.

But how in the world does SAP software touch all that? What does it do? While in recent years SAP has acquired a number of SaaS (Software as a Service) companies to broaden its portfolio and make shareholders richer, it began with its core focus on ERP: enterprise resource planning.

SAP started in Germany in 1972 under the sexy moniker Systemanalyse und Programmentwicklung. Running under DOS on IBM servers, the first functionality was a back-office financial accounting package. Modules soon followed for purchasing, inventory management, and invoice verification. You can see the theme emerging: doing the common stuff that businesses need to do.

That list of functionality may seem rather dull at first, especially to us cool hipster data scientists with Python modules and TensorWhatsits who know how to make a computer tell us that a picture has a dog (but not an airplane) in it. It's not magic like searching Google or using Siri on your iPhone. But SAP added a twist to those first few boring modules: integration. Inventory management directly affected purchasing, which directly affected financials, which directly affected...well, everything. That sin-

---

1 For a taste of how expansive the R package landscape is, see this blog post (*http://bit.ly/2kIobHy*) for perspective on package list growth and search strategies for finding the right ones.

gle SAP ERP system contained all of these modules. Now, instead of having to purchase and run separate financial/inventory/invoicing systems, companies saved loads of money. When one system gave them all the answers to business questions, customers started buying in droves. That was the value and the win of ERP. By the time Gartner coined the term ERP in the 1990s, SAP was doing over a billion Deutsche marks in yearly sales.

Acronyms for SAP Insiders

Since the 1970s, SAP has expanded into other areas of the back-office business. A modern SAP ERP implementation contains the option to run complex modules for many business functions. They have acronyms that SAP insiders know very well:

SD: Sales and Distribution
Manage sales, shipping, and billing activities.

QM: Quality Management
Manage quality inspections and notifications raised from there.

PM: Plant Maintenance
Planning maintenance of plant equipment, and tasks to perform during that maintenance.

FICO: Financial Accounting, Controlling
Vital organizational financial data, managing profit/cost centers and internal orders.

HCM: Human Capital Management
Everything you think of when you think "HR."

PP: Production Planning
Capacity planning, material planning, and activities related to actually making the things you make.

MM: Materials Management
Inventory, procurement, and master data for materials.

PS: Project System
Project and portfolio management, for both internally and externally financed projects.

When you consider all the other capabilities that SAP's satellite products bring, this list doesn't even scratch the surface. There's Customer Relationship Management, Transportation Management, Supplier Relationship Management, and acquired cloud offerings like Ariba (B2B network and marketplace) and Concur (travel and expense management).

No single book could possibly capture all of this functionality. In this book, we focus on data scenarios in a couple of the ERP modules and in SAP CRM.

 Since such a high percentage of large companies around the world use SAP for so many business-critical functions, is it any wonder that so much business can be conducted inside it?

Getting Data Out of SAP

Like most large business applications, SAP ERP uses a relational database to house transactional and master data. It's designed such that customers can choose from many relational database management systems (RDBMS) to function as the SAP application database. Microsoft SQL Server, IBM DB2, Oracle, and SAP's MaxDB are all supported. In the last few years, SAP has rapidly introduced another proprietary database technology, HANA, as an RDBMS solution with in-memory technology. While future versions of SAP's core ERP product will one day require HANA, most SAP installations today still use one of the other technologies as their database.

 In this book, we will introduce several ways of getting data out of your SAP system, none of which will require you to know exactly which DB your SAP system runs on. But if you're a true nerd, you'll find out anyway.

The relational databases that power the SAP instances at your company are huge and full of transactional and master data. They fully describe the shape of the vital business information stored and processed by SAP. The databases at the heart of your SAP systems are the source of truth for the discoveries you can make.

And unless it's your absolute last resort, you should never directly connect to them.

All right, we're being a little facetious here. You will find valid times to directly query data from the SAP databases with SQL statements. But the sheer size and incredible complexity of the data model make it so that fully understanding the structure of a simple sales order can involve over 40 tables and 1000+ fields. Even SAP black belts have difficulty remembering all the various tables and fields they need to use, so imagine how inefficient it would be for a data scientist who is new to SAP to unpack all the various bits of requisite data.

BAPIs: Using the NetWeaver RFC Library

Data nerds who don't know SAP that well should start by examining the available Business Application Programming Interfaces (BAPIs) in the SAP system. BAPIs are remote-callable functions provided by SAP that expose the data in various business information documents. Instead of figuring out which of the 40+ sales order tables apply to your particular data question, you can look at the structure of various sales order BAPIs and determine if they fill that gap. The trouble of reverse engineering the data model is gone.

BAPIs also help by covering over system limitations from earlier versions. During the early period of SAP's core product development, the various modules restricted the number of characters that could denote a table or field. With SAP's remarkable stability over the years, those table and field names have stuck around. Without living inside SAP, how could you possibly know that "LIKP" and "VBELN" have anything to do with delivery data? BAPIs are a later addition, so they have grown up with interfaces that better describe their shape and function.

OData

SAP NetWeaver Gateway represents one of SAP's many ways of breaking into the modern web era. It's an SAP module—in some cases running enough of its own stuff to be worth a separate system—that allows SAP developers to quickly and easily establish HTTP connections to SAP backend business data. We predict that you'll see examples of using SAP NetWeaver Gateway in Chapter 6.

The foundational layer of transport is known as OData. OData represents many tech companies coming together to put forward a standard way of communicating over the web via RESTful APIs. It provides a common format for data going over the web using either XML or JSON, ways for clients to indicate the basic create/read/update/delete operations for server data, and an XML-based method for servers to specify to clients exactly the fields, structure, and options for interacting with data that the servers provide via metadata.

Using OData through SAP NetWeaver Gateway requires programming in SAP's native backend language, ABAP. Some of our SAP-native readers may be well versed in this language and can produce Gateway OData APIs. Other readers will likely be unfamiliar, but should take solace: if your company runs SAP in any meaningful way, your company will have people who know ABAP. These people will either know how to create OData services, or will be able to quickly learn since it's not difficult.

Choose OData when you can't find a BAPI that meets your data needs. It's a great middle ground that provides SAP administrators with the flexibility to meter and monitor its usage. It also gives developers the ability to put together data in any way they choose. Another benefit of using OData is that it doesn't require a NetWeaver connector like the BAPI method: any device that can make HTTP requests safely inside the corporate network will be able to make OData requests.

Other ways to get data

If you can't find the right BAPI and you can't find the resources to make an OData service, there are always a few other routes you can take. We'll cover those more briefly, since they aren't things we typically recommend.[2]

Web services. SAP allows you to create web services based on its Internet Communication Manager (ICM) layer. These web services allow you to work even more flexibly than OData, but they still require ABAP knowledge. The space between OData with Gateway and a totally custom SAP web service is small—consider carefully whether your data question can't be answered with OData.

Direct database access. Everyone says you shouldn't, but we've all also encountered one or two times when it was the only thing that would work. If you need to go this route, a key task will be ensuring that the data you extract matches up with what SAP provides on the screen to end users. Many times there are hidden input/output conversions and layers of data modeling that don't become apparent when just browsing through a data model.

Seriously. Picking directly from an SAP database is like driving a Formula One car with brake problems. You'll get where you need to go really fast, but you'll probably smash into a wall or two on the way.

Screen dumps to Excel. Sometimes an end user will know exactly which screen has the right data for them. Many times this screen will have a mechanism for exporting data to Excel.

Which Way?

A simple set of rules for deciding how to get your SAP data from the system:

BAPI
I know what data I want, and SAP provides the exact right remote function to get it.

OData
I know what data I want, but SAP doesn't provide the exact right function for it— or I want to be able to extract this data with a simple web call.

Web services
I know what data I want, but OData doesn't quite let me shape the data exactly as I want.

---

2 However, this book couldn't be called "Practical" if we didn't acknowledge that the worst hacks and ill-advised duct-tape solutions make up at least 50% of any real-world environment.

Direct DB access
> I know what data I want, and I know exactly what the SAP application data model provides for this, but I don't have ABAP skills to build it myself.

Screen dumps to Excel
> Somebody else knows what data I want, and can only provide it by going to a screen to get it for me.

Roles and Responsibilities

Data science combines a range of skill sets. These often include statistics, programming, machine learning, analysis, architecture, and engineering. Many blogs and posts online discuss the differences between data science roles. There are innumerable job titles and delineations. One camp defines roles into data analysts, data engineers, data architects, data scientists, and data generalists. Other groups have their own delineations.

Readers should understand something very important. Unless you are at a very large company with a data science team, you will be lucky to have one person on your team with some of these skills. These job delineations exist in theory for all, but in practice for only a small percentage. Be prepared to wear many hats. If you apply some of these forays into data science at your company, be prepared to do the work yourself. Don't have a SQL database and want to extract and store some SAP data? We'll introduce this. Want to automate a workflow for extraction? Here you go. Everything from the SAP data to the presentation layer will be covered.

Our intention is clear: we want to create citizen data scientists who understand what it takes to make data science work at their organizations. You may not have any resources to help you, and you may get resistance when you ask for some of these things. Often, you must prove your theory before someone helps. We understand that the roles and responsibilities are not well defined. We hope to give you an overview of the landscape. If you're reading this book, you've already rolled up your sleeves and are ready to do everything from building SQL databases to presenting machine learning results in PowerBI.

Summary

A huge part of getting value is communicating it. We went over how to tell great stories with the data you find in SAP: identify your story, find the audience, discover the data, and apply rigorous tooling to that discovered data. Sometimes all it takes to communicate the story is one simple graph. Other times it may require detailed lists of results. But no matter what visual method conveys your findings, be prepared to tell a story with it.

SAP professionals looking to tell stories about their data should look at tools such as programming languages like Python and R, and visualization tools like Tableau and Power BI. Look at Chapter 2 to dive deeper.

Data scientists looking to discover what's in SAP should look at ways of getting that data out. BAPIs provide a function-based approach to retrieving data, OData sets up repeatable and predictable HTTP services, and you can always dump screen data to Excel or directly query the SAP database as a last resort. Look at Chapter 3 to find out more.

We want you to get the most out of the SAP data that's ripe for the picking in your enterprise, and the best way to get value out of raw data is by applying data science principles. This book will show you how to marry the world of SAP with the world of data science.

## CHAPTER 2

Data Science for SAP Professionals

 If you're a data scientist, you may not need much of the information in this chapter. We're trying to get SAP professionals up to speed on things that you probably already know.

As a SAP business analyst, Fred is always looking for process improvements. That's his job, and he is good at it. He's heard a lot of buzz about data science, but to him, it is just that...buzz. Data science is creating the self-driving car, beating world champions at Go, and translating languages. Fred works at a US manufacturer, and data science has no real relevance to him.

Or does it?

If Fred knew the basic concepts around data science, he would understand how it could be leveraged to provide business value. He recently worked with the product development team, which is looking to IT for help in streamlining their processes. They have lots of unorganized data. They present Fred with an idea, a dashboard to help them track their process. When Fred evaluates the project his first response is to put the data in a SQL database. Once there he can use a presentation tool like PowerBI to create a dashboard. It is a solution that everyone likes.

Fred doesn't know the basics of data science. There are features in this data that might help the company make better, data-driven decisions. If he knew the basic concepts of regression and clustering, he would see it. He would know that he could do more with this business data than the project team requested.

Therein lies the point of this chapter. We're not trying to create data scientists. We are trying to get business analysts to think a little like a data scientist; we're trying to create *citizen data scientists*. These are business analysts and professionals who understand enough about data science to ask questions about how it can be applied to their data (in particular, useful to their *SAP* data). To do that, we need to introduce the fundamentals of data science, including the different types of learning models: machine learning and neural networks.

What follows is a rabbit race through the subject that will leave you with, at the very least, enough information to think about business processes in a slightly different way...in a data science way. Ideally you can think about your projects and data and say to your data scientist or developer, "Maybe a classification algorithm like Naive Bayes might work on this." Imagine the jaws that will drop to that response!

This is a conceptual chapter that provides an overview of the main data science concepts, and as such we will not discuss tactical ideas such as exploratory data analysis (EDA) or data preparation. We've covered the topics we feel are most relevant, but one could easily argue that we left out things of importance, such as automated machine learning (autoML) and ensemble methods; however, we had to draw a line in the sand somewhere to keep this chapter manageable. Nonetheless, we will later take a look at tactical concepts such as EDA (discussed in Chapter 4), so stay tuned.

Machine Learning

The syntax in data science can be confusing and overlapping. Deep learning is a component of machine learning by definition, but we refer to deep learning as those models that use more complex neural networks. Deep learning requires more computing power, more time, and more data to be successful. Often, simpler machine learning models perform equally, and sometimes better. Don't overlook them in the face of shiny and fancy neural networks.

 Most data scientists spend the majority of their time finding, cleaning, and organizing huge amounts of data. Some estimates say that data scientists spend 80% of their time (*http://bit.ly/2NBXPTJ*) on this unrewarding task. We have good news for the data scientist looking at SAP data. SAP is an ERP system. The millions of rows of business data are already in a relational database. While this does not end the need to do some cleaning and reorganizing, it does reduce that effort. We will show how to find and extract this data, but often there is very little cleaning or organizing needed.

Machine learning falls roughly into four categories:

- Supervised
- Unsupervised
- Semi-supervised
- Reinforcement

 Deep learning includes these categories as well. It is considered a subset of machine learning. For the purposes of this book, here we refer to machine learning and not the subset of deep learning. We will present deep learning a little later. There is a lot of overlap and confusion in the terminology. If you follow news about machine learning, you'll see that no two people on Earth are using the same terminology in the same way—so don't feel bad about getting confused.

Supervised Machine Learning

Supervised machine learning is done on labeled data. It works well on classification, which is a method to classify or predict categorical labels for a set of data. In marketing, for instance, it may be determining the customer who will buy a product. Supervised machine learning also works well on prediction. Prediction is a method to determine a numerical value from a set of data. Using the same analogy as for classification, in marketing it may be used to try and determine how much a customer will spend. For example, the well-known Iris dataset includes information about the petal length, petal width, sepal length, and sepal width of 150 iris flowers, and identifies their species. Once we train a model against this data, it can accurately predict the species of a new iris flower, given its sepal and petal data. Let's take a closer look at some of the different types of supervised machine learning models.

Linear regression

Linear regression is an approach to modeling the relationship between a dependent variable and one or more explanatory variables. The relationship between a home's value and its square footage is a good example (Figure 2-1). If you have several home values and their respective square footage you could surmise the value of an unknown home if you know its size. Granted, there's more to a home's value than that, but you get the point.

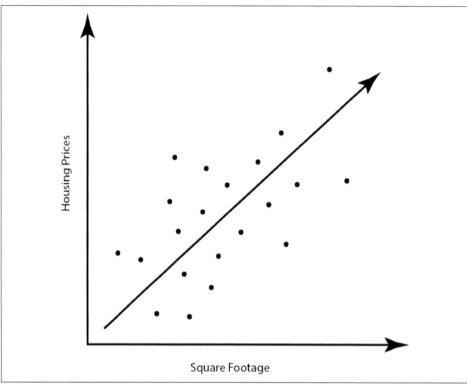

Figure 2-1. Linear regression of housing prices by square footage

Logistic regression

Logistic regression, like linear regression, uses the same basic formula. However, logistic regression is categorical while linear is continuous. Using the same home value example, linear regression would be used to determine the home value, whereas logistic regression could be used to determine if it would sell.

Decision trees

Decision trees are a type of model that simply asks questions and makes decisions. The nodes of the decision tree ask questions that lead to either other nodes, or to end nodes (leaves) which are classifications or predictions (Figure 2-2).

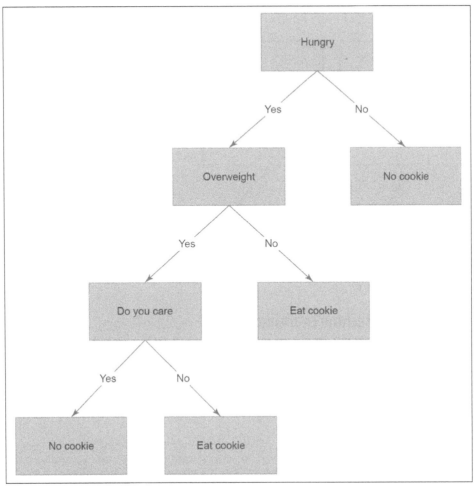

Figure 2-2. Decision tree for eating a cookie

Random forest

Random forests are groups of decision trees that help solve one of the biggest problem of decision trees: overfitting (Figure 2-3). Overfitting a model means that it is very good at solving problems it knows, but when introduced to new data it will fall short. Think of it as training yourself to be a world-class Formula One driver—but never learning to park.[1]

---

1 The authors recommend learning to park *before* Formula One racing, but we did not analyze this using any of the techniques in this book. So who knows? Maybe it *is* better to be an Formula One driver but not learn to park! More data is needed.

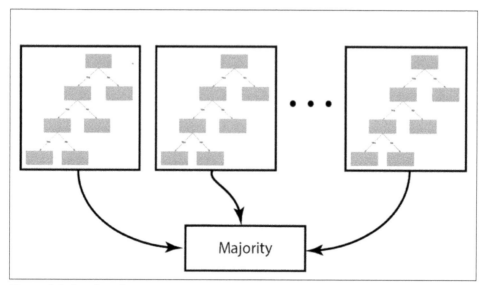

Figure 2-3. Random forest

Unsupervised Machine Learning

Unsupervised machine learning, as you may have guessed, does not have labeled data. That is, you have a pile of data, but you do not know the output label. For example, you have a set of voting records with age, sex, income, occupation, and other features. What you do not know is how they relate. Let's take a look at some of the different types of unsupervised machine learning.

k-means clustering

k-means clustering takes data and groups it into a given set of points (Figure 2-4). An example would be to segment or cluster a group of customers into groups representing their buying frequency. One way it does this by grouping them with the nearest mean value. It also works on words if you use a non-Euclidean[2] distance, such as Levenshtein. We will go more into this in Chapter 7.

---

2 Euclidean distance is simply the ordinary straight-line distance between two points, either on a plane or in three-dimensional space. Why say "straight-line" when you can say "Euclidean distance" and sound scholarly? Bonus points if you have a pipe or tweed jacket.

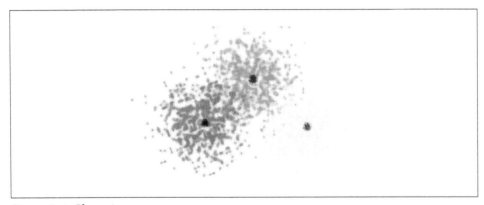

Figure 2-4. Clustering

Naive Bayes

Naive Bayes is not a single algorithm but a collection of classification algorithms within the *Bayes' theorem* family (Figure 2-5). The common concept is that every feature of the data is classified as independent of every other feature. For example, a car has a hood, a trunk, wheels, and seats. Naive Bayes sees all of these as independent contributors to the probability the object is a car. Naive Bayes is extremely fast and is often the first classifier tried for machine learning tasks.

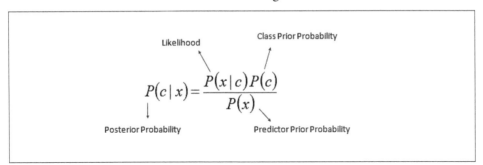

Figure 2-5. Bayes' theorem

Here are the terms of Bayes' theorem, in plain language:

$P(c \mid x)$
> The probability the hypothesis (c) is true given the data (x).

$P(x \mid c)$
> The probability of the data (x) if the hypothesis (c) is true.

$P(c)$
> The probability the hypothesis (c) is true regardless of the data.

$P(x)$

The probability of the data (x) regardless of the data.

This is a common explanation of Bayes; it's found everywhere. However, it's a bit tricky to understand so let's simplify.

There is a very common and intuitive explanation of Bayes using breast cancer as an example. Consider this scenario: a patient goes to the doctor for a checkup and the results of a mammogram come back abnormal. What are the odds the patient has cancer? You might intuitively think that cancer must be present because of the test results, but applying Bayes to the situation shows something different. Let's take a look.

Consider these statistics:[3]

- 1% of women age 40 who participate in routine screenings have breast cancer. 99% do not.
- 80% of mammograms will detect cancer when present and 20% miss it.
- 9.5% of mammograms return a false positive; they detect cancer when it is not there. Meaning 89.5% do not detect cancer and it is not there (true negative).
- The probability of the event is the event divided by all possibilities.
  $P(c|x) = .01 * .8 / (.99 * .095) + (.01 * .8) = .0776$

Intuitively you hear that the mammogram is 80% accurate, so a positive result would mean you have an 80% chance of having cancer. But the truth is...you only have a 7.8% chance even if you get a positive result.

Hierarchical clustering

Hierarchical clustering is a method of grouping results into a dendrogram, or tree (Figure 2-6). If it starts from many clusters and moves to one it is called *divisive*. If it starts from one cluster and moves to many clusters it is *agglomerative*. A divisive method partitions a given cluster by computing the greatest difference (or distance) between two of its features. An agglomerative method does the opposite. It computes the differences between all clusters and combines the two with the least common distances between their features. They both continue until they are either out of data or the dendrogram splits the predefined number of times. We will go into more detail in Chapter 7.

---

3 A much more detailed explanation of this scenario can be found at *http://yudkowsky.net/rational/bayes#content*.

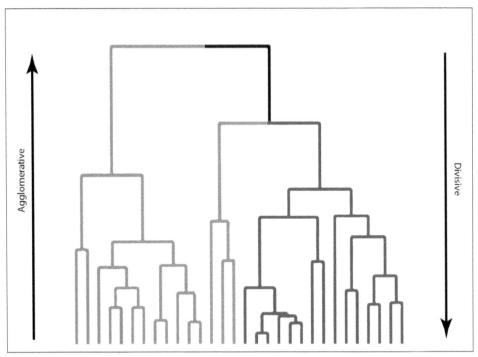

Figure 2-6. Agglomerative and divisive hierarchical clustering

Semi-Supervised Machine Learning

Semi-supervised machine learning is a combination of supervised and unsupervised learning. In this scenario you have a lot of data but not all of it is labeled. Consider the scenario for fraud detection. Credit card companies and banks have huge amounts of transaction data, some of which has been properly labeled as fraudulent. However, they do not know of all the fraudulent transactions. Ideally, they would properly label all of the fraudulent transactions manually. However, this process is not practical and would take far too much time and effort. There exists a small set of labeled data and a very large set of unlabeled data. In semi-supervised learning one common technique is called *pseudo-labeling*. In this process the labeled data is modeled using traditional supervised learning methods. Once the model is built and tuned, the unlabeled data is fed into the model and *labeled*. Finally, the labeled data and the newly pseudo-labeled data is used to train the model again (Figure 2-7).

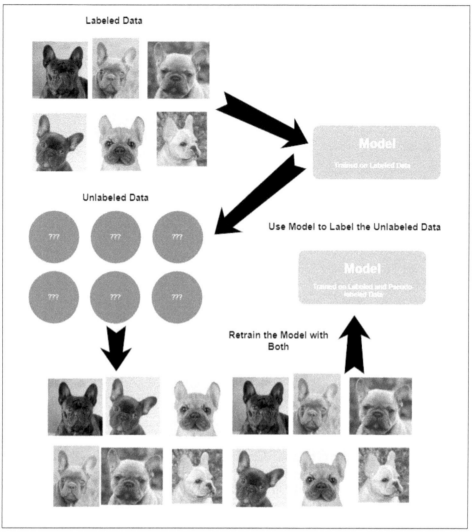

Figure 2-7. Pseudo-labeling for semi-supervised learning

Reinforcement Machine Learning

Reinforcement machine learning is when you train a model to make decisions based on trial and error. This model interacts with its environment by learning from past successes and failures. It then determines a course of action for the next attempt or iteration. It works on the premise of maximizing a reward. The most common example of this is training a machine to play a game. Let's take a closer look at some of the different types of reinforcement learning.

Hidden Markov models

Hidden Markov models (HMMs) are a series of observable *emissions*. These are the results of a given state that a model passed through to make those emissions. This is a bit confusing so let us clarify. In a HMM you cannot directly observe the state, but you can observe the results of those states. You work in an office without windows and you cannot see the weather outside. You can see what people are wearing when they show up to the office. Say 75% of people are carrying umbrellas...you can surmise that it's raining outside. HMMs are popular ways to identify sequences and time series. They do not look at the true state; rather, they look at the emissions from the true states. The simplest models assume that each observation is independent of the next. However, HMMs assume a relationship between the observations. As another example, a series of data is observed for weather. That data has features in it like barometric pressure, temperature, and day of the year. The corresponding *emission* data has the binary feature of "not cloudy" or "cloudy." Observing many days in succession, the model predicts the state of the weather not only on today's observable features, but on the previous days' features. HMMs attempt to identify the most likely underlying unknown sequence to explain the observed sequence.

The concept is a bit tricky so let's use another example. Say you're wanting to use a HMM to determine if there is going to be an increase or decrease in the number of purchase orders placed at your company for widgets. SAP has a history of purchase order data with timestamps. It also has other *states* that might influence when widgets are purchased. There are sales orders, time of year (seasonality), warehouse inventory levels, and production orders. Each of these could be used by the HMM. Think of it in this way: "past behavior predicts future behavior."

Q-learning

Q-learning is a value-based reinforcement learning algorithm. It is based on the *quality* of an action. Q-learning goes through steps where it learns to optimize its outcome (Figure 2-8). In a way, it builds a secret cheat sheet of how it should behave. In the example of game play, it takes an action, evaluates that action, updates its cheat sheet with whether it was good or not, and then tries again. It iterates on this incredibly fast.

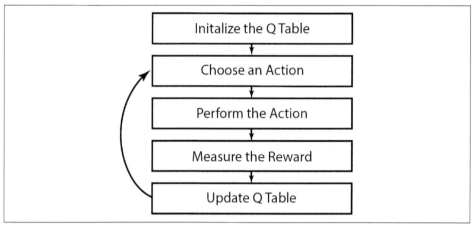

Figure 2-8. Q-learning steps

A common illustration is to imagine a game where you are a dog and you must find the pile of bones. Every step you take costs one bone. If you run into that pesky cat you lose 10 bones and die (Figure 2-9). The goal is to maximize the number of bones.

Figure 2-9. Q-learning dog optimizes for most bones

It may seem like a simple game to us, but a computer doesn't know how to start. So first it goes down and gets two bones. Yaaaah! Man, that was a good move. It records that and takes a step to the right. Damn that cat...game over. It updates the cheat sheet with that information. Next time it takes a right step first, then another right, and then it only has the option of down. Yes—a motherlode of bones!! Remember there is a −1 bone price per step. The result is −1 +2 −1 −1 +1 −1 −1 +10 = 8. It logs the results and tries again. This time it takes a right because it knows there is a +1 there. It takes another right and then a down to hit the motherlode. The result is −1 +1 −1 −1 +10 = 8. Both paths are equally as valuable, but if there is a bonus or limit on the number of steps option 2 wins.

You may be thinking, "Pretty cool, but how would this apply to anything but games?" Take the image of the bulldog finding the path to the motherlode. Now imagine it is a simple warehouse...expand it greatly (Figure 2-10). Reinforcement learning could reduce transit time for picking, packing, and stocking as well as optimizing space utilization. It is more complex, but fundamentally the same as the dog and bones game.

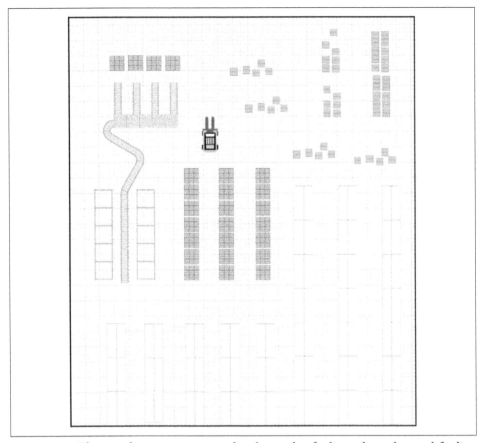

Figure 2-10. This warehouse is more complex than a dog finding a bone, but pathfinding through reinforcement learning works here, too

Neural Networks

Both of us authors have been programming for many years and have experienced some wonderful "wow" moments along the way. Greg learned to program using Basic on the Apple IIe. He had been programming for about a year before learning the PEEK, POKE, and CALL commands. The first time he used these evocations and ran his program, he sat back and thought, "Wow!"; he's been programming in one form or another ever since. Greg and Paul both had that feeling when they wrote their first few deep learning programs. "Wow!" is all we could say.

Let's talk about deep learning and what that term means.

Traditional programming follows a tale of straightforward, predefined logic. IF this THEN perform that action 10 times. It's so powerful that we can simulate beautiful scenery and create games that transport us to magic, imaginary realms. But it makes tasks such as language translation near impossible. Imagine the program it would take to translate English to Korean. That program would need to have conditions for words, phrases, negations, syntax, vernacular, punctuation, and on and on, ad infinitum. Imagine nesting all that in linear logic. Along comes machine learning. Now you input a set of English texts and their translated Korean equal. You train the model by showing it the input and the expected output. The more data you have, the more you can train your model. Finally, you input a set of English texts that do not have a Korean translation and kazam! It performs the translation as it has learned.

That is remarkable in itself, but it gets better. Google built a deep learning algorithm (*https://tcrn.ch/2Pcz2YJ*) in 2016 that translated from English to Korean, Korean to English, Japanese to English, and English to Japanese. Pretty incredible by itself—but that's not the amazing part. The network was able to translate from Japanese to Korean and Korean to Japanese *without first translating through English* (*https://tcrn.ch/2Lc0KAM*). Let that sink in. What is happening in the network to allow for such a thing to happen? The network learned a *metalanguage*—a type of linguistic mapping that transcended simple one-to-one language translation.

When translating from Japanese to Korean one would expect the model to go through the English first (the curved lines); see Figure 2-11. After all, the model was not trained to go from Japanese to Korean. However, the model did not do this. It went directly from Japanese to Korean (the dotted line). Amazing! Kind of spooky actually.

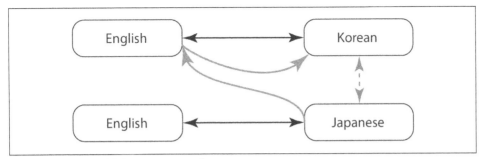

Figure 2-11. Google's language translator

Google's language translator is a neural network in action. Let's take a look at a few basic neural network architectures. This is a gentle introduction to neural networks and deep learning. We hope it piques your curiosity enough for you to want to take a deeper dive. At its foundation, a neural network is a series of interconnected processing modules that work together to take inputs and solve for a given output. They are inspired by the way neurons and synapses in the brain process information. They have been instrumental in solving problems ranging from image classification[4] to language translation. We will go into more depth on this in Chapter 9.

There are three basic layers to a neural network:

The input layer
    This is where the data is input into the network.

The hidden layer(s)
    This layer performs basic computation and then transfers weights to the next layer. The next layer can be another hidden layer or the output layer.

The output layer
    This is the end of the network and where the model outputs results.

Neural networks have six foundational concepts, as described in the following sections.

Feed-forward propagation

Data (weights and biases) flows forward through the network from the input layer through various hidden layers and finally to the output layer (Figure 2-12).

---

4 Image classification refers to the process of extracting information from an image and classifying it; for example, to identify when a picture is of a Chihuahua or a blueberry muffin (*http://bit.ly/2U6fpAt*).

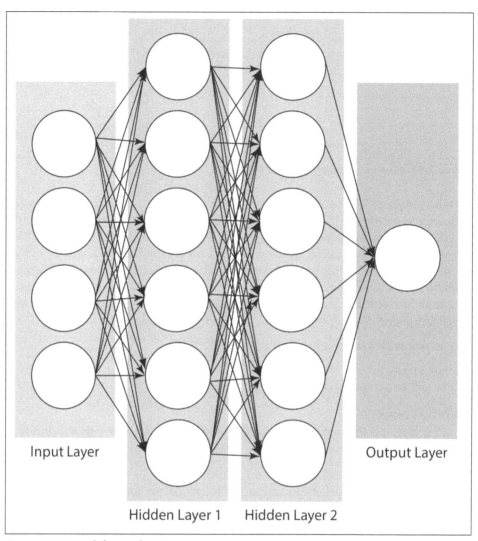

Figure 2-12. Feed-forward propagation

Backward propagation

After data is fed forward through the network, the error (desired value minus the obtained value) is fed backward through the network to adjust the weights and biases with the aim of reducing the error (Figure 2-13).

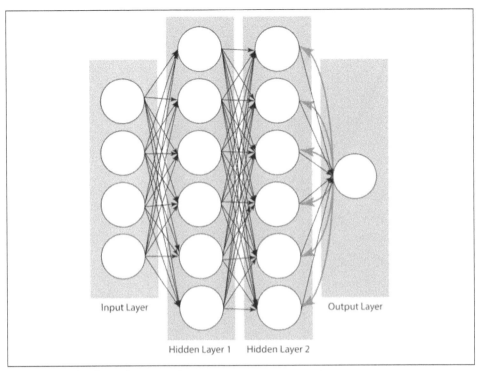

Figure 2-13. Backward propagation

Gradient descent

An optimization function that attempts to find the minimum value of a function. Another way of saying it is that gradient descent has the goal of minimizing the cost function as much as possible (Figure 2-14). When this is achieved, the network is optimized. A common analogy is a man walking down a mountain. Every step he takes he wants to head in a downward direction until he reaches the lowest possible point; it is here where the cost function is at a minimal. When this is achieved the model has the highest accuracy.

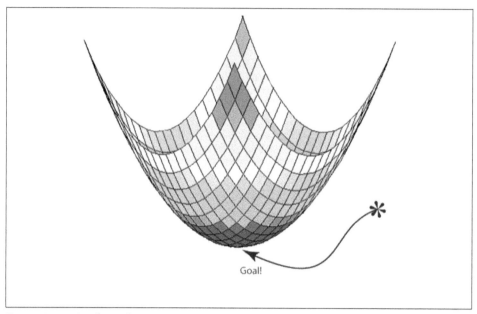

Figure 2-14. Gradient descent

Learning rate

The learning rate is the size of the steps we take to achieve the minimum of gradient descent (bottom of the mountain). If the learning rate is too large, it will pass the minimum and potentially spin out of control. If it is too small, the process takes far too long (Figure 2-15).

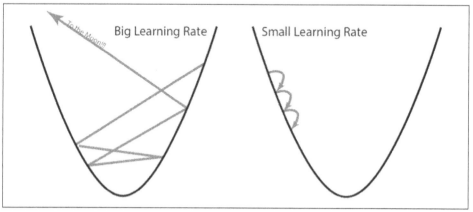

Figure 2-15. Learning rates

Neuron

A neuron is the foundation of a neural network. It takes an input, or inputs, applies a function to those inputs and renders an output. It is loosely based on the human neuron (Figure 2-16).

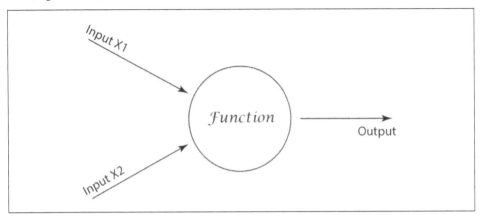

Figure 2-16. Neuron

Functions

A function is a mathematical equation within a neuron that takes the input values and decides whether it should activate (or fire). There are many activation functions, but these are the are most common in neural networks:

Sigmoid
    Takes the input value and puts it in a range from 0 to 1 (Figure 2-17).

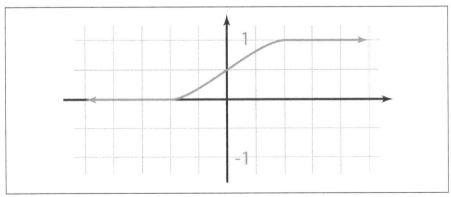

Figure 2-17. Sigmoid

Tanh

Takes the input value and puts it in the range of −1 to 1 (Figure 2-18).

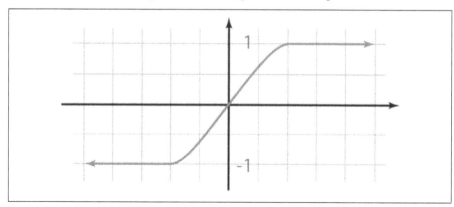

Figure 2-18. Tanh

ReLU

Rectified Linear Unit takes the input value and puts it in the range of 0 to infinity. It makes all negative values 0 (Figure 2-19).

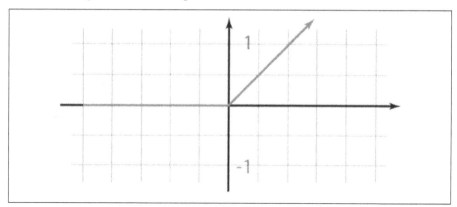

Figure 2-19. Rectified Linear Unit

Leaky ReLU

Takes an input value and puts the range from a very small negative value to infinity (Figure 2-20).

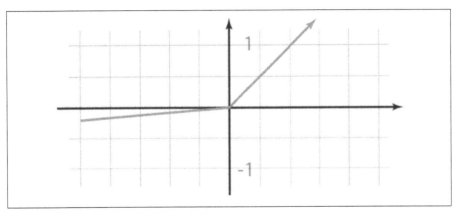

Figure 2-20. Leaky Rectified Linear Unit

Softmax

Takes the inputs and predicts a result over a certain set of possibilities. For instance, in digit recognition the softmax function returns a result of 10 possibilities (0-9) with probabilities for each. If you have five different sodas, it would return five possibilities with probabilities for each (Figure 2-21).

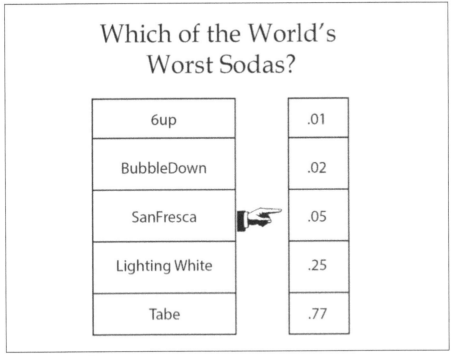

Figure 2-21. Softmax Function

ReLUs have the problem of "dying"—getting stuck on the negative side and always outputting a value of 0. Using Leaky ReLUs with their slight negative slope can remedy the problem, as can lowering the learning rate.

As business analysts we recommend taking a high-level view of machine learning and, in particular, neural networks. You can go down many rabbit holes here trying to understand the exact difference between sigmoid or tanh, or how exactly to determine gradient descent. You can dig into the math of this to such an extent you could write many doctoral theses on it. Our goal with this overview is to impart to SAP business analysts the sheer depth of this beautiful science. Furthermore, a basic understanding of this science will allow you to leverage it for real-world results.

Now that we have some of the fundamentals, what are some of the basic neural networks we see in practice today?

Single layer perceptron

A *Single layer perceptron* is the simplest form of a neural network (Figure 2-22). It has no hidden layers. It has only an input and output layer. You might think that diagram has two layers, but the input layer is not considered a layer because it does no computation. A single layer perceptron receives multiple input signals, sums them, and if the value is above a predetermined threshold it fires. Because they either have a value or not, they are only capable of discerning between two linearly separable classes. What's the big deal? In themselves, the single layer perceptron is quite limited. However, they comprise other neural networks. Imagine: the average human brain has 100 billion neurons. Each neuron has a simple function, as simple as this single layer perceptron. It is the concert of these neurons in our brains that makes the music of who we are.

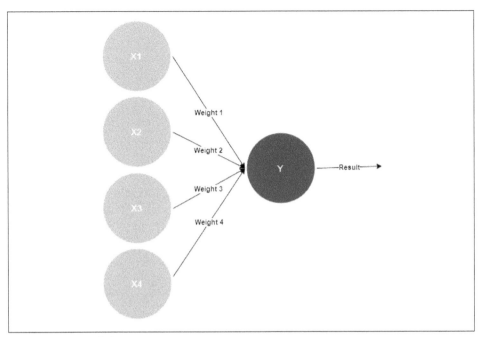

Figure 2-22. Single layer perceptron

Multilayer perceptron

A *Multilayer perceptron* is composed of multiple layers (Figure 2-23). They are normally interconnected. Nodes in the first hidden layer connect to the nodes in the input layer. A bias node can be added in the hidden layer that is not connected to the input layer. Bias nodes increase flexibility of the network to fit the data and their value is normally set to 1. In more advanced neural networks the process of *batch normalization* performs this function.

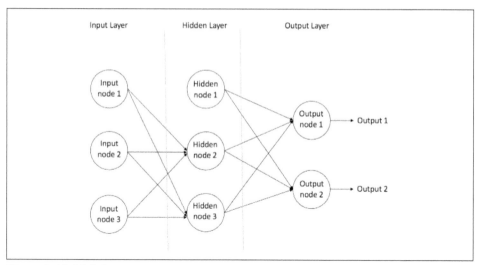

Figure 2-23. Multilayer perceptron

Convolutional network

A *convolutional neural network* (CNN) is a multilayer network that passes weights and biases back and forth through the layers. CNNs assume that the inputs are images and therefore there are special layers and encoding to these networks. Why not use a multilayer perceptron for image classification? Well, image data is big...it would not scale well. CNNs use three-dimensional tensors composed of width, height, and depth as their input.

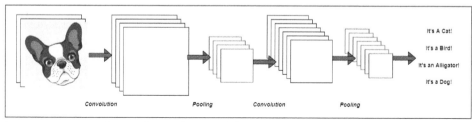

Figure 2-24. Convolutional neural network layers

There are three unique layers to a CNN:

Convolutional Layer
 The primary purpose is to extract features from the input. Every image is a matrix of pixel values, which are converted to features using a *filter* which slides over the image and computes a dot product.

Pooling Layer
 This layer is also sometimes called downsampling or subsampling. It reduces the dimensionality of the features presented by the convolutional layer by using either Max, Average, or Sum values.

Fully Connected Layer
 Similar to a multilayer perceptron that uses a SoftMax activation function to deliver to the output layer a probability distribution.

CNNs can become very complex. Check out Google's Inception model, shown in Figure 2-25.

Figure 2-25. Google's Inception model

The field of neural networks is undergoing rapid and exciting change. Brilliant minds are working ardently to push this field forward incredibly fast. Along come researchers Sara Sabour, Nicholas Frost, and Geoffrey Hinton with a proposal called CapsNets (*http://bit.ly/2lQr9dl*) (Capsule Networks). (Hinton is an icon in this field; when his name is on a paper...you read it.) In a multilayer neural network you add more and more layers depending on your needs. In a CapsNet you add a neural network inside another layer.

As Hinton says, "The pooling operation used in convolutional neural networks is a big mistake and the fact that it works so well is a disaster."

What makes capsule networks so exciting is they, like our own image processing, do not take into account the orientation of the image. When a child looks at a dog, the orientation of the dog does not affect his/her perception of the image.

CapsNets are too new at this time, but if they continue to gain traction we will discuss them more fully in future editions of this book.

Recursive neural network

A *recursive neural network* is a multilayer network that leverages time-series or sequential data. They perform very well and are often the go-to model for natural language processing (NLP) tasks and time-series data. We will see them in action in the chapter *Language and Text Processing*. In our other neural networks, once data is passed to the next layer the previous layer is forgotten. However, when trying to make predictions along a sequence of data it is important to *remember* what came before it. These networks are *recurrent* in that they double back and look at the previous input or inputs. In a sense, they have a memory.

The arrows circling back show the recurrence in the RNN (Figure 2-26). As you can see, this recurrence is very short; it only circles back on the same layer. In essence, it has only a short-term memory. This problem is overcome by introducing to the network a long short-term memory (LSTM).

LSTMs allow the network to learn over a long period of time. They have three gates: input, output, and forget. The input gate determines what data is let in. The output gate determines what data is let out. Finally, the forget gate decides what data should be forgotten. Their architecture can be difficult for the beginner so suffice it to say that LSTMs allow the network to remember over a long period. If you are interested in a deeper dive into them, read this blog (*http://bit.ly/2kjzC8A*).

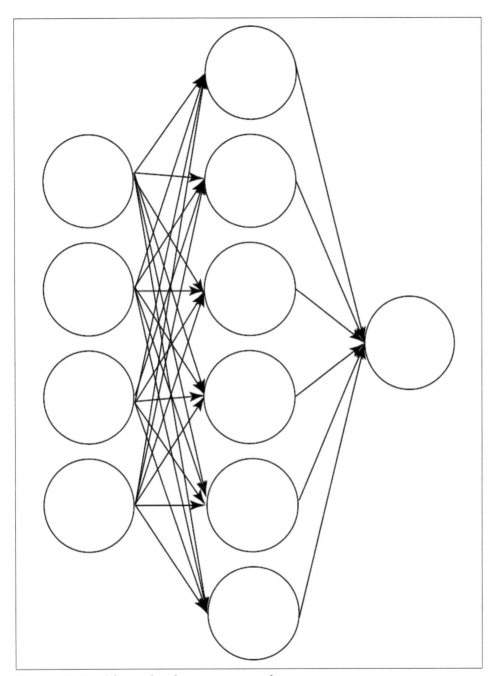

Figure 2-26. Feed forward and recurrent networks

Temporal networks

A *temporal convolutional network* (TCN) is a multilayer network that has the advantages of a convolutional network while also considering placement and position.

Convolutional networks are generally very good at image recognition and language classification. They do not however, care about placement. For instance, a CNN wants to know if the image contains a tail, a brown button nose, and floppy ears. Then it classifies that image as a dog. It does not care about the positioning of the image. In language classification, a CNN wants to know the presence of certain key-words that will indicate if it is looking at a legal document, a comic book, or a Hemingway novel. The position, again, does not really matter. What if you want to work on data in which position and placement *is* important, such as time-series data? Time-series data is simply a dataset on a timeline with date and/or timestamps. As we mentioned earlier, the industry go-to model for such tasks is the RNN. However, like many things in data science, that model has recently been unseated...by the mighty TCN.

Compared to RNNs, TCNs have the advantage of being computationally less expensive and using a simpler architecture. RNNs need resources, the LSTM layers, to *remember*. TCNs use input steps that map to outputs that are used in the next layer of the input (Figure 2-27). Instead of using recurrence, they use the results of one layer to feed the next layer.

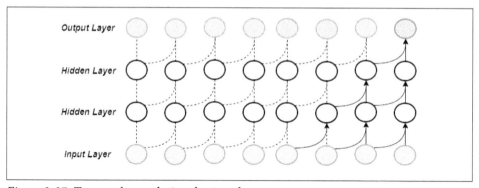

Figure 2-27. Temporal convolutional network

In Chapter 6, we do a simple sales forecast. TCNs seem like the proper model to use for such a task; we will attempt to use it to forecast the sales for a particular product from an SAP system.

Autoencoder

The Autoencoder is a feed-forward-only neural network with a deceptively simple definition. It is a network that takes input data and tries to copy it as the output. It is comprised of two parts:

Encoder

Deconstructs the input data.

Decoder

Reconstructs the data for output.

The most common use for this type of network is image denoising and image generation. The real value in the autoencoder is not the output, which is the case for our other neural networks. The real value is in the representation that the neural network has of the output in the compressed data. To clarify this further, the model at its most compressed has learned the salient features of the object. Let's say it is looking at the image of a dog. The salient features are ears, eyes, mouth, snout, dog-like nose, and so on. If the model compresses too far it may think the only salient features are eyes and won't be able to tell the difference between a dog and any other animal. If the model is not compressed enough such that it recognizes too many features (such as coloring and facial shape) it will know only one type of dog. The trick in this model is knowing the balance. As a recap, the neural network is optimized not when the output is closer to the input, but when the output still represents the key features of the input and the data is *compressed* as much as possible.

 A key concept with Autoencoders is that the output dimension must be smaller than the input dimension for the network to learn the most relevant features.

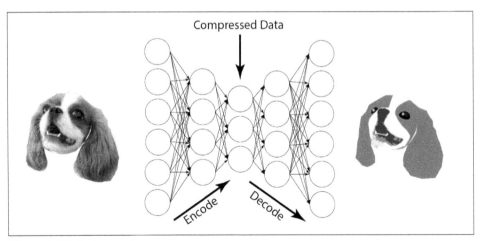

Figure 2-28. Autoencoder

Autoencoders are typically used for reducing the dimensionality of the data and feature learning. They are commonly part of another neural network where it helps reduce feature dimensionality.

Generative adversarial network

A generative adversarial network (GAN) is a neural network architecture where two networks, to put it frankly, fight. Hence the term *adversarial*. The two networks are referred to as the Generator and the Discriminator. Imagine this commonly used scenario. The GAN wants to make fake money. The generator creates a bill and sends it to the discriminator for testing. Well, the discriminator knows what bills look like because it has learned from a set of real-world images. The generator's first attempt is woeful, it fails and it gets feedback on its failure. Then it tries again, and again, and again until it is able to produce a bill that the discriminator thinks is real. Then it is the discriminator's turn to learn. It finds out that it was wrong and learns not to accept that fake bill again. This bickering goes back and forth until a point where the networks fairly evenly fail and succeed...a point where no more learning is happening on either side.

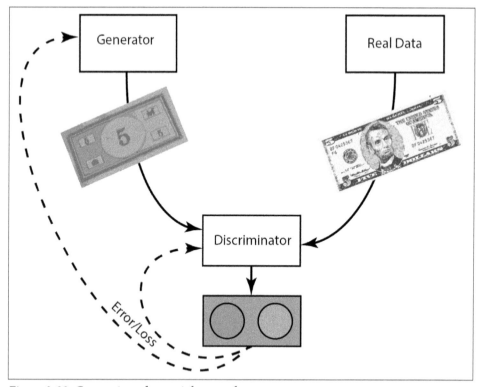

Figure 2-29. Generative adversarial network

You may wonder how a network like this would be used. Well, these networks like to mimic data. Therefore they have been taught to mimic art, music, images, and even poetry. They can be taught to merge concepts in images. For instance, you train the network on images of men wearing hats, women wearing no hats and ask the GAN to generate images of women wearing hats, and it does a pretty good job. Sounds nifty, but what is the use in our business scenarios? Well, GANs have been used to detect anomalies in data and also to generate training data for other networks when a limited amount is available. In the introduction to neural networks we provide here, we would be remiss to not mention GANs. However, we admit it is harder to apply them to business applications. Presenting them here is illustrative of our goal of creating a type of *Citizen Data Scientist* within the SAP business analyst community. Keep in mind all the concepts, including GANs, and perhaps you will identify a business scenario where a GAN could be employed.

Summary

If this was your first introduction to data science concepts, we understand it was a lot to take in. If you are an experienced data scientist you may have asked questions such as "Where is XGBoost?" or "Why not AutoML?" Remember our main intent, we want to get business analysts to think a little like data scientists. The creation of citizen data scientists if you will. There are many other areas of data science that we did not cover in this chapter but will address later such as exploratory data analysis and data visualization. Business analysts, we hope that you found in this chapter ideas that will get you thinking about your own data—and in particular for this book, your SAP data. In the following chapters we will go into detailed business scenarios using SAP data and the concepts we introduced in this chapter.

## CHAPTER 3

SAP for Data Scientists

 If you're an SAP professional, you may not need much of the information in this chapter. We're trying to get data scientists up to speed on things that you probably already know.

At Big Bonanza Warehouse, Greg and Paul[1] make up the entire data science team. They're surrounded by delicious data everywhere they look: plant automation systems, transportation records for customer shipments, marketing campaign data, and the copious spreadsheets and Microsoft Access databases that seem to sprout up everywhere at big enterprises. They can't get up to get coffee without hearing about another fascinating data opportunity. They're simultaneously overjoyed and swamped: they get to come in and work on interesting problems every day, but there's no way they can ever catch up to the insane backlog of data requests.

Well, of course, there's one way they could catch up. They could dive in and learn SAP.

Because SAP is the leviathan that continues to swallow other Big Bonanza Warehouse systems whole. As Big Bonanza moves to consolidate its enterprise software resources into the SAP portfolio, more of that delicious data disappears into the belly of the beast. Greg and Paul know the amount of data—and therefore opportunity—in SAP boggles the mind. They just have no idea how to go poking around to get it. Talking to SAP end users doesn't reveal the true data model, and talking to SAP administrators hardly goes anywhere, because they're so incredibly overworked. Greg and Paul need a way in.

---

1 Please permit us this one instance of authorial hubris.

Data scientists, listen up. This chapter lays out the SAP basics that will get you where you need to go. SAP professionals spent many years becoming familiar with the waters of SAP. You will not be able to navigate like Magellan after one chapter of a book. This is your way of becoming conversant enough to work with your SAP team and SAP data.

If you've ever heard the expression "I know just enough to be dangerous"—that's our goal.

Getting Started with SAP

SAP is enterprise resource planning (ERP) software with multiple highly configurable capabilities. Enterprises that install and run SAP choose from many possible modules (see Chapter 1 for a partial list), but the most common release of SAP in use is R/3 ERP, a client/server architecture that places heavy application processing requirements on application servers.

The application servers will almost certainly be set up and maintained by a set of administrators known within the SAP community as SAP Basis administrators. They specialize in installing and configuring SAP systems to run with high availability. SAP Basis administrators perform database administration, server administration, scheduling and troubleshooting batch jobs, managing low-level security, patching both the application and the base OS that runs the application, and many other technical tasks.

Working with SAP means you'll use the powerful (if a bit antiquated-looking) SAP GUI. It's likely that you will have to get it installed by—or get instructions from—your corporate IT department. Most often there are connection settings maintained by the Basis team that point your installation to the right servers. Once the GUI is installed, you start SAP by opening the SAP GUI Logon Pad (Figure 3-1).

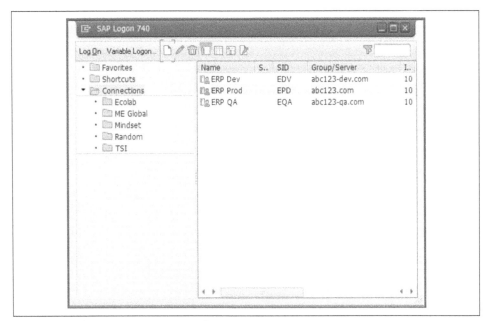

Figure 3-1. The SAP GUI Logon Pad

If your SAP logon pad has lots and lots of system connections in it, don't fret. This is normal. When you consider that separate systems can be installed for many of the SAP R/3 applications, and that each system is present in sandbox, development, QA, pre-prod, and production environments, you can see: often there are hundreds of possible systems to log into. Knowing where the data you need exists among all these systems will probably require at least one initial pointer from the SAP experts in your company.

But once you find the right system, and you get the proper access, you're ready to sign in. Remember: just like in any enterprise system, getting this access usually goes through a team of security pros and approvals, and can take anywhere from seconds to weeks. Once that's squared away and you enter your credentials, you'll see something like Figure 3-2 (though some companies choose to put other pictures in the righthand side of the GUI screen).

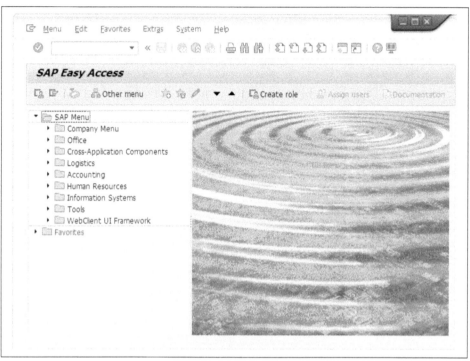

Figure 3-2. The SAP Easy Access screen, ready to run transactions

Now you're ready to do some real exploration. The screen you find yourself at initially lets you launch into any of the SAP GUI functionality via the use of *transaction codes* (you'll hear SAP pros refer to them as "t-codes"). The command field at the top allows you to manually type t-codes, and all the files and folders on the lefthand side are shortcuts to t-codes.

Think of t-codes as SAP's internal shortcuts to programs. Entering t-code VA03 as in Figure 3-3 will start the SAP program to view sales orders, SE37 will take you to the editor for SAP functions, and so on. End users have alternative ways of viewing their business t-codes, like web interfaces or mobile apps—but data scientists will need to explore the administrative side of the SAP application suite.

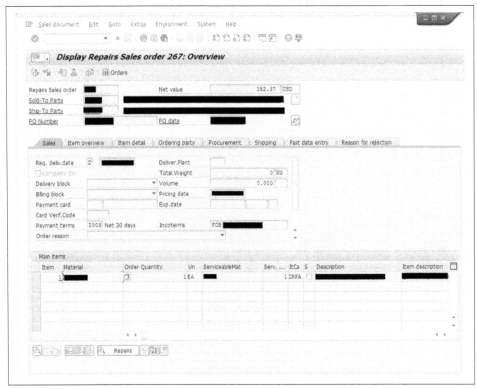

Figure 3-3. The first screen for displaying and editing sales orders

As you can see from the VA03 screenshot shown in Figure 3-3, the SAP end user experience can get incredibly confusing. A typical SAP user will only need to use a small subset of the available fields for an order. In some cases, entering data into a normally unused field can trigger unintended functionality.

This is part of what makes the SAP and data science intersection so weird yet so interesting. There's *so much* data to be had from SAP. Where do you find it? How would you even know it's there?

For you data scientists, this book will help you answer some of those questions, some of the time. For you SAP gurus, rest assured that all that hard-won experience and domain knowledge has *immense* value to the data science process.

The ABAP Data Dictionary

One of the great powers of SAP systems is their built-in flexibility for customers to add or change delivered functionality. This allows SAP to deliver support packs and enhancements that customers can implement for themselves, but also allows customers to create their own data objects and programs *inside* the SAP system.

SAP systems lay out a process for letting customers define custom data objects. The collection of tools, objects, and processes is commonly referred to as the *ABAP Data Dictionary*. Data scientists and other programmers are probably familiar with common SQL commands for creating data types and tables. SAP provides the same functionality in concept, but in fact turbo-charges it. Data definition changes instantly impact the system's raw application functionality. For example, by altering the definition of a field in an SAP table, you can make a screen immediately give the user a friendly drop-down list of values for an input field.

We'll go over some of the main pieces of the ABAP Data Dictionary here, since they are of great use in sleuthing out what data is in the systems you can access.

With great power comes great responsibility! You data scientists out there peeking into SAP for the first time should avoid the temptation to edit SAP data dictionary objects. If your administrators have given you developer access, you may find that you have the right permissions to do this. Don't!

Changing data dictionary objects can lead to instability across many areas of the system. The authors have seen an unwise data dictionary change require an entire SAP instance to be restored from a backup. It should tell you something that the most seasoned SAP veterans are also the most paranoid to touch data dictionary objects.

Tables

In most SAP systems the application runs on top of a traditional RDBMS like Microsoft SQL Server, Oracle, or IBM DB2. Rather than directly editing those database systems to make changes to them, SAP gives users several t-codes that can view and change the system DB. In the last few years SAP has released its own RDBMS, called HANA. It's gaining a foothold in SAP environments around the world, but as of this writing it's not a majority shareholder of the market for SAP databases. Later in this chapter we'll show an example of creating a data service for HANA systems.[2]

Let's examine a couple of SAP tables in depth. Go to t-code SE11 and enter VBAK into the Database Table field. Click the Display button, and the table definition is displayed as in Figure 3-4.

---

2 Just because we're nice like that.

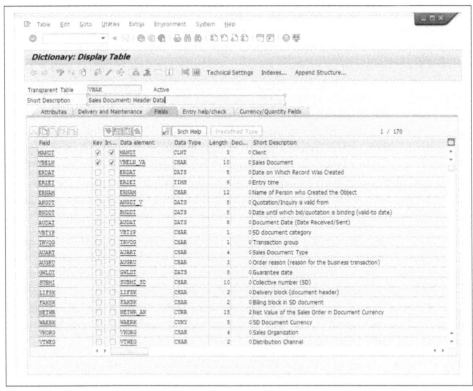

Figure 3-4. *The VBAK table definition in t-code SE11*

VBAK is a *transparent table*, which means that the fields and other information presented on the screen match one-to-one with the table in the lower-level RDBMS. This is way better than staring at some DDL statement in SQL. SAP also allows two other sorts of tables: pooled and cluster. For the purposes of this book we don't need to go into a lot of details, but understand that SAP pooled and cluster tables are not one-to-one with the lower-level RDBMS tables, so the screen does not show a perfect representation of how the data is physically stored in the database. For most programming tasks in SAP, this distinction doesn't matter much.[3]

VBAK is the sales order header table. VBAP is a sales order item table. As you hunt around SAP tables, remember: SAP is German software. Ks often stand for "Kopf" or head. Ps often stand for "Position" or item.

---

3 In the newest SAP releases of HANA, pooled and clustered tables have been de-pooled and de-clustered. So if you don't understand them, don't bother—they're going away.

The SAP GUI lists out the fields that are part of this table in the lower section, with their data types and lengths. The Field column gives you the name of the field in the database—MANDT in our first example row. Rows that have the Key checkbox checked are enforced to be unique together, so in our example MANDT and VBELN must be unique in combination before a record is written to this table. The Data Element column identifies the referencing data object type, further specified by the Data Type, Length, and Decimals columns. For data scientists trying to identify a field's purpose, the Short Description column gives you just that. If you scroll to the bottom of the list of fields, you may see one or more fields with Y or Z prefixes to their names. This indicates fields that the company has added to the delivered database tables, since data scientists may need to collect other unique data inside the SAP system.[4] SAP segments these fields by using a Y or Z to name them. But those new fields do actually become part of the underlying database table when they are added.

T-code SE11 gives you another valuable feature when searching for SAP data. There's an "Indexes..." button near the top. This lets you know which fields are optimized for searching this table, an incredibly important note when considering some of the larger SAP tables. Indices are another key point of flexibility—the SAP application lets you add your own indices to the base system tables to improve search performance. Indices aren't perfect, though. They can incur a performance cost, so be cautious and pragmatic when adding your own to the SAP tables.

If our intrepid data scientists Greg and Paul need to examine a particular set of sales orders to see what sort of data exists in their system, they can use t-code SE16 (General Table Display) or the newer SE16N as shown in Figure 3-5. Knowing that VBAK is the order header table on a tip from their SAP colleagues, they can enter search criteria in the lower section, and view results. Note that they can restrict the number of records returned—great for discovering if they're searching for the right things without having to wait for 30 million rows to return to the screen. SE16/SE16N are better designed for viewing the data in tables, whereas SE11 is better for inspecting setup details of the tables.

---

4 We weren't kidding with that note at the beginning of the chapter—only do this if you are an SAP system administrator, have system backups, and have performed the required rituals.

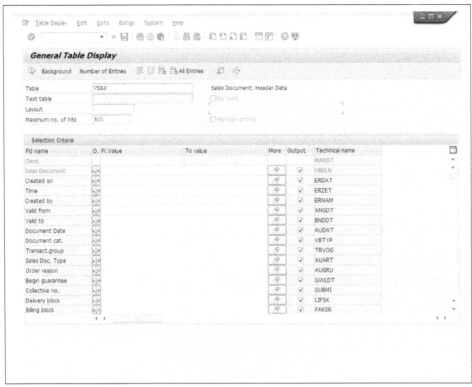

Figure 3-5. The VBAK table displayed in SE16N, for querying

Structures

SE11 is also used to define SAP structures. Structures are groups of fields defined in the dictionary that provide common ways to refer to data in SAP ABAP code. In "OData Services" on page 68, we use a dictionary-defined structure to hold SAP physical plant data. If you define a structure in the dictionary as in Figure 3-6, programs all over the SAP system can use that structure to create internal variables. Structures do not persist data permanently in and of themselves; they're just the cookie-cutter that stamps out data cookies.

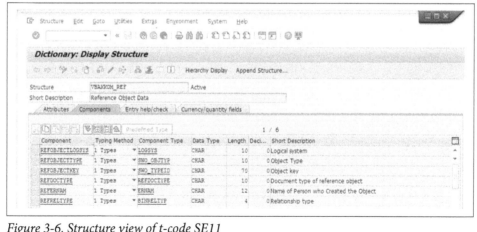

Figure 3-6. Structure view of t-code SE11

The visual is very similar to the table view. You can review the field names, data types, and some basic descriptions. As a data scientist you probably won't find yourself defining new structures very often, but the nice thing is that defining your own structures carries far less risk than redefining the base application tables. For an example, in Chapter 5, you'll learn about anomaly detection, where we define our own structure to use for extracting data from SAP.

Data Elements and Domains

The SAP application layer uses data elements as the lowest-level piece of structures and table definitions (outside of elementary types like integers and strings). They can be used in structures, tables, and programs all over the system, making them a key part of the flexibility of available in custom dictionary definitions.

Data elements are also defined in SE11 (Figure 3-7).

Here, you define a data element as made up of either a predefined elementary type or of a domain. In the screenshot shown in Figure 3-8, the SAP-provided LOGSYS data element uses the same-named LOGSYS domain. This comes installed with the base system. Whenever possible, use a domain to give your data elements some extra power.

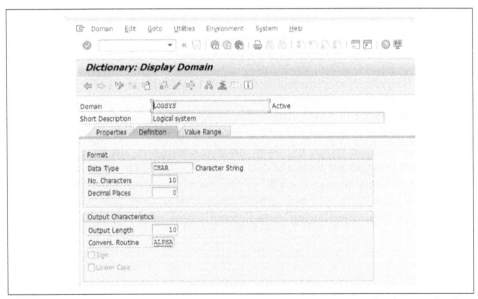

Figure 3-7. A data element defined in t-code SE11

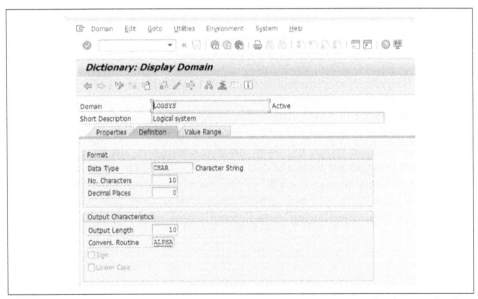

Figure 3-8. Domain definition for LOGSYS (in this case, LOGSYS is the domain for the LOGSYS data element)

Domains can act as a kind of sensibility layer on top of data elements. Most power-fully, you can define a list of acceptable values for that domain, either by hardcoding your list (as shown in Figure 3-9 for the VBTYP domain), or by specifying an SAP table as the definition of possible values for that domain (as shown in Figure 3-10 for the LOGSYS domain).

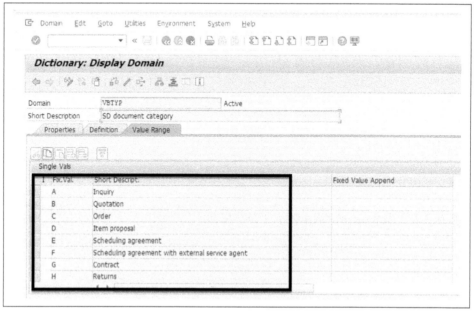

Figure 3-9. Hardcoded list of acceptable values for the VBTYP domain

As you sleuth around in SAP trying to find information about the data, having data elements defined with domains can be extremely helpful for finding possible values. Knowing the possible values and their meaning grants an immediate boost to the insight you're trying to get about the data at your fingertips. For example, if Greg and Paul extract information from the VBTYP field seen in Figure 3-9, the data comes out of SAP with those A, B, C... and so on shortcut values. Greg and Paul can quickly translate those values by referring to the domain definition of VBTYP.

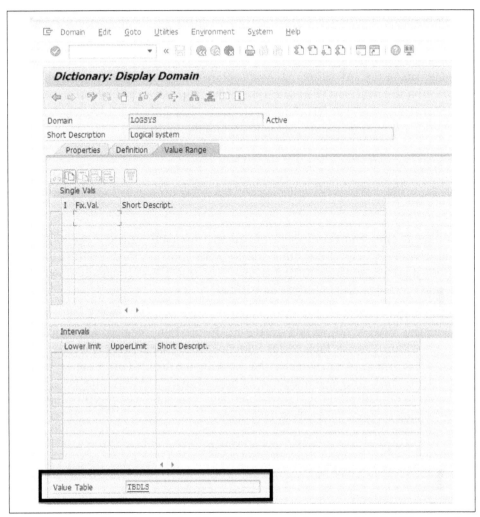

Figure 3-10. Possible values for the LOGSYS domain defined in table TBDLS, as configured in SE11

Where-Used

We've talked about tables, structures, data elements, and domains as the key points of defining data in the SAP system. As you explore things and hunt for the right set of information to science up your data, one of the most powerful tools available is the where-used list, available for all those elements. The little weird-looking box with arrows (Figure 3-11) means you can hunt around for related information.

Figure 3-11. The "where-used" button, to find references to the ABAP object you're looking at

For example, Greg and Paul came to know that the table VBAK is the sales order header table. They suspect that other system tables contain valuable related information, but don't know where to find them. They read the short descriptions of the fields and decided to drill in further on VBELN.

To see how they'd do this, click to highlight the field VBELN, then double-click the data element VBELN_VA as in Figure 3-12. In the Data Element screen, click the where-used icon. Choose Table Fields from the dialog that appears as in Figure 3-13, and voila! A listing of other tables that contain the VBELN field appears like in Figure 3-14. Then, with a combination of further analysis through the general table display in t-code SE16 and finding related data, you can piece together the model you're looking for from the available table data.

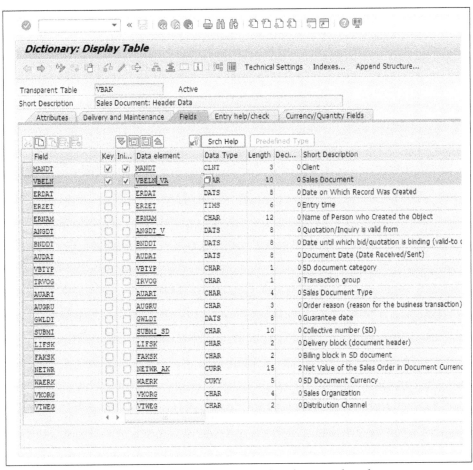

Figure 3-12. Choosing data element VBELN_VA for where-used analysis

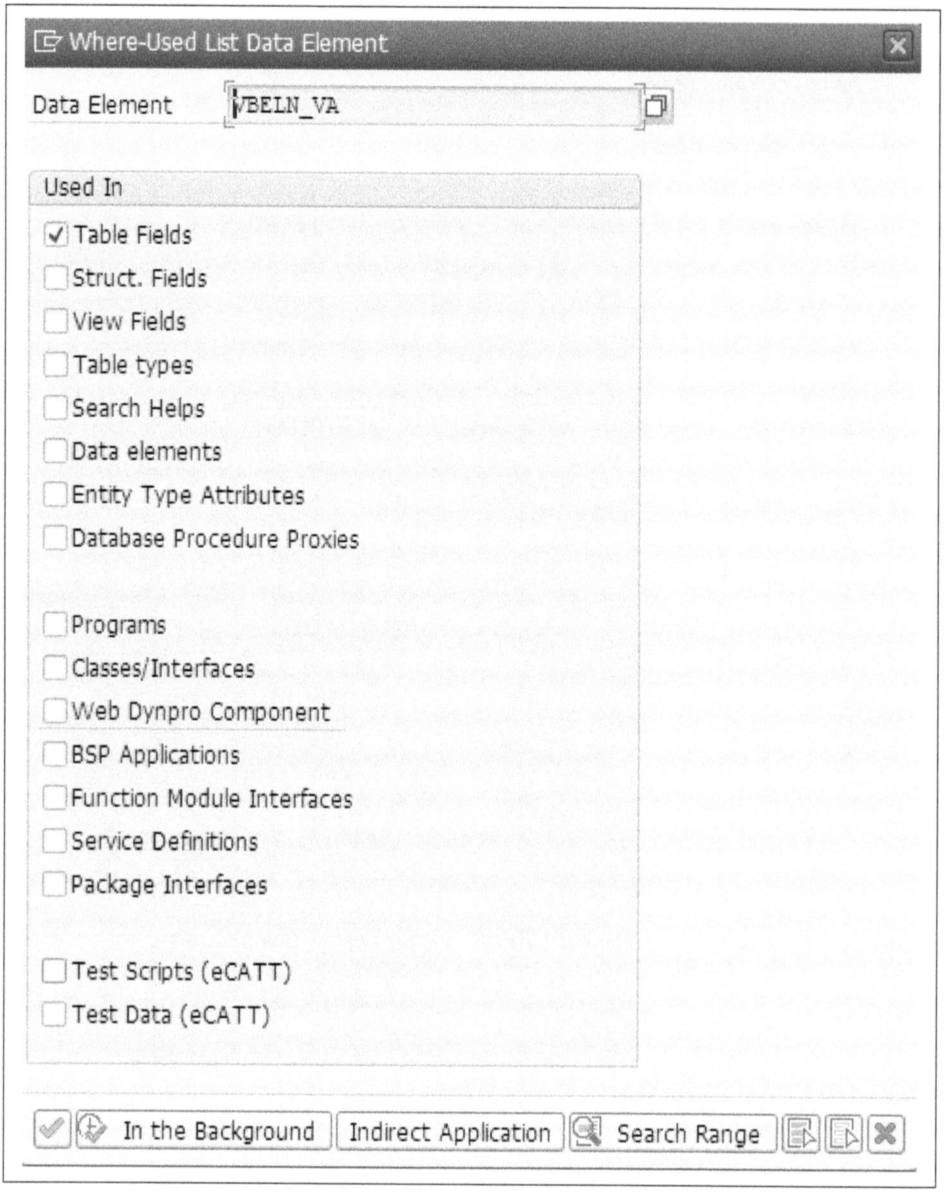

Figure 3-13. Restricting the where-used search to just table fields

Table Fields	Short descriptn
/BEV1/BO_DATA	Proof Table for Rebate Processing
AUBEL	Sales Document
/BEV1/EMLGBWDP	Empties Movement Account Customer
AUBEL	Sales Document
/BEV1/RBVBAK	Sales Document: Header Data
VBELN	Sales Document
/BEV1/RBVBAP	Sales Document: Item Data
VBELN	Sales Document
/BEV1/RBWE	Itemized Proof Rebate Settlement
AUBEL	Sales Document
/BEV1/REMIETE	Rental Items: Shadow Table for VBAK/VBAP/VBEP
VBELN	Sales Document
/BEV1/SRRUE02	Sales Returns
VBELN	Sales Document
/BEV3/CH1030BSG1	Document Segment CH Event Ledger Part1
VBEL2	Sales Document
/BPR3MI/MIN_CBP	Mining - Contract additional parameters

Figure 3-14. A partial list of VBELN_VA results for where-used in tables

The same goes with individual domains and data elements. If your investigation has led you to find a data element that you suspect is vital to your data sleuthing, you can *where-used* that little guy and find out where else the system uses this field. In this way you can find the table in which that data element is used; hopefully that table has the data you need.

In addition to uncovering the model structure of SAP tables, you can also often discover program elements that support your search. By searching functions, classes, and other program objects for your chosen dictionary object, you gain access to possible utility functions and reusable code. In several of the later chapters, we'll use SAP functions and tables to show these relationships, but teaching you how to write SAP ABAP code is not a main objective of this book.[5]

ABAP QuickViewer

Most often you'll want to view data from multiple tables. For instance, you may want to see purchase order data—but like most data in SAP, it's split out by the header and the item. If you were to use SE16 or SE16N you'd need to query data from both EKKO and EKPO[6]—not the most effective method. To further complicate things, there are hundreds of fields on each of these tables—the vast majority of which you won't want.

There's a better tool to look at multiple related tables: ABAP Quick Viewer. This tool allows you to make quick queries that you can view in the SAP GUI or extract for another tool. Let's take a look at a quick example.

Enter t-code **SQVI** into the command bar. You will see the Quick Viewer Initial Screen as in Figure 3-15. Put in a name for your query, Purchasing, and click on the Create button.

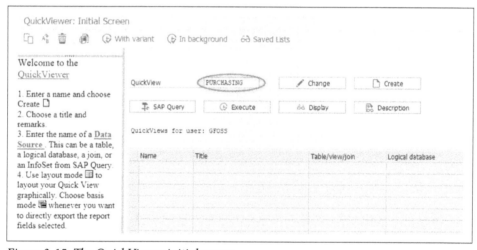

Figure 3-15. The QuickViewer initial screen

Enter a Title and change the Data Source to Table join. Click on the Enter button (the one with a checkmark inside a green circle).

---

5 Which is good, because it's not as fun as Python or R.

6 EKKO is the purchase order header table and EKPO is for the line items. Notice the "K" and the "P" as mentioned earlier?

You will see a blank canvas where you can visualize the tables you work with. Click on the Insert Table button (Figure 3-16).

Figure 3-16. The Insert Table button

In the Add Table dialog (Figure 3-17) enter the primary table EKKO for the query. Click on the Enter button.

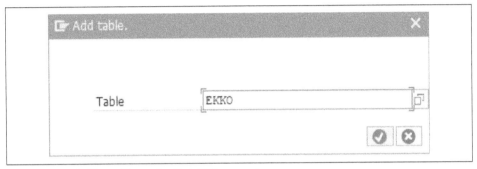

Figure 3-17. Add a table to the QuickViewer setup

You will now see on the canvas the primary table you selected. Click on the Insert Table button again to add another table—EKPO. Click on the Enter button again to accept it.

SAP tries to detect the proper relationship between the two tables and displays the result on the canvas; however, it doesn't always get it quite right. Figure 3-18 shows that there are two relationships between EKKO and EKPO—specifically, EKKO-EBELN to EKPO-EBELN and EKKO-LPONR to EKPO-EBELP. The second of these is not correct (for our purposes) and needs to be removed.

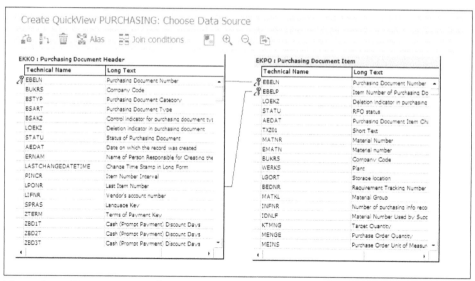

Figure 3-18. Two automatically proposed relationships between EKKO and EKPO

Right-click the connection to be removed and select "Delete Link" from the context menu.

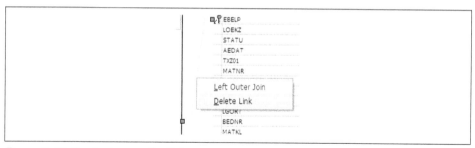

Figure 3-19. Context menu for link

Now that the relationship is correct, click on the Back button to see a screen like Figure 3-20, and select the fields. On the right is a list of the available fields. There are hundreds of them, but we only want a few. Click on the ones desired and then click on the Add Field button.

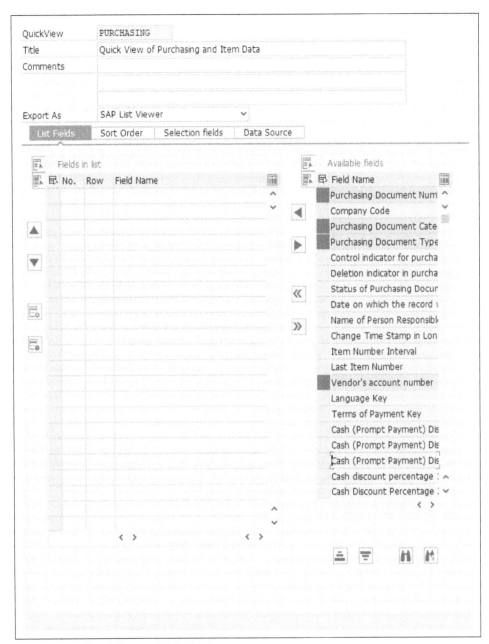

Figure 3-20. QuickViewer field selection

The selected fields (Figure 3-21) will move to the left panel.

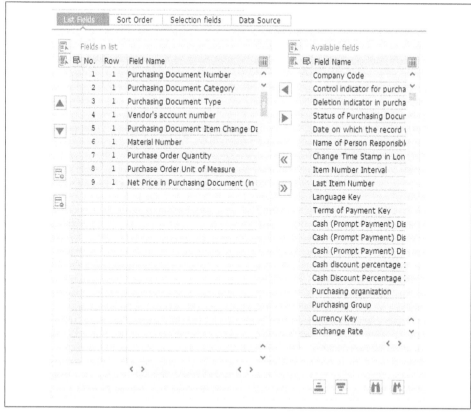

Figure 3-21. Fields selected in QuickViewer

Click on the "Selection fields" tab shown in Figure 3-21, and select those fields by which you want to query the data (Figure 3-22). For instance, we only want to filter our data by date so we'll select "Date on which the record was created" and move that value to the left as we did earlier.

Figure 3-22. Selecting the fields for display

That's it! The query is ready to go! Click on the Save button to save your work. Next click on the Execute button to test it.[7] You will see a simple report with only the selection criteria we specified. Put in a date range for purchase orders and then click on the Execute button. SAP shows a simple table report (as in Figure 3-23) of the purchasing details you requested.

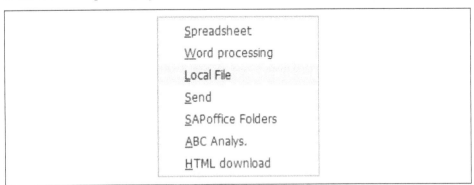

Figure 3-23. Results of QuickViewer query

This toolbar is found throughout SAP and is part of nearly all standard reports.

Notice in particular the Export button. When you click on it you are given a number of options for exporting the data (Figure 3-24). Selecting Local File will then take you to the local file options (Figure 3-25).

Spreadsheet
Word processing
Local File
Send
SAPoffice Folders
ABC Analys.
HTML download

Figure 3-24. Query export options

---

7 At this point you may see a log detail dialog box. Just click through it.

Figure 3-25. Local file options

As a data scientist you already know how to import tab-delimited files into R, Python, or Weka. The ABAP Quick Viewer provides an easy way to do some initial data exports and crucial exploratory data analysis. By using this technique, you can quickly get data out of SAP and perform proof-of-concept without too much effort.

SE16 Export

Now that you can see the data in SAP you want to do some exploratory data analysis and visualization in your tool of choice. Perhaps you plan to use R and R Studio or the Jupyter Notebook. Maybe even Weka! Let's get this tabular data pulled out from the SAP GUI.

The General Table Display t-code SE16 comes with this handy toolbar (Figure 3-26).

Figure 3-26. SE16 General Table Display toolbar options

There are two buttons of interest to the data scientist: "Open in Excel" (left circle) and "Local file" (right circle). They both do what you would expect. The "Local file" button offers options on formatting before export.

A data scientist that has access to a raw data file is a happy data scientist.

OData Services

Now that you know a bit about how to find the right data and manually pull it out, let's look at how to reproduce that data pull and make it externally available. Recall from Chapter 1 that OData services have advantages for data extraction.

- They fit the popular REST paradigm.

- They expose data services to any device/client that can make HTTP calls.

- They allow for filtering and paging through result data.

Now that we know how data dictionary objects are defined, we can use that to build the components of a simple OData service using SAP NetWeaver Gateway. A few things to keep in mind before we begin:

Gateway architecture

Some SAP installations use a separate system to run the Gateway component, and others use Gateway installed right into the same system as all the ERP modules. For simplicity, we'll assume we're on the same system as all the modules, and just note when there may be some differences.

ABAP programming

We'll minimize the amount of code written for our example. As mentioned earlier, this book is not an ABAP primer. Hopefully you data scientists out there won't have to spend a lot of time learning the language when all you really need is the data.

Security matters

By default, most companies that run NetWeaver Gateway run it behind the corporate firewall. You will likely need a computer running inside the corporate network to make use of the OData services you create. It is possible to expose them to the broader internet, but do heed the advice of your security team in coming up with the best way to secure and monitor the APIs as they're created.

Other OData capabilities

OData also allows for the full RESTful set of operations—create/read/update/delete—if they're programmed in. We will only make use of and explain the read capabilities as they're most pertinent to this book, but if your scenarios expand to other data gathering and analysis, OData is a great place to start creating those capabilities.

Since we'll use OData for other use cases throughout this book, let's do a simple example just to show how to set things up. We'll make a simple service that returns a listing of all the plants configured in the SAP ERP system.

First, we'll create a structure to define the shape of the data we'll serve out. Start by going to t-code SE11 and clicking on the radio button next to "Data type." Enter **ZEX AMPLE_PLANT** in the field next to it, and then click the Create button, as in Figure 3-27.

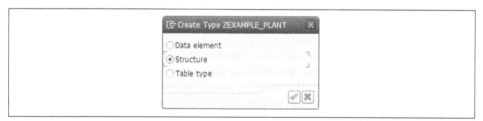

Figure 3-27. Defining a new structure in SE11

When you click Create, you'll see an option for one of three kinds of types: Data Element, Structure, and Table Type. Choose Structure as in Figure 3-28 and click the checkmark to continue.

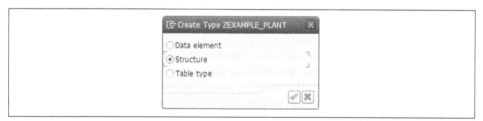

Figure 3-28. Structure type selection

On the next screen (Figure 3-29), you define the actual fields that go into the structure. Keep it simple and define only plant and description fields. When you're done, click the magic wand button to activate this structure. This will make it so that the structure is available to outside programs. Note that you're required to enter a description of the structure itself in the top section.

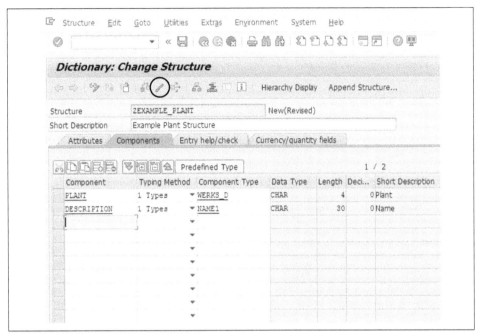

Figure 3-29. Plant and Description fields defined for our new ZEXAMPLE_PLANT structure

How did we know what types and data elements to use for this structure? We discovered that plants are stored at the line item level of sales orders in table VBAP. Using SE11 to view that table, we found the plant field (WERKS) and its associated data element (WERKS_EXT). By clicking into the data element, we found the domain that defines WERKS_EXT to be WERKS. We used the properties of that domain to discover the table that underlies it: T001W (Figure 3-30). By then opening T001W in its own SE11 session, we found the WERKS and NAME1 fields to contain the information that we wanted. Just like we showed you for the data dictionary stuff! So for our two fields, PLANT and DESCRIPTION, we use the same data elements as the corresponding fields in T001W.

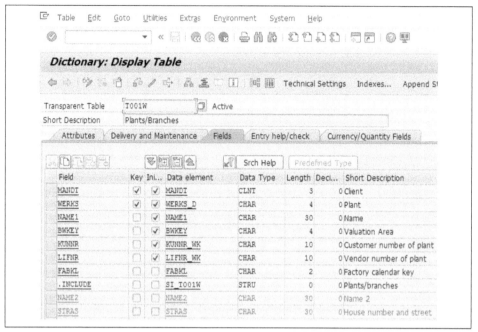

Figure 3-30. T001W table defining plants and branches viewed in t-code SE11

Now that we have the right shape of our returned data, let's set up the OData service to feed it. Enter t-code SEGW. This is the Gateway Service Builder (Figure 3-31), your one stop to set up and maintain OData services. Click the little white paper button to start building our service.

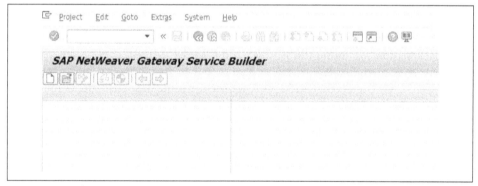

Figure 3-31. The Gateway Service Builder

In the pop-up, enter the values as shown in Figure 3-32. Make sure to replace *[YOUR_USER]* with your actual user ID (it should be filled in by default), then click the checkmark. You'll see that there's a skeleton of your service created. Now we can plug in the structure we created and automatically make it into a part of the service.

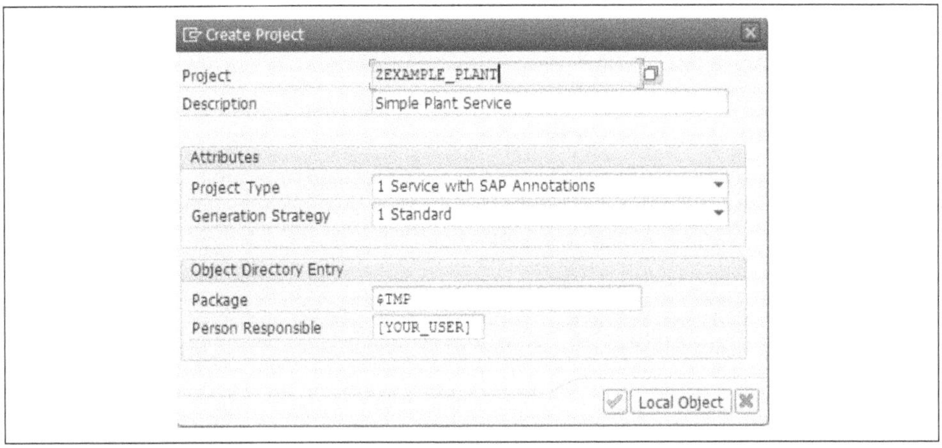

Figure 3-32. Naming and defining the SEGW project

OData services can have multiple sources of data plugged in to them. These sources of data are referred to as *entities* and *entity sets*. Think of an entity as defining the single-record structure of a data source endpoint, and an entity set as a collection of records matching that structure. A single service can have multiple entities and entity sets attached to it, and each entity can choose whether to implement some or all of the create/read/update/delete operations. We will turn our plant information into one of the available entity sets in our service, and only implement the read functionality.

Right-click the Data Model folder and choose "Import...DDIC Structure" (DDIC means "data dictionary"), as shown in Figure 3-33.

In the first step of the wizard (Figure 3-34), enter **Plant** as the name of the entity, enter **ZEXAMPLE_PLANT** as the ABAP Structure (remember we just created that structure), and make sure Create Default Entity Set is selected.

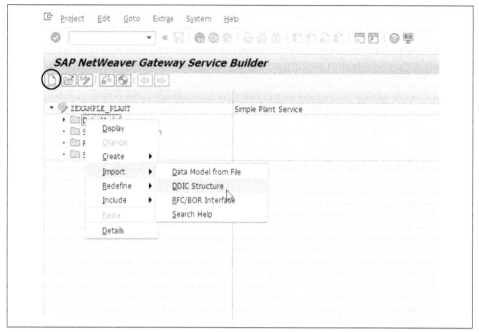

Figure 3-33. Import DDIC structure

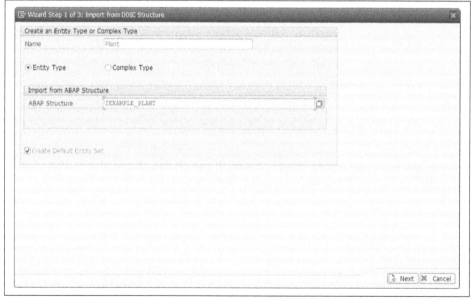

Figure 3-34. OData setup wizard step 1

In the second step (Figure 3-35), check all the available fields from the structure as imports, and click the Next button.

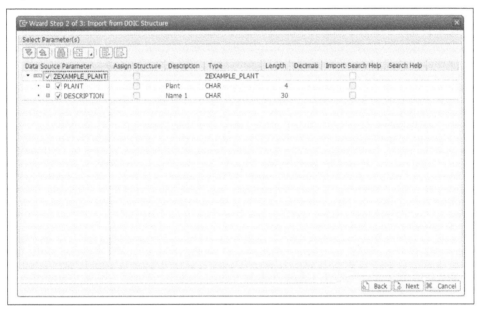

Figure 3-35. OData setup wizard step 2

In the final step (Figure 3-36), mark the Plant field as the key field, as this will be the uniquely identifying piece of information for these records. Click Finish.

What we just did ensures that the structure we created is imported into the service as the definition of the Plant entity. The SAP system uses information from the structure to ensure that the OData service is properly type-defined.

Next, we generate some data extraction classes. SAP Gateway uses generated classes to handle default behavior of the OData services when particular actions (create/read/update/delete) are called, and developers can use those generated classes as hooks to implement their own unique code and features for the OData services. To generate those classes, click the little checkerboarded circle icon (circled in Figure 3-37).

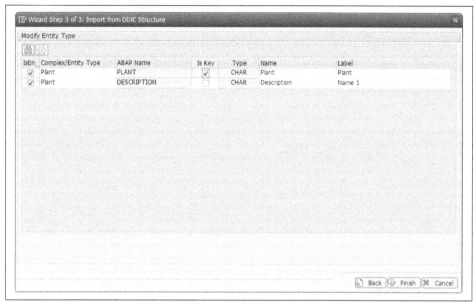

Figure 3-36. OData setup wizard final step

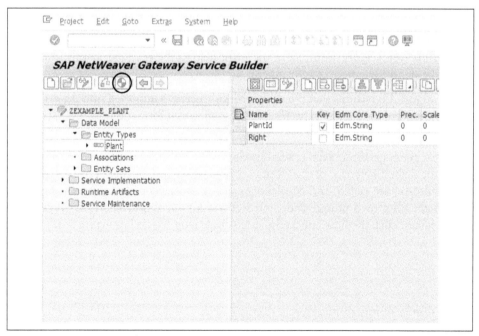

Figure 3-37. Generating base OData classes

When this completes, we're ready to write some brief data retrieval code. Open the Service Implementation folder and expand the PlantSet item. Right-click on GetEntitySet (Query) and choose Go to ABAP Workbench (Figure 3-38). You will get a nasty-sounding information popup indicating that a method has not yet been implemented. That is OK—that's what we're going to do!

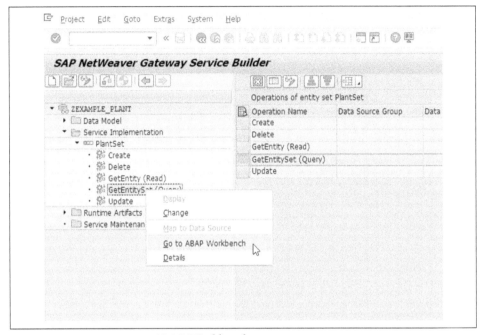

Figure 3-38. Navigating to ABAP Workbench

You'll be taken to the class builder screen. Using the lefthand side of the screen, navigate to the inherited method PLANTSET_GET_ENTITYSET. Right-click on it and choose Redefine, as in Figure 3-39.

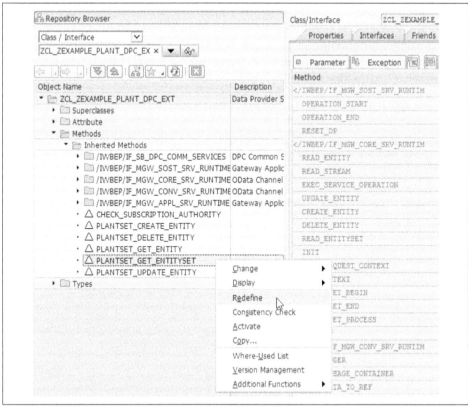

Figure 3-39. Preparing to redefine OData ABAP code

On the righthand side of the screen, you'll be greeted with a text editor allowing you to edit the code of the method. We're not going to dive all the way into ABAP programming here, so just trust us and input the following code and click the magic wand to activate the code:

```
METHOD plantset_get_entityset.

SELECT werks AS plant
name1 AS description
INTO CORRESPONDING FIELDS OF TABLE et_entityset
FROM t001w
ORDER BY werks ASCENDING.

ENDMETHOD.
```

By entering this code, we've done enough to set up the service to have runnable code. Now we have to do a couple more steps to get it working as a web service. Go to t-code /N/IWFND/MAINT_SERVICE and click the Add Service button near the top of the catalog. The next screen will allow you to search, and you may have to talk to your local SAP expert to understand your system environment to know whether you have to use the local system as the Gateway or if you have a separate Gateway server. If you have to use the local system you'll enter a system alias of LOCAL or similar, whereas if you have to use a Gateway hub system then you'll have to find out the right alias to use.

Click Get Services after entering the alias, and scroll down to our service: ZEXAMPLE_PLANT_SRV. Click on the service to see a single-screen activation wizard—just accept its defaults and go back to the main service catalog. Now your new service will be in the main catalog and ready to test.

Scroll down in the list to find ZEXAMPLE_PLANT_SRV, and click on it. At the bottom of the screen, you'll see an "ICF Nodes" section expand like in Figure 3-40. Click the Gateway Client button in that section to be taken to the SAP GUI Gateway testing tool.

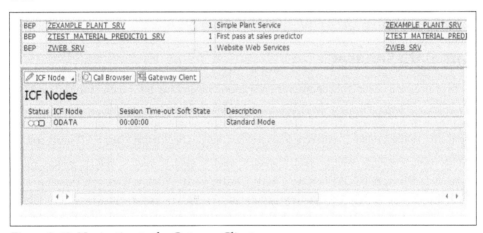

Figure 3-40. Navigating to the Gateway Client

Change the request URI to */sap/opu/odata/sap/ZEXAMPLE_PLANT_SRV/PlantSet? $format=json* and click Execute. You'll see JSON-formatted data appear as results of your service call as in Figure 3-41. There you go! You've set up a simple, web-callable service for getting SAP plant data. OData services we set up in later chapters will have more complexity to them, but this initial process will get you off on the right foot.

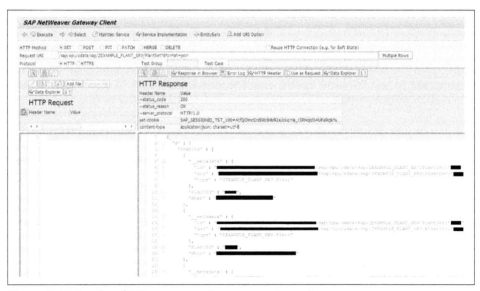

Figure 3-41. Results of OData request for our sample service

Core Data Services

As promised earlier in this chapter, here's a look at making SAP data stored in HANA available. Remember, HANA is the new backend database that the latest SAP ERP systems run on top of. If your system is new (or newly updated) you may have this capability ready to use. If you're a data science nerd, check with your SAP nerd colleagues.

Core Data Services (CDS) is a new SAP feature with which a user can develop data models that can be exposed to client requests via HTTP. These models can be tables, SQL views, associations, and user-defined structures. Think of them like the NetWeaver Gateway…but no gateway. They are incredibly powerful and useful ways of exposing, modeling, and analyzing SAP data. Their capabilities are one of the most compelling reasons for an SAP shop to upgrade to HANA.

While there are many features to CDS, we'll stick to a simple sales order data extraction example. In order to create these views you will need to install and modify Eclipse such that it can be used with SAP. Most ABAP developers have already migrated to Eclipse for their development needs, but that was a choice not a requirement. CDS views *require* Eclipse.

Download the latest version of Eclipse from *www.eclipse.org* and follow the wizard instructions to install it. You will need to install the *Eclipse IDE for Java Developers* as a minimum.

Eclipse IDE for Java Developers

The essential tools for any Java developer, including a Java IDE, a Git client, XML
Editor, Mylyn, Maven and Gradle integration

Once installed, you will need to add some additions to make it work with SAP.
Launch Eclipse and navigate to the menu path Menu → Install New Software as in
Figure 3-42.

Figure 3-42. Installing new add-ons to Eclipse

In the dialog that displays (Figure 3-43) enter the URL *https://tools.hana.onde
mand.com/photon*. Replace *photon* with the version of Eclipse you are using.

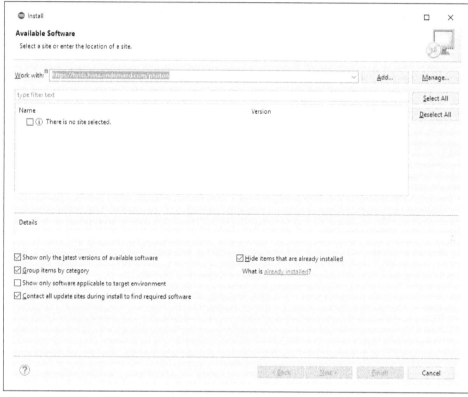

Figure 3-43. Choose Eclipse version to download add-ons

Hit Enter to see the options for installation. Then select the components you'd like to install. In our example, we are selecting all the SAP options in Figure 3-44.

Name
> ☑ ▫▫▫ ABAP Development Tools for SAP NetWeaver
> ☑ ▫▫▫ Modeling Tools for SAP BW/4HANA and SAP BW powered by SAP HANA
> ☑ ▫▫▫ SAP Cloud Platform Tools
> ☑ ▫▫▫ SAP HANA Tools
> ☑ ▫▫▫ UI Development Toolkit for HTML5

Figure 3-44. Software selections for installing into Eclipse

Click on the Next button and wait for the components to install. When finished, it will display all the software components it added to the Eclipse environment. Click Next again to accept the license agreement and then click on the Finish button.

When the software is done installing you will need to restart Eclipse. Once restarted, click on the Open Perspective button to open up your new SAP environment. Select the ABAP perspective as in Figure 3-45 and then click on the Open button.

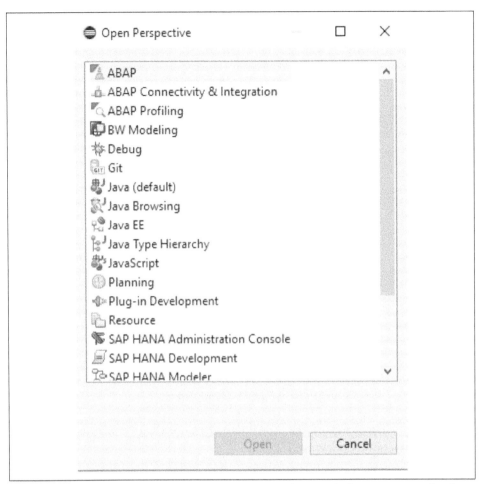

Figure 3-45. Choose the ABAP perspective to open Eclipse with the correct SAP development settings

The first step is to create a CDS document. These are design-time source files that contain the DDL (Data Definition Language) code describing the model.

In Eclipse, follow the menu path File → New → Other (Figure 3-46).

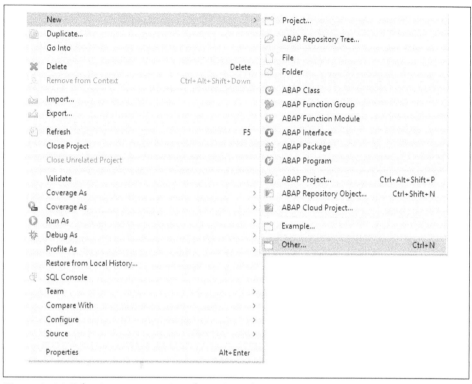

Figure 3-46. Selecting a new project for a CDS document

In the dialog window expand the ABAP and the Core Data Services and select the Data Definition option (Figure 3-47).

Click on the Next button and accept the default project.

Enter a package for the development objects. For our purposes, we will use $TMP, which is SAP's designation for a local/nontransportable object.

Enter a name for your service and a description, then click on the Finish button (Figure 3-48).

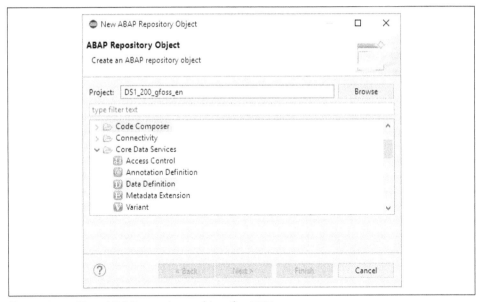

Figure 3-47. New ABAP repository object for CDS

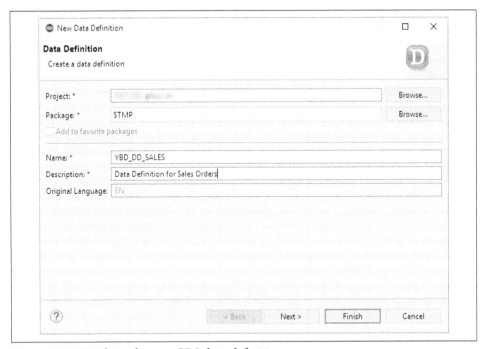

Figure 3-48. Finishing the new CDS data definition

In the workspace there are some default annotations. We will change a few and add some new ones.

The annotations begin by default:

```
@AbapCatalog.sqlViewName: 'sql_view_name'
@AbapCatalog.compiler.compareFilter: true
@AbapCatalog.preserveKey: true
@AccessControl.authorizationCheck: #CHECK
@EndUserText.label: 'Data Definition for Sales Orders'
```

Change the sqlViewName and the authorizationCheck:

```
@AbapCatalog.sqlViewName: 'Sales_Orders'
@AccessControl.authorizationCheck: #NOT_REQUIRED
```

Two new annotations are needed:

@VDM.viewType: #CONSUMPTION
  Indicates that we want to consume this data definition.

@OData.publish: true
  Indicates that we want the definition to be published automatically.

The annotations section should now look like this:

```
@AbapCatalog.sqlViewName: 'Sales_Orders'
@AbapCatalog.compiler.compareFilter: true
@AbapCatalog.preserveKey: true
@AccessControl.authorizationCheck: #NOT_REQUIRED
@EndUserText.label: 'Data Definition for Sales Orders'
@VDM.viewType: #CONSUMPTION
@OData.publish: true
```

Now you can set up the shape and relationships of the data. First, define the main table to be read:

```
define view YBD_DD_SALES
  as select from vbak as header
```

If there are other tables that are associated with the main table, identify and name them:

```
    association[0..*] to vbap as line
      on header.vbeln = line.vbeln
```

Identify and name the fields to be extracted from the SAP system. Note we've included a calculated line to show on-the-fly output for NetPrice:

```
{
  key header.vbeln as SalesDocument,
  key line.posnr as SalesDocumentLine,
  header.erdat as CreateDate,
  header.erzet as CreateTime,
```

```
    header.vbtyp as DocumentCategory,
    header.auart as DocumentType,
    header.kunnr as Customer,
    line.matnr as Material,
    @Semantics.quantity.unitOfMeasure: 'UoM'
    line.kwmeng as Quantity,
    line.meins as UoM,
    line.kdmat as CustomerMaterial,
    line.pstyv as ItemCategory,
    round(line.netpr * line.kwmeng,2) as NetPrice
}
```

Add any conditions to the selection:

```
where header.auart = 'ZOR'
```

The complete final definition:

```
@AbapCatalog.sqlViewName: 'Sales_Orders'
@AbapCatalog.compiler.compareFilter: true
@AbapCatalog.preserveKey: true
@AccessControl.authorizationCheck: #NOT_REQUIRED
@EndUserText.label: 'Data Definition for Sales Orders'
@VDM.viewType: #CONSUMPTION
@OData.publish: true

define view YBD_DD_SALES
  as select from vbak as header
    association[0..*] to vbap as line
      on header.vbeln = line.vbeln

{
  key header.vbeln as SalesDocument,
  key line.posnr as SalesDocumentLine,
  header.erdat as CreateDate,
  header.erzet as CreateTime,
  header.vbtyp as DocumentCategory,
  header.auart as DocumentType,
  header.kunnr as Customer,
  line.matnr as Material,
  @Semantics.quantity.unitOfMeasure: 'UoM'
  line.kwmeng as Quantity,
  line.meins as UoM,
  line.kdmat as CustomerMaterial,
  line.pstyv as ItemCategory,
  round(line.netpr * line.kwmeng,2) as NetPrice
}

where header.auart = 'ZOR'
```

Click on the Save button, and then click on the Activate button to publish the data definition.

Test the service by pressing F8. The results are shown in another tab (Figure 3-49).

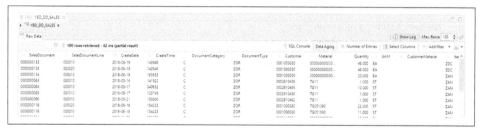

Figure 3-49. CDS data results in Eclipse

The service should properly activate. If you happen to receive the following warning next to the OData annotation then the service did not actually publish. The following steps allow you to manually do so.

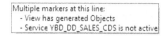

```
Multiple markers at this line:
 - View has generated Objects
 - Service YBD_DD_SALES_CDS is not active
```

Within Eclipse, click on the SAP GUI button (Figure 3-50). Select the project to be launched and click the OK button. This is the same project where the data definition is made.

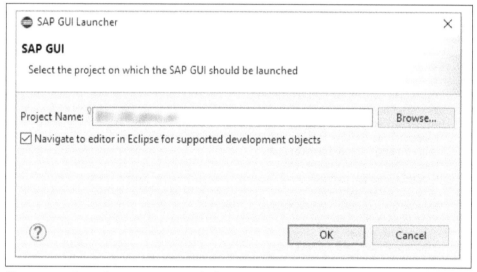

Figure 3-50. Launching SAP GUI with the CDS project

In the transaction field, enter the transaction code **/n/iwfnd/maint_service** (Figure 3-51).

Figure 3-51. Enter the transaction code for maintaining services

Click the Enter button (circled), then click on the Add Service button.

Enter the System Alias, which in our case will be LOCAL, and the Technical Service Name as in Figure 3-52. This is the name of the data definition with "_CDS" appended. Then click on the Get Services button.

Figure 3-52. Settings for starting the technical service

The service definition will appear in the report. Highlight the appropriate service and click on the Add Selected Services button.

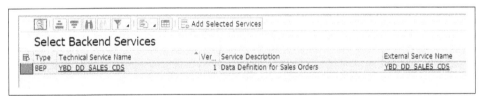

Figure 3-53. Adding the new service to the Gateway backend services

The last "Add Service" screen appears, as shown in Figure 3-54. Accept the default settings and add the package assignment, which in our case is $TMP.

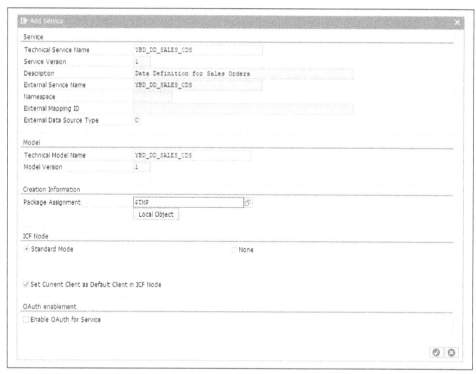

Figure 3-54. Accept defaults and add $TMP package assignment to add the service to Gateway

Click on the Enter button (circled). If all was done correctly, you'll see the message shown in Figure 3-55.

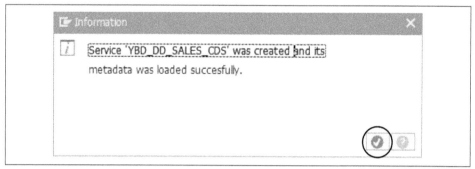

Figure 3-55. Successfully creating the CDS OData service

Return to the data definition screen with the CDS annotations and click on the Activate button (Figure 3-56).

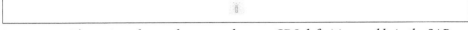

Figure 3-56. The activate button let you make your CDS definition usable in the SAP system

There is a new *Generated OData Service* indicator next to the OData annotation. Put your cursor over that symbol to show a pop-up with the OData-Service details. Click on the OData-Service highlighted link like the one in Figure 3-57 to see the OData service definition in your browser.

Figure 3-57. OData service publishing results

Summary

Having exhaustively perused the data dictionary, data export, OData, and CDS information, Greg and Paul feel ready to dive in to create their SAP data science stories!

Data scientists working with SAP data should never forget the real live resources available to them. SAP teams working in the enterprise are filled with people who know the data model intimately. They also have that wonderfully helpful tribal knowledge of how their particular enterprise has customized SAP for its own business purposes. Just like hackers who socially engineer passwords from people before attempting to crack difficult encryption, data scientists working with SAP should seek knowledge from those experienced with SAP before trying to reverse engineer all the nooks and crannies of the SAP data model. Inspecting the data dictionary as we've laid out here will eventually allow you to navigate to the data you need for business answers, but it will take serious time. A human being sitting right behind you may very likely have all those goofy SAP table names in her head.

## CHAPTER 4

Exploratory Data Analysis with R

Pat is a manager in the purchasing department at Big Bonanza Warehouse. His department specializes in the manufacture of tubing for a variety of construction industries, which requires procuring a lot of raw and semi-raw materials. However, Pat has a problem; he receives up to a hundred purchase requisitions per day in SAP, which need approval before becoming purchase orders. It is a burdensome and time-consuming process he would like help streamlining. He decides to ask his IT department and the SAP team if anything can be done to help.

The SAP team has already configured the system to be optimal for the purchase requisition process. When Pat and the SAP team reach out to their colleagues on the data science team, they immediately wonder: "Could we build a model to learn if a purchase requisition is going to be approved?" There is ample data in the SAP system —nearly 10 years of historical data—for which they know all the requisition approvals and rejections. It turns out to be millions of records of labeled data. All those records indicate approval or rejection. Doesn't this fall into supervised learning? It certainly does!

We introduced four different types of learning models in Chapter 2. Those are:

- Supervised
- Unsupervised
- Semi-supervised
- Reinforcement

We are inclined to think that the scenario mentioned here is a supervised one because we have data that is labeled. That is, we have purchase requisitions that have been approved and rejected. We can train a model on this labeled data, therefore it is a supervised scenario. Having identified the type of learning model we are working, the next step is to explore the data.

One of the most vital processes in the data scientist's workflow is exploratory data analysis (EDA). The data scientist uses this process to explore the data and determine whether it can be modeled, and if so, how. EDA's goal is to understand the data by summarizing the main characteristics, most often using visualizations. This is the step in the data science process that asks the data scientist to become familiar with the data.

Readers who know SAP well: if you think you're familiar with your data, go through this exercise. You'll be surprised how much you learn. There's a vast difference between knowing the general shape of the relational data and knowing the cleaned, analyzed, and fully modeled results of EDA.

In this chapter we will walk through the EDA process. To make it more understandable, we will go through it in real time. That is, we will not manipulate data to make this lesson easy to write; rather, we're going to make this as realistic and relatable as possible. We will run into problems along the way, and we will work through them as a real scenario. As shown in Figure 4-1, EDA runs through four main phases: collection, cleansing, analysis, and modeling. Let's break down each phase briefly before we dive deeper into our scenario.

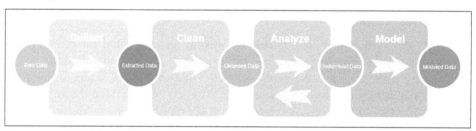

Figure 4-1. Workflow for exploratory data analysis

The Four Phases of EDA

In the *Collect Data* phase, we start with our source system's data. It's important to understand how the source system records data. If, for example, we don't know what purchase requisitions look like in SAP tables, we can't pull them out for later analysis.

Once we've understood the source data, we choose the methods and tools to get it out and examine it. In this chapter, we use a flat-file extraction from SAP as an intermediate storage, and the R data analysis language as the method to process and play with the data. In EDA that focuses on business scenarios it's important to iterate on hypotheses quickly. Therefore, choose tools that you are comfortable and familiar with.

If you're not familiar with any tools yet, fear not! Many options exist for extracting and analyzing. Chapter 3 discusses several alternative SAP data extraction methods and later chapters of this book use many of them. The R language is a favorite among statisticians and data scientists, but Python also has a very strong community. In this book we'll use examples and tools from both languages.

After successfully extracting the data, we enter the *Clean Data* phase. The source system's database, data maintenance rules, and the method we choose to extract can all leave their own unique marks on the data. For example, as we'll see sometimes a CSV extract can have extra unwanted header rows. Sometimes an API extraction can format numbers in a way incompatible with the analysis tool. It can—and often does—happen that when we extract years' worth of data the source system's own internal rules for governing data has changed.

When we clean the data right after extracting, we're looking for the things that are obviously wrong or inconsistent. In this chapter we use R methods to clean the data whereas you may feel more comfortable in another language. Whatever your approach, our goal for this phase is having the data stripped of obviously bad things.

Having met the goal of removing those bad things, it's time to proceed to the *Analysis* phase. This is where we begin to set up hypotheses and explore questions. Since the data is in a state we can trust after cleansing, we can visualize relationships and decide which ones are the strongest and most deserving of further modeling.

In this phase, we will often find ourselves reshaping and reformatting the data. It's a form of cleansing the data that is not focused on removing bad (or badly formatted) data; rather, it's focused on taking good data and shaping it so that it can effectively be used in the next phase. The Analysis phase often presents several opportunities for this further reshaping.

The final phase is *Modeling*. By this phase, we've discovered several relationships within the data that are worth pursuing. Our goal here: create a model that allows us to draw insightful conclusions or make evidence-supported predictions. The model ought to be reliable and repeatable. By modeling this purchasing scenario, the SAP team seeks to arm Pat the purchasing manager with information and tools that have an insightful impact on his business processes.

Greg and Paul know this process well, so let's get started!

Phase 1: Collecting Our Data

An easy way to get data out of SAP is by using the ABAP QuickViewer. This transaction allows the user to view fields of a table or a collection of tables joined together. For the purchase requisition to purchase order scenario we need two tables: EBAN for purchase requisitions and EKPO for purchase order lines. Use transaction code SQVI to start the QuickViewer transaction.

Enter a name for the QuickView (Figure 4-2).

Figure 4-2. QuickView first screen

Click on the Create button and give the QuickView a title (Figure 4-3).

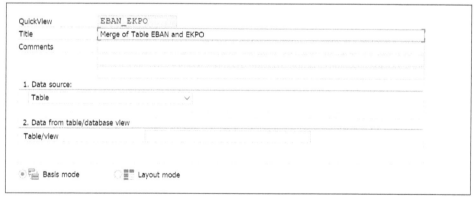

Figure 4-3. QuickView title

Change the "Data source" to "Table join" (Figure 4-4).

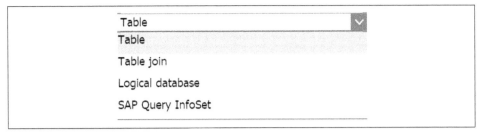

Figure 4-4. QuickView type options

Click on the Enter button, then click on the Insert Table button (indicated in Figure 4-5).

Figure 4-5. QuickView Insert Table button

Enter the name of the first table and click Enter (Figure 4-6).

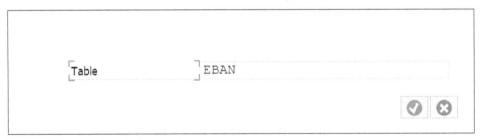

Figure 4-6. First QuickView Table

Repeat the process, click on the Insert Table button, and then click Enter (Figure 4-7).

Figure 4-7. Second Quick View Table

The tables will be displayed on the screen with their default relationships determined (Figure 4-8). Always check these relationships to make sure they are what is wanted. In this case, four relationships were determined but only two are needed.

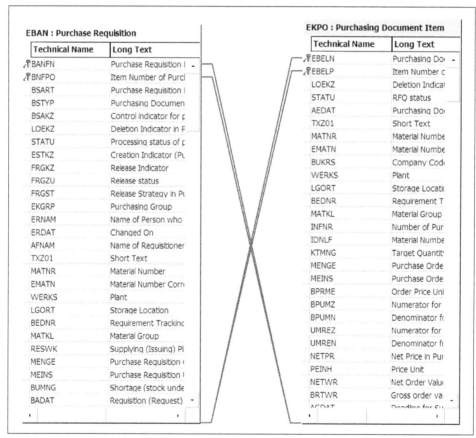

Figure 4-8. QuickView default join properties

Right-click on the links for BANFN and BNFPO and select Delete Link (Figure 4-9).

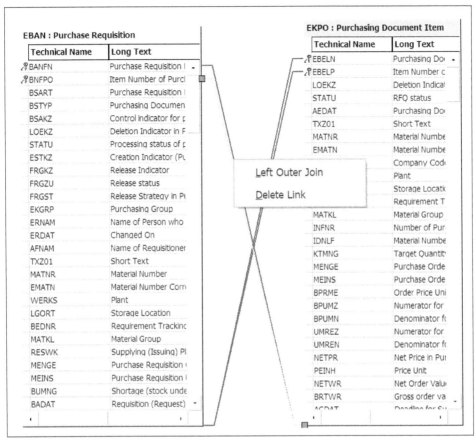

Figure 4-9. Removing a default join in a QuickView

Double-check the remaining two relationships to make sure they are correct. Tables EBAN and EKPO should be linked by EBELN and EBELP (Figure 4-10); these are the purchase order number and the purchase order item.

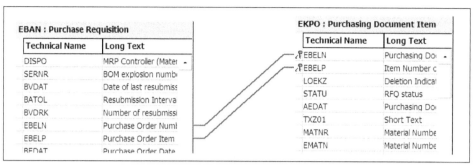

Figure 4-10. Confirming remaining joins in a QuickView

Click on the Back button. The next screen allows for the selection of fields for the report. Open the caret on the left to show all the fields for a table (Figure 4-11).

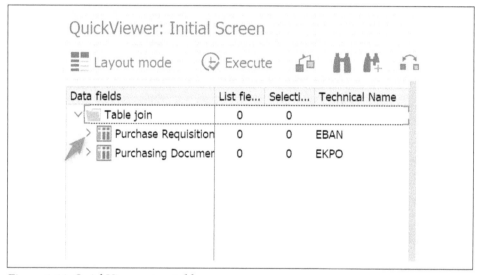

Figure 4-11. QuickViewer open table

Select the fields to be seen in the first column and the selection parameters for the table in the second column (Figure 4-12). Choosing fields as selection parameters enables those fields for filtering the overall results.

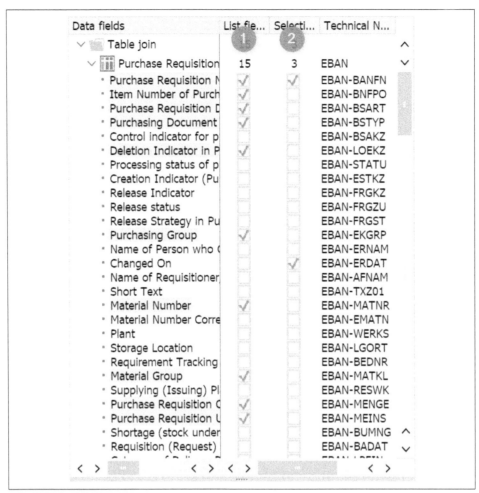

Figure 4-12. Selection and list options for a QuickView

Next, repeat the process for the Purchase Document Item table.

Click on the Execute button to run the report. Because the data may be very large, we made one of the selection criteria the Changed On date. This allows us to narrow the result data. Set the date range and then click on the Execute button. For our example, we will select a small one-month set of data just to see if the results are what we expect. Then we will rerun the report for the full 10 years of data.

Figure 4-13. QuickView test report

The report is displayed with the fields selected (Figure 4-14).

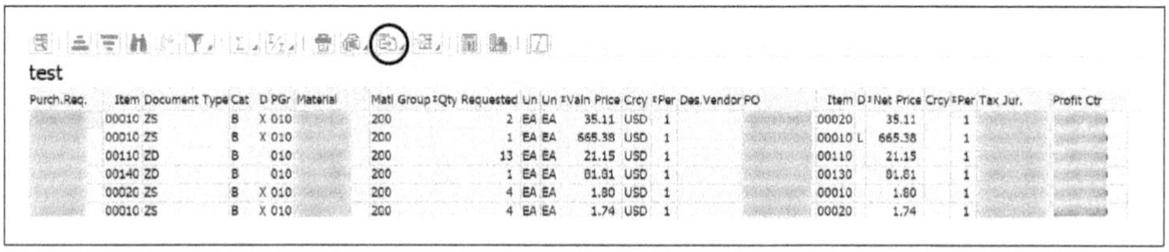

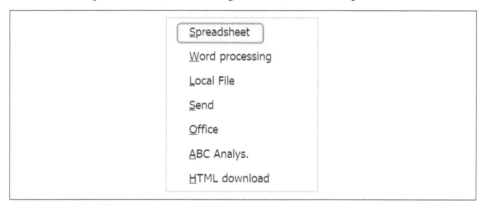

Figure 4-14. QuickView ALV (ABAP List Viewer) report

Click on the Export button (circled in Figure 4-14) and select Spreadsheet.

Spreadsheet

Word processing

Local File

Send

Office

ABC Analys.

HTML download

Figure 4-15. QuickView export options

Accept the default setting for Excel and click Enter (Figure 4-16).

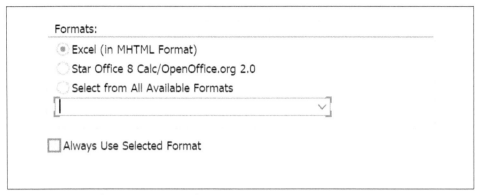

Figure 4-16. QuickView export to xlsx

Format options here will depend on the SAP version, so the screen may look slightly different. Whatever other formats are visible, make sure to choose Excel.

Name the file and save it (Figure 4-17).

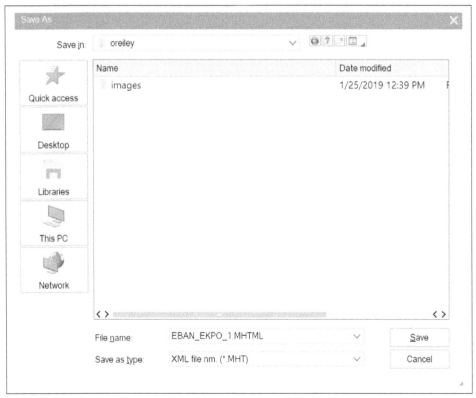

Figure 4-17. QuickView Save As dialog box

Excel will open automatically. Save it as a CSV file so it can easily be loaded into R or Python.

Importing with R

If you have not yet done anything with R or R Studio,[1] there are many excellent resources online with step-by-step installation guides. It is no more difficult than installing any other software on your computer. While this book is not intended to be a tutorial in R, we will cover a few of the basics to get you started. Once you have installed R Studio, double-click on the icon in Figure 4-18 to start it.

Figure 4-18. R Studio icon

One of the basic concepts in R is the use of packages. These are collections of functions, data, and compiled code in a well-defined format. They make coding much easier and consistent. You will need to install the necessary packages in order to use them. One of our favorites is tidyverse (*https://www.tidyverse.org/*). There are two ways to install this package. You can do it from the console window in R Studio using the install.packages() function as shown in Figure 4-19. Simply hit Enter, and it will download and install the package for you.

```
Console   Terminal
~/

Using the Intel MKL for parallel mathematical computing (using 4 cores).

Default CRAN mirror snapshot taken on 2018-04-01.
See: https://mran.microsoft.com/.

[Workspace loaded from ~/.RData]

> install.packages("tidyverse")
```

Figure 4-19. Install packages from the console window

The other method of installation is from the menu path Tools → Install Packages as shown in Figure 4-20.

---

1 For instructions on how to install R Studio and R, go to *https://www.rstudio.com/products/rstudio/download/*.

Figure 4-20. Install packages from the menu path

Start typing the package name in the Packages line and then select it from the options, as in Figure 4-21.

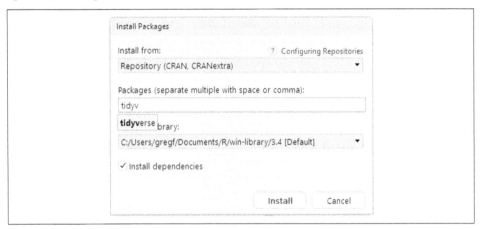

Figure 4-21. Select package from the drop-down options

Finish by clicking on the Install button.

Now that you've installed one package, let's start a new script. Click on the New button and select R Script from the drop-down menu, as in Figure 4-22.

Figure 4-22. Starting a new R Studio script

Now you will have a blank canvas from which to start your data exploration using the R programming language.

Now, let's get started. It is easy to import data into R or R Studio using the read.csv() function. We read the file with the following settings: header is set to TRUE because we have a header on the file. We do not want the strings set to factors so stringsAsFactors is set to FALSE.

It often makes sense to set your strings to factors. Factors represent categorical data and can be ordered or unordered. If you plan on manipulating or formatting your data after loading it, most often you will not want them as factors. You can always convert your categorical variables to factors later using the factor() function.

Finally, we want any empty lines or single blank spaces set to NA:

```
pr <- read.csv("D:/DataScience/Data/prtopo.csv",
          header=TRUE,
          stringsAsFactors = FALSE,
          na.strings=c("", " ","NA"))
```

Once the data has loaded we can view a snippet of the file using the head command, as shown in Figures 4-23 and 4-24.

```
head(pr)
```

```
> head(pr)
  X.2    X Purch.Req.   Item Document.Type Cat    D PGr Material Matl.Group Qty.Requested Un Un.1 Valn.Price
1   1 <NA>   10000051  00010 ZD             B  <NA> 030 75025637 200                    1 EA  EA       50.00
2   2 <NA>   10000013  00010 ZD             B  <NA> 010 75024180 100                   12 EA  EA        4.59
3   3 <NA>   10000007  00010 ZD             B  <NA> 030 75005776 200                    1 EA  EA      115.56
4   4 <NA>   10000007  00020 ZD             B  <NA> 030 75005713 200                    1 EA  EA       40.85
5   5 <NA>   10000007  00030 ZD             B  <NA> 030 75005722 200                    1 EA  EA       94.70
6   6 <NA>   10000132  00470 NB             B  <NA> 010 75038005 1000                   1 EA  EA       55.74
> |
```

Figure 4-23. Viewing header dataframe in R

```
Crcy Per Des.Vendor          PO Item.1 D.1    Net.Price Crcy.1 Per.1  Tax.Jur. Profit.Ctr X.1
USD  1              4500000213 00010 <NA>         50.00           1 1509706701 11004450    NA
USD  1              4500000214 00010 <NA>                         1 1509706701 11004450    NA
USD  1              4500000215 00010 <NA>        115.56           1 1509706701 11004450    NA
USD  1              4500000215 00020 <NA>         40.85           1 1509706701 11004450    NA
USD  1              4500000215 00030 <NA>         94.69           1 1509706701 11004450    NA
USD  1              4500000445 00020 <NA>         55.73           1 1509706701 11004450    NA
```

Figure 4-24. Viewing header dataframe in R continued

We can quickly see that some cleanup is in order. The row numbers came in as columns and some formatting problems created some arbitrary columns such as X and X.1. Cleaning them up is our first task.

Phase 2: Cleaning Our Data

Our goal in this phase is to remove or correct the obvious errors within the extraction. By taking the time to clean the data now, we greatly improve the effectiveness of our analysis and modeling steps. Greg and Paul know that cleaning can take up a major portion of the EDA time so they hunker down with R Studio at the ready.

Null Removal

First, we remove all rows where there is no purchase requisition number. This is erroneous data. There may not actually be any rows to remove, but this is a good standard process. Making sure that the key features of the data actually have entries is a good start:

```
pr <- pr[!(is.na(pr$Purch.Req.)), ]
```

Binary Indicators

Next, the D and the D.1 columns are our deletion or rejection indicators for the purchase requisition. Making that a binary will be a true or false indicator. We can easily do that by making blanks equal to 0 (false) and any other entry equal to 1 (true). Why use a binary and not just put in text as "Rejected" or "Not Rejected"? Keep in mind that you will be visualizing and perhaps modeling this data. Models and visualizations do not do well with categorical variables or text. However, visualizing and modeling 0 and 1 is easy:

```
pr = within(pr, {
  deletion = ifelse(is.na(D) & is.na(D.1), 0, 1)
})
```

Removing Extraneous Columns

Let's get rid of the worthless and erroneous columns. Why do this? Why not simply ignore those columns? Keeping the data free of extra columns frees up memory for processing. In our current example, this is not truly necessary. However, later if we build a neural network we want to be as efficient as possible. It is simply good practice to have clean and tidy[2] data. We create a list of column names and assign them to the "drops"variable. Then we create a new dataframe that is old dataframe with the "drops" excluded:

```
drops <- c("X.2","X", "Un.1", "Crcy.1", "Per.1", "X.1",
           "Purch.Req.", "Item", "PO", "Item.1", "D", "D.1",
           "Per", "Crcy")
pr <- pr[ , !(names(pr) %in% drops)]
```

There are many different types of data structures in R. A dataframe is a table in which each column represents a variable and each row contains values for each column, much like a table in Excel.

Whitespace

A common problem when working with data is whitespace. Whitespace can cause lookup and merge problems later. For instance, you want to merge two dataframes by the column *customer*. One data frame column has "Smith DrugStore" and the other has " Smith DrugStore". Notice the spaces before and after the name in the second dataframe? R will not think that these two customers are the same. These spaces or blanks in the data look like legitimate entries to the program. It is a good idea to remove whitespace and other "invisible" elements early. We can clean that up easily for all columns in the dataframe with the following code:

```
pr <- data.frame(lapply(pr, trimws), stringsAsFactors = FALSE)
```

What is that `lapply()` function doing? Read up on these useful functions (*http://bit.ly/2khPSHb*) to get more out of your R code.

---

2 We have referenced this before, but we'll link to it again (it is that good): *https://vita.had.co.nz/papers/tidy-data.pdf*.

Numbers

Next, we modify the columns that are numeric or integer to have that characteristic. If your column has a numeric value then it should not be stored as a character. This can happen during the loading of data. Simply put, a value of 1 does not equal the value of "1". Making sure the columns in our dataframe are correctly classified with the right type is another one of the key cleaning steps that will solve potential problems later:

```
pr$deletion <- as.integer(pr$deletion)
pr$Qty.Requested <- as.numeric(pr$Qty.Requested)
pr$Valn.Price <- as.numeric(pr$Valn.Price)
pr$Net.Price <- as.numeric(pr$Net.Price)
```

Next, we replace NA values with zeros in the numeric values we just created. NA simply means the value is not present. R will not assume discrete variables such as quantity will have a value of zero if the value is not present. In our circumstance, however, we want the NAs to have a value of zero:

```
pr[,c("Qty.Requested", "Valn.Price", "Net.Price")] <-
    apply(pr[,c("Qty.Requested", "Valn.Price", "Net.Price")], 2,
        function(x){replace(x, is.na(x), 0)})
```

Finally, we clean up those categorical variables by replacing any blanks with NA. This will come in handy later when looking for missing values...blanks can sometimes look like values in categorical variables, therefore NA is more reliable. We already treated whitespace earlier, but this is another good practice step that will help us to avoid problems later:

```
pr <- pr %>% mutate(Des.Vendor = na_if(Des.Vendor, ""),
                    Un = na_if(Un, ""),
                    Material = na_if(Material, ""),
                    PGr = na_if(PGr, ""),
                    Cat = na_if(Cat, ""),
                    Document.Type = na_if(Document.Type, ""),
                    Tax.Jur. = na_if(Tax.Jur., ""),
                    Profit.Ctr = na_if(Profit.Ctr, ""))
```

Phase 3: Analyzing Our Data

We've cleaned up the data and are now entering the analysis phase. We'll recall two key goals of this phase: asking deeper questions to form hypotheses, and shaping and formatting the data appropriately for the Modeling phase. Greg and Paul's cleanup process left them with data in a great position to continue into the Analysis phase.

DataExplorer

Let's cheat and take some shortcuts. That is part of the glory of all the libraries that R has to offer. Some very quick and easy data exploration can be done using the Data Explorer library.[3]

Install and include the library using the following R commands:

```
install.packages("DataExplorer")
library(DataExplorer)
```

Perform a quick visualization of the overall structure of the data (Figure 4-25):

```
plot_str(pr)
```

Figure 4-25. Viewing overall structure of data using DataExplorer

---

3 Dive deep into DataExplorer using the vignette available at *https://cran.r-project.org/web/packages/Data Explorer/vignettes/dataexplorer-intro.html.*

We can use the `introduce` command from the `DataExplorer` package to get an overview of our data:

```
introduce(pr)
      rows columns discrete_columns continuous_columns
   3361850      13                9                  4
   all_missing_columns total_missing_values complete_rows
                     0                    0      3361850
   total_observations memory_usage
             43704050    351294072
```

We see that we have over three million rows of data with thirteen columns. Nine of them are discrete and four of them are continuous.

It is important to see if any of the columns are missing a lot of data. In general, columns that are largely empty (over 90%) don't have any value in modeling (Figure 4-26):

```
plot_missing(pr)
```

Because of the large number of missing entries for the `Des.Vendor` field we will remove it:

```
pr$Des.Vendor = NULL
```

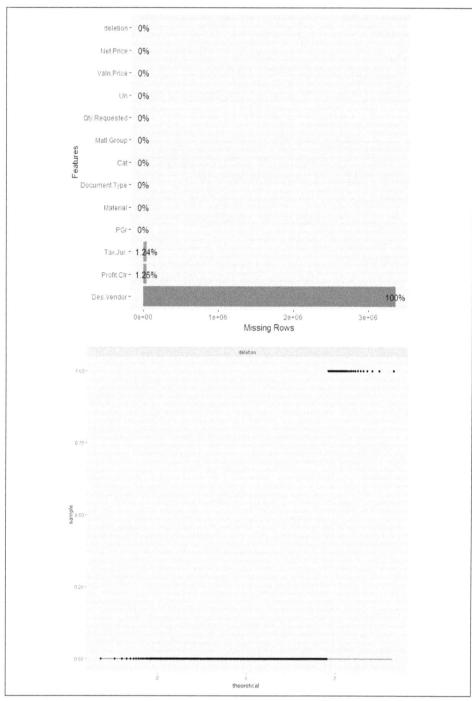

Figure 4-26. Identifying missing or near missing variables with DataExplorer

Discrete Features

Understanding the discrete features[4] helps in selecting data that will improve model performance, and removing data that does not. We can plot the distribution of all discrete features quite easily (Figures 4-27 through 4-29):

```
plot_bar(pr)
```

 Discrete variables with more than 50 entries are excluded.

What we notice right away is that there is a mysterious and obvious erroneous entry. In the distribution for Document Type there is a document type called…"Document Type." Same with all the other discrete features. Let's find out where that line is and take a look at it:

```
pr[which(pr$Document.Type == "Document Type"),]
count(pr[which(pr$Document.Type == "Document Type"),])
```

What we see is a list and count of 49 entries where the document type is "Document Type" and all other columns have the description of the column and not a valid value. It is likely that the extraction from SAP had breaks at certain intervals where there were header rows. It is easy to remove:

```
pr <- pr[which(pr$Document.Type != "Document Type"),]
```

---

4 Remember from Chapter 2 that discrete or categorical features are features with definable boundaries. Think *categories* such as colors or types of dogs.

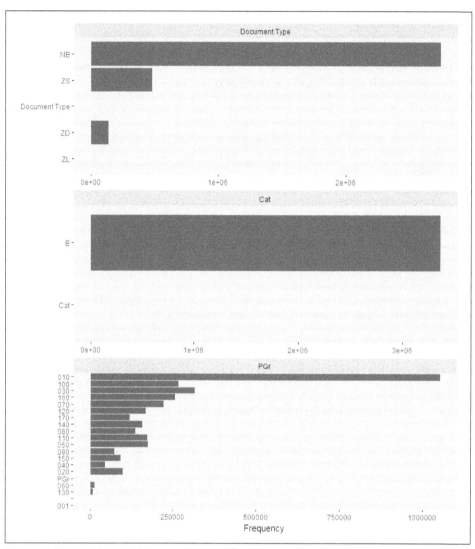

Figure 4-27. Bar charts of discrete features (part I)

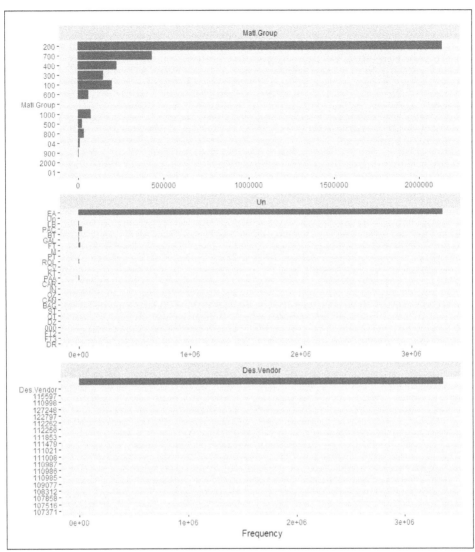

Figure 4-28. Bar charts of discrete features (part II)

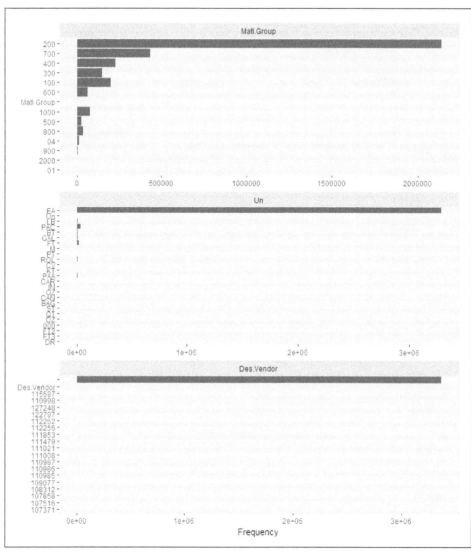

Figure 4-29. Bar charts of discrete features (part III)

When we run `plot_bar(pr)` again we see that these bad rows have been removed.

We also noticed that some of the variables were not plotted. This is because they had more than 50 unique values. If a discrete variable has too many unique values it will be difficult to code for in the model. We can use this bit of code to see the count of unique values in the variable `Material`:

```
length(unique(pr$Material))
```

Wow, we find that we have more than 500,000 unique values. Let's think about this. Will the material itself make a good feature for the model? We also have a variable `Matl.Group`, which represents the grouping into which the material belongs. This could be office supplies, IT infrastructure, raw materials, or something similar. This categorization is more meaningful to us than an exact material number. So we'll remove those material number values as well:

```
pr$Material = NULL
```

We also notice from this bar plot that the variable `Cat` only has one unique value. This variable will have no value in determining the approval or disapproval of a purchase requisition. We'll delete that variable as well:

```
pr$Cat = NULL
```

Continuous Features

Next we want to get to know our numeric/continuous variables, such as Net.Price. Do our continuous variables have a normal bell-shaped distribution? This is helpful in modeling, because machine learning and neural networks prefer distributions that are not skewed left or right. Our suspicions are that the continuous variables are all right skewed. There will be more purchase requisition requests for one or two items than 20 or 30. Let's see if that suspicion is correct.

 Nature loves a uniform/Gaussian distribution. School grades, rainfall over a number of years or by country, and individual heights and weights all follow a Gaussian distribution. Machine learning and neural networks prefer these distributions. If your data is not Gaussian, it is a good choice to log transform, scale, or normalize the data.

We can see a distribution of the data with a simple histogram plot. Using the `Data Explorer` package in R makes it easy to plot a histogram of all continuous variables at once (Figure 4-30):

```
plot_histogram(pr)
```

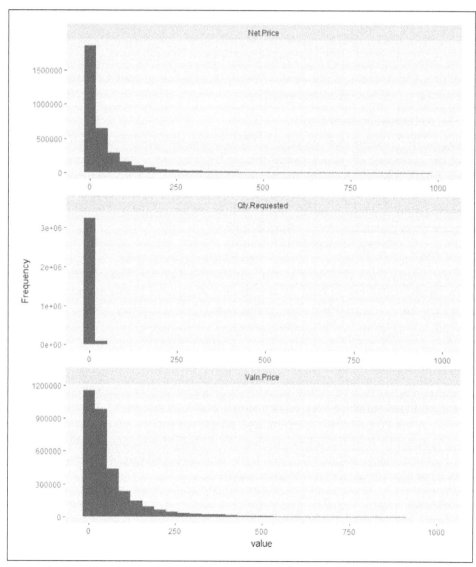

Figure 4-30. Histograms of continuous features

We are only concerned with the histograms for Qty.Requested, Valn.Price, and Net.Price. The deletion column we know is just a binary we created where 1 means the item was rejected (deleted) and 0 means it was not. We quickly see that all histograms are right skewed as we suspected. They have a tail running off to the right. It is important to know this as we may need to perform some standardization or normalization before modeling the data.

Normalization reduces the scale of the data to be in a range from 0 to 1:

$X_{normalized} = X-X_{min} / (X_{max}-X_{min})$

Standardization reduces the scale of the data to have a mean(μ) of 0 and a standard deviation(σ) of 1:

$X_{standardized} = X-\mu / \sigma$

Another test is the QQ plot (quantile-quantile). This will also show us if our continuous variables have a normal distribution. We know that the distributions were not normally distributed by the histograms. The QQ plot here is for illustration purposes.

A QQ plot will display a diagonal straight line if it is normally distributed. In our observations we can quickly see that these variables are not normally distributed. The QQ plot in DataExplorer (see Figure 4-31 for interesting continuous features, and Figure 4-32 for the deletion flag) by default compares the data to a normal distribution:

```
plot_qq(pr, sample=1000L)
```

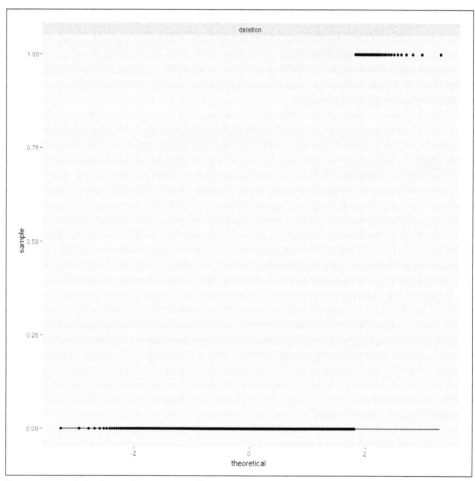

Figure 4-31. QQ plots of continuous features

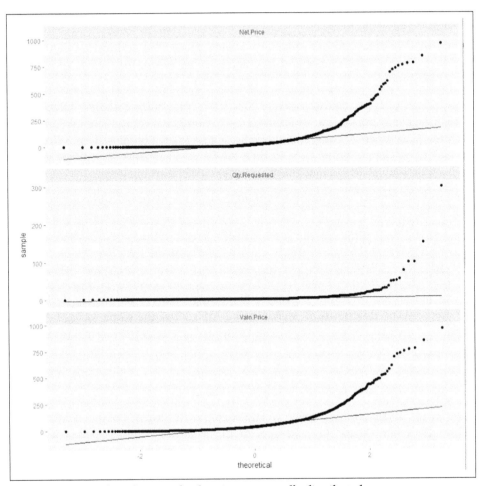

Figure 4-32. QQ plots showing the data is not normally distributed

Phase 4: Modeling Our Data

Now that we've familiarized ourselves with the data, it's time to shape and feed it into a neural network to check whether it can learn if a purchase requisition is approved or rejected. We will be using TensorFlow and Keras in R to do this. Greg and Paul know that the Modeling phase is where value actually gets extracted—if they approach modeling correctly, they know they'll glean valuable insight unlocked by following through on the Collect, Clean, and Analyze phases.

TensorFlow and Keras

Before we dive deep into our model, we should pause a bit and discuss TensorFlow and Keras. In the data science and machine learning world, they're two of the most widely used tools.

TensorFlow is an open source software library that, especially since its 1.0.0 release in 2017, has quickly grown into widespread use in numerical computation. While high-performance numerical computation applies across many domains, TensorFlow grew up inside the Google Brain team in their AI focus. That kind of pedigree gives its design high adaptability to machine learning and deep learning tasks.

Even though TensorFlow's hardest-working code is highly tuned and compiled C++, it provides a great Python and R API for easy consumption. You can program directly using TensorFlow (*http://bit.ly/2mfiwsY*) or use Keras. Keras is a higher level API for TensorFlow that is user-friendly, modular, and easy to extend. You can use Tensor-Flow and Keras on Windows, macOS, Linux, and Android/iOS. The coolest piece of the TensorFlow universe is that Google has even created custom hardware to super-charge TensorFlow performance. Tensor Processing Units (TPUs) were at the heart of the most advanced versions of AlphaGo and AlphaZero, the game-focused AIs that conquered the game of Go—long thought to be decades away from machine mastery.

Core TensorFlow is great for setting up powerful computation in complex data science scenarios. But it's often helpful for data scientists to model their work at a higher level and abstract away some of the lower-level details.

Enter Keras. It's extensible enough to run on top of several of the major lower-level ML toolkits, like TensorFlow, Theano, or the Microsoft Cognitive Toolkit. Keras' design focuses on Pythonic and R user-friendliness in quickly setting up and experimenting on deep neural network models. And as data scientists, we know that quick experiments provide the best results—they allow you to fail fast and move toward being more correct!

Quick pause over. Let's dive back into the scenario. We will be using TensorFlow and Keras in a bit, but first we'll use basic R programming.

Training and Testing Split

The first step of the process is to split the data into training and testing sets. This is easy with the library *rsample* (*http://bit.ly/2mk4iHr*).

```
tt_split <- initial_split(pr, prop=0.85)
trn <- training(tt_split)
tst <- testing(tt_split)
```

Looking in the global environments of R Studio shows there are two new dataframes: TRN for training and TST for testing (Figure 4-33).

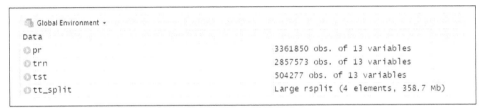

Figure 4-33. View of the training and testing dataframes

Shaping and One-Hot Encoding

We are still in the process of shaping our data for TensorFlow and Keras. We continue with basic R programming in the next steps. The next steps are to shape the data such that it will work well with a neural network. Neural networks, in general, work best on data that is normally distributed. The data that we are feeding into our network needs to be nominal: we can't feed the categorical variables we find in our purchase requisition data into the model. The network wouldn't know what to do with something such as "Material Group." We will convert our categorical data to sparse data using a process called *one-hot encoding*.[5] For instance, the result of a one-hot encoding for the Matl.Group column would look like Figure 4-34.

01	1	0	0	0	0	0	0	0	0	0	0	0
04	0	1	0	0	0	0	0	0	0	0	0	0
200	0	0	1	0	0	0	0	0	0	0	0	0
300	0	0	0	1	0	0	0	0	0	0	0	0
400	0	0	0	0	1	0	0	0	0	0	0	0
500	0	0	0	0	0	1	0	0	0	0	0	0
600	0	0	0	0	0	0	1	0	0	0	0	0
700	0	0	0	0	0	0	0	1	0	0	0	0
800	0	0	0	0	0	0	0	0	1	0	0	0
900	0	0	0	0	0	0	0	0	0	1	0	0
1000	0	0	0	0	0	0	0	0	0	0	1	0
2000	0	0	0	0	0	0	0	0	0	0	0	1

Figure 4-34. Visualization of one-hot encoding

We know that we want to one-hot encode our categorical variables, but what do we want to do with the others, if anything? Consider the Qty.Requested column, and the number of options on a purchase requisition for quantity requested. A purchase requisition for a new vehicle would likely not be more than one. However, the quantity requested for batches of raw materials might be a thousand pounds. This makes us curious, what is the range of values in the Qty.Requested column? We can see that easily with these commands:

---

5 Sometimes called creating "dummy variables."

```
max(pr$Qty.Requested)
min(pr$Qty.Requested)
```

We see that the values range from 0 to 986. What? Quantities of zero? How many of them are there?

```
count(pr[which(pr1$Qty.Requested == 0),])
```

We see that there are 313 rows with a quantity of 0! What could this mean? We are confused about this data, so do we throw it out? Data science is not a vacuum, as much as us coders would like it to be. We have to return to the business with a couple examples of purchase requisitions with quantities of zero and ask them if they know why. If they don't, then we'll toss the rows with zero quantities.

We learned something through this process. When Pat is asked about these strange requisitions he says, "Sometimes when I'm not at my computer and someone calls about a purchase requisition that I reject, they zero out the quantity because they don't have authority to reject the line." In essence, zero quantity purchase requisitions are rejected purchase requisitions. We have to convert the deletion indicator on these to 1 to indicate they are rejected:

```
pr = within(pr, {
    deletion = ifelse(Qty.Requested == 0, 1 ,0)
})
```

Now that we've properly dealt with zero quantity purchase requisitions we return to the task at hand. The model will not perform optimally on individual variables from 0 to a thousand. Bucketing these order quantities into groups will allow the model to perform better. We will create three buckets of values. We've chosen this value rather arbitrarily and can change it later as we test the performance of our model.

Recipes

We've decided to one-hot encode our categorical variables and scale and bucket our numeric ones. To do this we will use the recipes (*http://bit.ly/2NHJ9SY*) library in R. This very convenient library allows us to create "recipes" for our data transformation.

The *recipes* concept is intuitive: define a recipe that can be used later to apply encodings and processing. The final result can then be applied to machine learning or neural networks.

We've already decided what we want to do with our data to prepare it for a network. Let's go through the code from the recipes package that will make that happen.

First we want to create a recipe object that defines what we are analyzing. In this code we say we want to predict the deletion indicator based on the other features in our data:

```
library(recipes)
recipe_object <- recipe(deletion ~ Document.Type +
                PGr +
                Matl.Group +
                Qty.Requested +
                Un +
                Valn.Price +
                Tax.Jur. +
                Profit.Ctr,
                data = trn)
#We could also just use the . like this to indicate all, but the above is done
#for clarity. recipe_object <- recipe(deletion ~ ., data = trn)
```

 If you run into memory errors such as "Error: cannot allocate vector of size x.x Gb" you can increase the memory allowed by using the following command (the first two numbers indicate how many gigs you are allocating; in this case, it's 12):

```
memory.limit(1210241024*1024)
```

Our next step is to take that `recipe` object and apply some ingredients to it. We already stated that we want to put our quantity and price values into three bins. We use the `step_discretize` function from `recipes` to do that:

 Some modelers prefer binning and some prefer keeping continuous variables continuous. We bin here to improve performance of our model later.

```
recipe_object <- recipe_object %>%
    step_discretize(Qty.Requested, options = list(cuts = 3)) %>%
    step_discretize(Valn.Price, options = list(cuts = 3))
```

We wanted to also one-hot encode all of our categorical variables. We could list them out one at a time, or we could use one of the many selectors that come with the `rec ipes` package. We use the `step_dummy` function to perform the encoding and the `all_nominal` selector to select all of our categorical variables:

```
recipe_object <- recipe_object %>%
    step_dummy(all_nominal())
```

Then we need to scale and center all the values. As mentioned earlier, our data is not Gaussian (normally distributed) and therefore some sort of scaling is in order:

```
rec_obj <- rec_obj %>%
    step_center(all_predictors()) %>%
    step_scale(all_predictors())
```

There are many normalization methods; in our example, we use min-max feature scaling and standard score.

Notice so far that we've not done anything with the recipe. Now we need to prepare the data and apply the recipe to it using the `prep` command:

```
recipe_trained <- prep( recipe_object, training = trn, retain = TRUE)
```

Now we can apply the recipe to any dataset we have. We will start with our training set and also put in a command to exclude the deletion indicator:

```
x <- bake(rec_obj, new_data = trn) %>% select(-deletion)
```

Preparing Data for the Neural Network

Now that we are done with our recipe, we need to prepare the data for the neural network.

Our favorite (and commonly excepted best) technique is to *not* jump directly into a neural network model. It is best to grow from least to most complex models, set a performance bar, and then try to beat it with ever more increasingly complex models. For instance, we should first try a simple linear regression. Because we are trying to classify approved and not-approved purchase requisitions we may then try classification machine learning techniques such as a support vector machine (*http://bit.ly/2Zzy7FX*) (SVM) and/or a random forest (*http://bit.ly/2ZDrK4u*). Finally, we may come to a neural network. However, for teaching purposes we will go directly to the neural network. There was no a priori knowledge that led to this decision; it is just a teaching example.

First we want to create a vector of the deletion values:

```
training_vector <- pull(trn, deletion)
```

If this is your first time using TensorFlow and Keras you will need to install it. It is a little different than regular libraries so we'll cover the steps here. First you install the package like you would any other package using the following command:

```
install.packages("tensorflow")
```

Then, to use TensorFlow you need an additional function call after the library declaration:

```
library(tensorflow)
install_tensorflow()
```

Finally, it is good process to check and make sure it is working with the common print hello lines below. If you get the "Hello, TensorFlow!"" statement, it's working:

```
sess = tf$Session()
hello <- tf$constant('Hello, TensorFlow!')
sess$run(hello)
```

Keras installs like any other R library. Let's create our model in Keras. The first step is to initialize the model, which we will do using the keras_model_sequential() function:

```
k_model <- keras_model_sequential()
```

Models consist of layers. The next step is to create those layers.

Our first layer is an input layer. Input layers require the shape of the input. Subsequent layers infer the shape from the first input layer. In our case this is simple, the input shape is the number of columns in our training set *ncol(x_trn)*. We will set the number of units to 18. There are two key decisions to play with while testing your neural network. These are the number of units per layer and the number of layers.

Our next layer is a hidden layer with the same number of inputs. Notice that it is the same as the previous layer but we did not have to specify the shape.

Our third layer is a dropout layer set to 10%. That is, randomly 10% of the neurons in this layer will be *dropped*.

 Dropout layers control overfitting, which is when a model in a sense has memorized the training data. When this happens, the model does not do well on data it has not seen...kind of defeating the purpose of a neural network. Dropout is used during the training phase and essentially randomly drops out a set of neurons.

Our final layer is the output layer. The number of units is 1 because the result is mutually exclusive. That is, either the purchase requisition is approved or it is not.

Finally, we will compile the model or *build* it. We need to set three basic compilation settings:

Optimizer
The technique by which the weights of the model are adjusted. A very common starting point is the Adam optimizer.

Initializer
The way that the model sets the initial random weights of the layers (*https://keras.io/initializers/*). There are many options; a common starting point is uniform.

Activation

Refer to Chapter 2 for a description of activation functions. Keras has a number of easily available activation functions (*https://keras.io/activations/*).

```r
k_model %>%
  #First hidden layer with 18 units, a uniform kernel initializer,
  #the relu activation function, and a shape equal to
  #our "baked" recipe object.
  layer_dense(
    units = 18,
    kernel_initializer = "uniform",
    activation = "relu",
    input_shape = ncol(x_trn)) %>%

  #Second hidden layer - same number of layers with
  #same kernel initializer and activation function.
  layer_dense(
    units = 18,
    kernel_initializer = "uniform",
    activation = "relu") %>%

  #Dropout
layer_dropout(rate = 0.1) %>%

  #Output layer - final layer with one unit and the same initializer
  #and activation. Good to try sigmoid as an activation here.
  layer_dense(
    units = 1,
    kernel_initializer = "uniform",
    activation = "relu") %>%

#Compile - build the model with the adam optimizer. Perhaps the
#most common starting place for the optimizer. Also use the
#loss function of binary crossentropy...again, perhaps the most
#common starting place. Finally, use accuracy as the metric
#for seeing how the model performs.
compile(
  optimizer = "adam",
  loss = "binary_crossentropy",
  metrics = c("accuracy"))
```

Setting the parameters of your neural network is as much an art as it is a science. Play with the number of neurons in the layers, the dropout rate, the loss optimizer, and others. This is where you experiment and tune your network to get more accuracy and lower loss.

To take a look at the model, type **k_model**:

```
Layer (type)                    Output Shape                Param #
=================================================================
dense_2 (Dense)                 (None, 18)                    2646

dropout_1 (Dropout)             (None, 18)                       0

dense_3 (Dense)                 (None, 18)                     342

edropout_2 (Dropout)            (None, 18)                       0

dense_4 (Dense)                 (None, 1)                       19
=================================================================
Total params: 3,007
Trainable params: 3,007
Non-trainable params: 0
```

The final step is to fit the model to the data. We use the data that we *baked* with the recipe, which is the x_trn:

```
history <- fit(
    #fit to the model defined above
  object = k_model,
      #baked recipe
  x = as.matrix(x_trn),
      #include the training_vector of deletion indicators
  y = training_vector,
      #start with a batch size of 100 and vary it to see performance
  batch_size = 100,
      #how many times to run through?
  epochs = 5,
      #no class weights at this time, but something to try
      #class_weight <- list("0" = 1, "1" = 2)
      #class_weight = class_weight,
  validation_split = 0.25)
```

The model displays a log while it is running:

```
Train on 1450709 samples, validate on 483570 samples
Epoch 1/5
1450709/1450709 [==============================]
- 19s 13us/step - loss: 8.4881e-04 - acc: 0.9999 -
val_loss: 0.0053 - val_acc: 0.9997
Epoch 2/5
1450709/1450709 [==============================]
- 20s 14us/step - loss: 8.3528e-04 - acc: 0.9999 -
val_loss: 0.0062 - val_acc: 0.9997
Epoch 3/5
1450709/1450709 [==============================]
- 19s 13us/step - loss: 8.5323e-04 - acc: 0.9999 -
val_loss: 0.0055 - val_acc: 0.9997
Epoch 4/5
1450709/1450709 [==============================]
- 19s 13us/step - loss: 8.3805e-04 - acc: 0.9999 -
val_loss: 0.0054 - val_acc: 0.9997
Epoch 5/5
1450709/1450709 [==============================]
- 19s 13us/step - loss: 8.2265e-04 - acc: 0.9999 -
val_loss: 0.0058 - val_acc: 0.9997
```

Results

What we want from our model is for the accuracy to be high and for it to improve over the number of epochs. However, this is not what we see. Note the second graph in Figure 4-35. We see that the accuracy is very high from the start and never improves. The loss function also does not decrease but stays relatively steady.

This tells us that the model did not learn anything. Or rather, it learned something quickly that made it very accurate and quit learning from that point. We can try a number of tuning options, perhaps different optimizers and loss functions. We can also remodel the neural network to have more or less layers. However, let's think at a higher level for a minute and turn back to the raw data with some questions.

Did we select the right features from SAP from the beginning? Are there any other features that might be helpful?

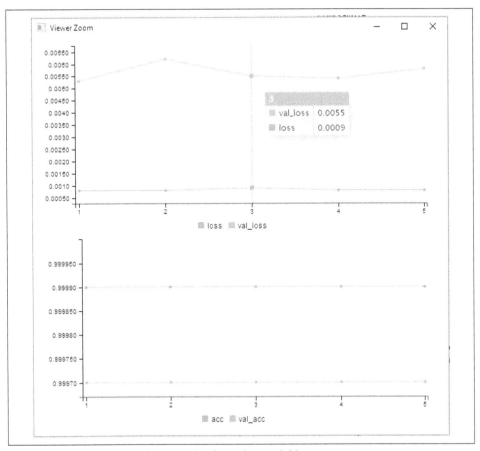

Figure 4-35. Accuracy and loss results from the model learning

Did we make mistakes along the way or did we make assumptions that were incorrect? This requires a review of the process.

Is this data that can be modeled? Not all data is model ready.

After going through these questions we stumble upon this. What if the number of approved purchase requisitions is overwhelming? What if the model just learned to say "Yes" to everything because during training it was nearly always the right answer? If we go back and look at the numbers before any modeling, we see that Pat approves over 99% of all purchase requisitions. We can try different models and different features in our data, but the likely truth to this data exploration saga is that this data cannot be modeled. Or rather it can be modeled, but because of the high number of approvals the model will learn only to approve. It will find it has great accuracy and low loss and therefore on the surface it is a good model.

Summary

Despite the failure to model the purchase requisition data, this example teaches a lot of good lessons. Sometimes data can't be modeled, it just happens...and it happens a lot. A model that has high accuracy and low loss doesn't mean it is a good model. Our model had 99% accuracy, which should raise a suspicious eyebrow from the start. But it was a worthless model; it didn't learn. A common role of a data scientist is to report on findings and to propose next steps. We failed, but we failed fast and can move past it toward the right solution.

It could be argued that Greg and Paul failed Pat. After all, we can't make any good predictions based on the data we found and explored. But just because we didn't find a way to predictively model the scenario doesn't mean we failed. We learned! If data science is *truly* science, it must admit negative results as well as positive. We didn't learn to predict purchase requisition behavior, but we did learn that trying to do so wouldn't be cost effective. We learned that Pat and his colleagues have created solid processes that make the business very disciplined in its purchasing behavior.

In exploratory data analysis, the only failure is failing to learn. The model may not have learned, but the data scientists did. Greg and Paul congratulate themselves with an extra trip to the coffee machine.

In this chapter we have identified a business need, extracted the necessary data from SAP, cleansed the data, explored the data, modeled the data, and drawn conclusions from the results. We discovered that we could not get our model to learn with the current data and surmised this was because the data is highly skewed in favor of approvals. At this point, we are making educated guesses; we could do more.

There are other approaches we could take. For instance, we could augment the data using encoders, which would be beyond the scope of this book. We could weight the variables such that the rejected purchase requisitions have greater value than the accepted ones. In testing this approach, however, the model simply loses all accuracy and fails for an entirely different reason. We could also treat the purchase requisitions that are rejected as anomalies and use a completely different approach. In Chapter 5, we will dig into anomaly detection, which might provide other answers if applied to this data.

We have decided that the final course of action to be taken in our example is not a data approach (much to our chagrin). The business should be informed that because over 99% of all purchase requisitions are approved, the model could not find salient features to determine when a rejection would occur. Without significantly more work, this is likely a dead end. Perhaps there are different IT solutions, such as a phone app that could help Pat do his job more efficiently. The likely solution, however, cannot be found through machine learning and data science.

## CHAPTER 5

Anomaly Detection with R and Python

McKesson Corporation (McKesson), one of the nation's largest distributors of pharmaceutical drugs, agreed to pay a record $150 million civil penalty for alleged violations of the Controlled Substances Act (CSA), the Justice Department announced today.

—Department of Justice, January 17, 2017

Upon reading those headlines, Janine's heart sank. She read the article with rapt attention; this affected her. She worked in the regulatory department at Big Bonanza Warehouse where she was responsible for maintaining corporate compliance. She was aware of Suspicious Order Monitoring Regulations (*http://bit.ly/2lRRCHu*) (21 C.F.R. 1301.74(b)). Lately the Department of Justice was hitting companies left and right for noncompliance with this regulation, much more than they had done in the past. The regulation loosely states that companies that manufacture and distribute controlled substances "know their customers." In the regulation's exact words,

> *It is fundamental for sound operations that handlers take reasonable measures to identify their customers, understand the normal and expected transactions typically conducted by those customers, and, consequently, identify those transactions conducted by their customers that are suspicious in nature.*
>
> —21 C.F.R. 1301.74(b)

But what exactly did this mean? She knew that her company had their sales orders in SAP. There were over 10 years of sales orders. But what did it mean to *understand the normal and expected transactions* of their customers? She decided to take this to the SAP team and discuss with them what, if anything, could be done to protect them from noncompliance and potential fines.

Duane, an analyst on the SAP team, was intrigued by her query. SAP contains/stores sales orders and sales order history, but it doesn't provide ordering patterns or a system to detect when there is an anomaly. The first question: "What is an anomaly?" It's not as simple as saying a customer typically orders 5 of a product one week and then suddenly orders 10. What if they missed a week? What if they had steadily been increasing their supply chain and now 10 was acceptable?

When Duane brought the problem to data scientists Greg and Paul, they immediately smelled an *anomaly detection* issue. Anomaly detection is fundamentally a method of identifying unusual patterns in data that do not conform to what is expected. Most of us have experienced anomaly detection using data science already. When you get that text message or call from your credit card company asking you about a recent transaction, you have experienced anomaly detection. Fraud detection is a sophisticated method of anomaly detection that credit card companies use to prevent loss.

Greg and Paul fired up their program editors, ready to find those anomalies. Duane stuck around, primarily to provide SAP insight to Greg and Paul—but also to check out how they went about doing what they did. Duane felt pretty sure that while he didn't have a PhD in statistics or computer science, he could follow along enough to start to understand.

Types of Anomalies

There are three general types of anomalies:

Point
Anomalies in data identified by a significant outlier. In our ordering pattern example, let's say a customer typically orders 10 of an item per week but one week they order 100. This increase of 10 times their typical order is a simple point anomaly.

Contextual
Anomalies within a condition. Often, this is an analysis within time-series data. Taking sales data as an example, let's say a customer orders many products throughout the year, but they order mittens in July. An order of mittens in December is not an anomaly, but in July it is.

Collective
Anomalies viewed within the context of a set of data. This relates to patterns overall in the data, like an EKG or sine wave. If a customer's ordering pattern breaks out of their typical wave or pattern, this would be anomalous.

Perhaps the simplest method of detecting anomalies is to flag data points as anomalous if they are a certain standard deviation from the mean or median. Sales data is over a time series so a rolling window will have to be taken into consideration. Defining the width of the rolling window would be determined by the business conditions, as each business's situation is a little different. In our case of suspicious order detection, a three-year window would be appropriate. The rolling window (or rolling average) flattens fluctuations over the short term and emphasizes long-term fluctuations.

In our current scenario, we could use a regression and fit the line with a tolerance. Anything that appears outside the tolerance is an anomaly.

However, this is a fairly static approach and for us...not enough. It would not take into consideration any context, such as seasonality. We do not know if there is seasonality in our sales order data; therefore, to be prudent we should at least check for it. We know that our requirement is to *know our customers* so we want to see ordering patterns over time. Simply put, we want to identify collective anomalies.

Tools in R

There are many well-documented techniques for detecting anomalies using static methods (like the ones discussed earlier), machine learning techniques, and neural network models. When considering which technique to use, answer the following questions:

- What type of data is it?

  For our scenario, it is time-series data.

- Is the data labeled?

  We don't have labeled data so we are in an unsupervised learning scenario.[1] If the data is labeled it can be broken into test and training sets and basically turned into a classification problem.

We have a number of tools in the data scientist's toolbox to conduct unsupervised learning with time-series data. We could go all sledgehammer on this and build a recursive neural network using TensorFlow/Keras. That would complicate things greatly and not necessarily (actually unlikely) return us any better results than a couple of R libraries and Python packages built for this very purpose.

In R there are vignettes. These are tutorials for packages and most of the time they are very informative and useful. To see the available vignettes for your packages, type **browseVignettes()** in the console of your R tool. To see a detailed tutorial on dplyr, for instance, type **browseVignettes("dplyr")**. In this case there are multiple tutorials for this essential package in R.

AnomalyDetection

This is a package that has been open sourced by Twitter. It is built to detect anomalies in time-series data...just what we are looking to do. It is based on a seasonal extreme

---

1 See Chapter 2 for a refresher on supervised and unsupervised learning.

studentized deviate (ESD), which in turn is based on the generalized ESD. The generalized ESD is a test to detect anomalies in univariate data that is approximately normally distributed. The advantage of the generalized ESD is that it does not require the number of outliers to be specified, just that there is an upper bound for the suspected number.

Given this upper bound, let's say u, the package essentially performs u number of tests, first a test for one anomaly, then two, and so on up to u anomalies.[2]

Anomalize

The `anomalize package` is yet another testament to the functionality and power of programming languages like R and Python. There is wonderful documentation (*http://bit.ly/2mkWhlB*) on this package on CRAN.

This package is designed to detect all types of anomalies: point, contextual, and collective. It is a scalable adaptation of the Twitter `AnomalyDetection` package developed by *Business Science*.[3] It is a time-series based anomaly detection package that is scalable from one to many time series.

We understand the scenario and the data needed from SAP. We have also identified some useful libraries in R for the detecting anomalies. Our mission is defined by the Justice Department. We need to understand our customers and their ordering patterns. Namely, we want to know when there are anomalies. The steps that follow will walk through the process of taking our SAP order data and turning it into a report of anomalies.

Getting the Data

There are many ways to get data out of SAP. For our anomaly detection scenario we could simply download the data in a CSV, read it through SAP Gateway, or use a CDS view. We may or may not need to house the data in a separate system, but for illustrative purposes, we will do so here. In our scenario, we will read data from SAP via the NetWeaver Gateway using SQL Server Integration Services (SSIS). We then pull that data from SQL into Power BI. Finally we'll use R and Python code to create an interactive dashboard for anomaly detection.

---

2 More details on the mechanics of how a generalized ESD works can be found at *https://www.itl.nist.gov/div898/handbook/eda/section3/eda35h3.htm*.

3 A wonderful presentation of this package can be found on *Business Science*'s website: *https://www.business-science.io/code-tools/2018/04/08/introducing-anomalize.html*.

SAP ECC System

Our first step is to define a structure of data that we would like to analyze. We want to see sales order line quantities by material and customer.

Enter transaction code **SE11** into SAP and give a name to the data structure and then click on the Create button (Figure 5-1).

Figure 5-1. SAP data dictionary

Select the Structure radio button and click on Enter (Figure 5-2).

Figure 5-2. SAP structure selection

We want to gather sales order, sales order item, material ordered, quantity, customer, and the order date. Enter a Short Description of the data and the fields (Figure 5-3). (Staying with the original SAP names as field names makes integration with the gateway simpler. We will rename them out of the gateway as something meaningful.)

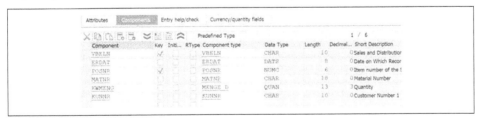

Figure 5-3. Components of a data structure

Click on the Currency/quantity fields tab to add a reference value for the quantity field.

If you do not know what the reference table and field are you can refer to the tables from which we will be reading. In this case those tables are VBAK (sales order header) and VBAP (sales order item).

Figure 5-4. Currency and quantity fields copied from the VBAP table for the quantity (KWMENG)

Follow the menu path Extras → Enhancement Category to enter whether this structure can be enhanced or not. We do not need enhancements, so we will choose Cannot be Enhanced (Figures 5-5 and 5-6).

Figure 5-5. Data structure enhancement category

Figure 5-6. Selection for enhancement category

Click on the Copy button, then click on the Activate button. The pop-up dialog is asking for a package to assign this structure. For our purposes we are using a $TMP object so it will not be transported.

Figure 5-7. Activating the SAP structure

If all is done correctly, you will get a confirmation "Object saved and activated" at the bottom of the screen.

Next, click on the Back button. A table type is needed for the function module. We will create that now.

Enter the same name as used for the structure but prepend a "_TT" to it, as shown in Figure 5-8.

Figure 5-8. Creating a table type in SAP

Click on the Create button. This time choose the "Table type" radio button and press Enter (Figure 5-9).

Figure 5-9. SAP table type selection

Enter a "Short text" and put in the structure previously created into the Line Type field (Figure 5-10).

Click on the Activate button. You will be asked again for a package and will get the confirmation "Object saved and activated" once finished.

Dictionary: Change Table Type

Hierarchy Display

Table Type   YGMF_SALES_DATA_TT   New(Revised)
Short text   Table Type for Sales Order Data

| Attributes | Line Type | Initialization and Access | Primary Key | Secondary Key |

● Line Type   YGMF_SALES_DATA

○ Built-in type
    Data Type
    No. of Characters   0   Decimal Places   0

○ Reference type
    ○ Referenced Type

    ○ Reference to built-in type
    Data Type
    Length   0   Decimal Places   0

Figure 5-10. Assigning the structure to the table type

The next step is to create a function module for reading the data. Enter transaction code **SE37** into the command line and hit Enter. Give the function module a meaningful name and then click on the Create button (#sap_function_builder). Enter a "Function group" and a "Short text" description and then click on the Save button. If you don't know a function group, you can get one from your Basis administrator or ABAP developer.

SE37

Function Builder: Initial Screen

Reassign...

Function Module   YGMF_SALES_ORDERS

| 🔍 Display | ✏ Change | 🗋 Create |

Figure 5-11. SAP Function Builder

You will get an information message (#sap_function_module_warning). Click Enter to move past it.

Figure 5-12. SAP function module warning

Click on the Attributes tab and ensure that the function module is remote-enabled (Figure 5-13). Without this, the NetWeaver Gateway will not be able to call this.

Function module	YGMF_SALES_ORD(
Attributes Import Export C	

Classification

Function Group	ZTTS_FI001
Short Text	TEXT

Processing Type
- ○ Regular Function Module
- ⊙ Remote-Enabled Module
- ○ Update Module
  - ⊙ Start immed.
  - ○ Immediate start (not updateable)
  - ○ Start Delayed
  - ○ Coll.run

Figure 5-13. SAP remote enabled function selection

Click on the Export tab and enter a Parameter Name and the Associated Type, which is the table type created earlier. Click on the Pass Value checkbox to ensure data is passed to this export parameter (Figure 5-14).

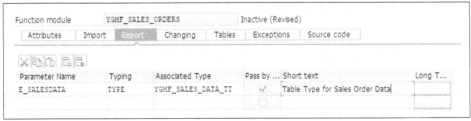

Function module	YGMF_SALES_ORDERS	Inactive (Revised)
Attributes	Import **Export** Changing Tables Exceptions Source code	

Parameter Name	Typing	Associated Type	Pass by ...	Short text	Long T...
E_SALESDATA	TYPE	YGMF_SALES_DATA_TT	✓	Table Type for Sales Order Data	

Figure 5-14. Parameters for function module

Click on the "Source code" tab. Enter the following code. It is going to read all sales order line items greater than 01/01/2014. Generally, it would be a good idea to add an import date parameter so it is more dynamic. However, for the purposes of illustration, we will keep this super simple:

```
SELECT DISTINCT vbak~vbeln
                vbak~erdat
                vbak~kunnr
                vbap~posnr
                vbap~matnr
                vbap~kwmeng
    INTO CORRESPONDING FIELDS OF TABLE e_salesdata
    FROM vbak JOIN vbap ON vbak~vbeln = vbap~vbeln
    WHERE vbak~erdat >= '2014101'.
```

Click on the Activate button, then click on the Test button to make sure it works and doesn't run too terribly long. Click on the Execute button. The function will return a table of data. If the table is large, like the one we have, do not click on the table button to view it. SAP will try to render the entire table and run into paging problems and simply quit.

Export parameters	Value
E_SALESDATA	1,094,982 Entries

Figure 5-15. Results of function module test

SAP NetWeaver Gateway

Now for the SAP NetWeaver Gateway. As pointed out earlier, the great function of this utility is to expose our newly found data in an OData feed (either XML or JSON). If your SAP environment has a separate NetWeaver Gateway server, log in and enter the transaction code **SEGW**. Click on the Create button to create a new project. Enter a name for the Project, a Description, and a Package. Then click on the Enter button (Figure 5-16).

Figure 5-16. Creating a new NetWeaver Gateway project in SAP

Your new project will appear below (Figure 5-17).

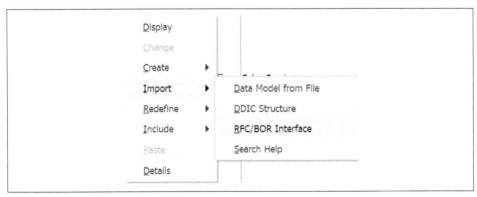

Figure 5-17. Project in transaction SEGW

Right-click on the Data Model node and select Import → RFC/BOR Interface from the context menu to read in the function definition we just created (Figure 5-18).

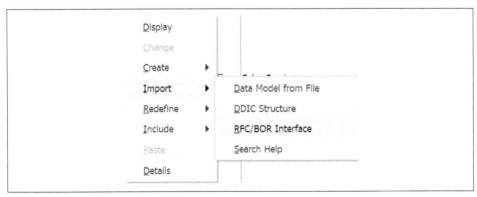

Figure 5-18. Importing the RFC into the model

Enter an Entity Type Name, select your target system, and enter the Name of the function module. In this example, since our gateway is embedded within SAP ERP, we use Local. Then click on the Next button (Figure 5-19).

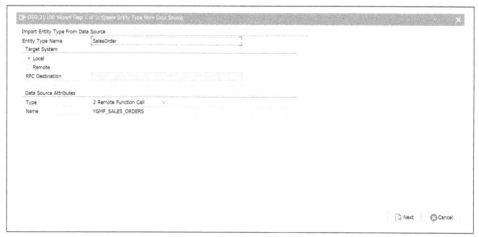

Figure 5-19. Defining the RFC for the gateway model

Select all the checkboxes for the elements to be used in the service. We want all of them so only the top node needs to be selected. Click on the Next button (Figure 5-20).

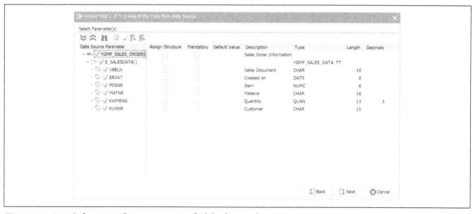

Figure 5-20. Selecting the necessary fields from the FM export

Identify what the key fields are for the structure, then click on the Finish button (Figure 5-21). The key fields are the unique fields for your structure—in this case, the sales order (VBELN) and the sales order item (POSNR). In an SAP system there will never be the same sales order number for the same sales order item.

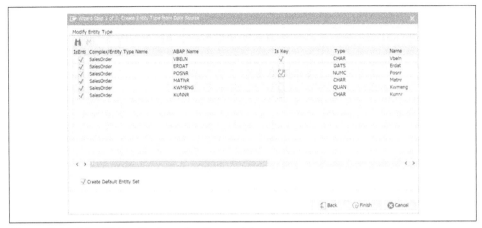

Figure 5-21. Identifying the keys for the model

Open the project folders Data Model → Entity Types → SalesOrder and click on the Properties folder. Add some meaningful names (as shown in Figure 5-22 to the service in the Name column and identify any values that can be Null by clicking in the checkbox in the Nullable column. When finished click on the Generate Runtime Objects button.

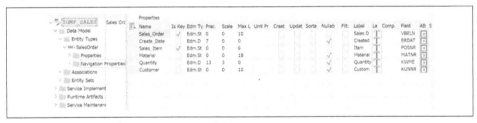

Figure 5-22. Giving the entity meaningful names

Accept the default values for the objects about to be generated. Click on the Enter button (Figure 5-23).

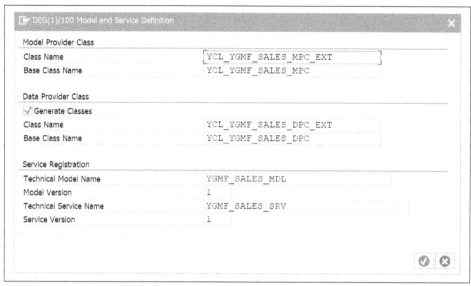

Figure 5-23. Generating the model and service definition

Again, assign this to a transport if necessary in pop-up dialog. Click on the Save button (Figure 5-24).

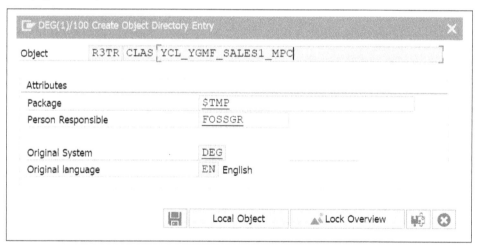

Figure 5-24. Selecting a package for the gateway project

Open the project folders Service Implementation → SalesorderSet and right-click on the GetEntitySet (Query) line (Figure 5-25). Select the Map to Data Source option, as shown in Figure 5-26.

Figure 5-25. Mapping the gateway to the data source

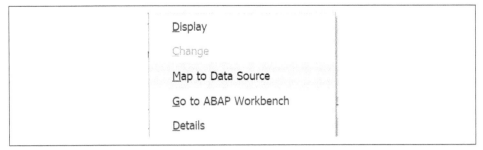

Figure 5-26. Selecting the Map to Data Source option

This will give the mapping option for our service and the backend function. Identify the Target System of the function module, the Type, and the Name. Press the Enter button (Figure 5-27).

Figure 5-27. Identifying the source function module

Map each field from the function module to the field in the service. If you've defined the function with common parameter types, you can make your life easier and click Propose Mapping (Figure 5-28). In this example, that works well.

Figure 5-28. Mapping using the propose mapping option

When finished click on the Generate Runtime Objects button (Figure 5-29).

Open the Service Maintenance folder, right-click on the hub to be used, and select Register (Figure 5-30).

Figure 5-29. Node for the service maintenance

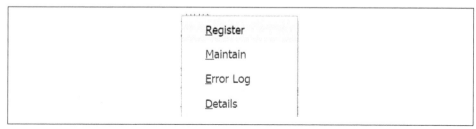

Figure 5-30. Selecting to register the gateway components

Select the system alias and then click on the Enter button (Figure 5-31).

Figure 5-31. Identifying a system alias for the gateway service

The system will now register the service. Accept the default entries, assign a package, and then click on the Enter button (Figure 5-32).

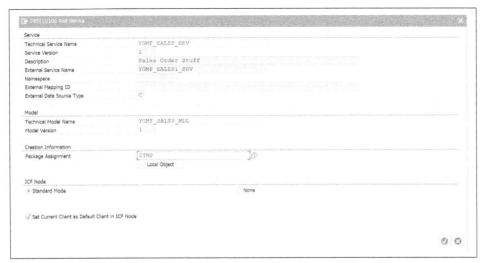

Figure 5-32. Generating and activating gateway services and components

 If you do not have a hub under the Service Maintenance folder then your system is not properly configured. Refer to your Basis Administration for help doing this. There are some excellent blogs at blogs.sap.com that walk through this very well.

Let's test this and see if it works. Right-click on the hub again but this time select Maintain (Figure 5-33).

Register

Maintain

Error Log

Details

Figure 5-33. Maintaining the gateway service

The service is displayed with some additional functionality. It is easiest to call the service in a browser so click on the Call Browser button (Figure 5-34).

Figure 5-34. Testing the gateway service in the browser

The default browser opens with the service and entity sets displayed:

```
<app:service xml:base="http://<host>:<port>/sap/opu/odata/sap/ZGMF_SALES_SRV/">
  <app:workspace>
  <atom:title type="text">Data</atom:title>
  <app:collection sap:creatable="false" sap:updatable="false"
     sap:deletable="false" sap:pageable="false"
     sap:content-version="1" href="SalesOrderSet">
     <atom:title type="text">SalesOrderSet</atom:title>
     <sap:member-title>SalesOrder</sap:member-title>
  </app:collection>
  </app:workspace>
  <atom:link rel="self"
    href="http://<host>:<port>/sap/opu/odata/sap/ZGMF_SALES_SRV/"/>
  <atom:link rel="latest-version"
    href="http://<host>:<port>/sap/opu/odata/sap/ZGMF_SALES_SRV/"/>
  </app:service>
```

To try the actual entityset and function module, copy out the entityset name (in our case, `SalesOrderSet`) and put it at the end of the URL between the / and ?. For our example, this URL would work:

```
https://[YOUR_SAP_HOSTNAME]/sap/opu/odata/sap/ZGMF_SALES_SRV/SalesOrderSet?
    $format=xml
```

And would produce an output like this:

```
...
<id>
  http://<host>:<port>/sap/opu/odata/sap/YGMF_SALES_SRV/SalesOrderSet
</id>
<title type="text">SalesOrderSet</title>
<updated>2019-04-25T17:39:37Z</updated>
<author>
  <name/>
</author>
<link href="SalesOrderSet" rel="self" title="SalesOrderSet"/>
<entry>
  <id>
http://<host>:<port>/sap/opu/odata/sap/YGMF_SALES_SRV/SalesOrderSet
  (Vbeln='5000000',Posnr='000010')
  </id>
  <title type="text">SalesOrderSet(Vbeln='5000000',Posnr='000010')</title>
  <updated>2019-04-25T17:39:37Z</updated>
  <category term="YGMF_SALES_SRV.SalesOrder"
scheme="http://schemas.microsoft.com/ado/2007/08/dataservices/scheme"/>
  <link href="SalesOrderSet(Vbeln='5000000',Posnr='000010')"
     rel="self" title="SalesOrder"/>
  <content type="application/xml">
    <m:properties>
      <d:Vbeln>5000000</d:Vbeln>
      <d:Erdat>2017-07-03T00:00:00</d:Erdat>
      <d:Posnr>000010</d:Posnr>
      <d:Matnr>12345678</d:Matnr>
      <d:Kwmeng>1.000</d:Kwmeng>
      <d:Kunnr>56789</d:Kunnr>
    </m:properties>
  </content>
</entry>
...
```

Now that we know our data feed is working, we can move onto reading with SSIS and putting it into SQL. For high volume and frequently accessed analytical data, storing it in an intermediate SQL database can save the SAP system from memory errors. At lower volumes or occasionally accessed frequencies, this could work just fine as an OData service read directly from PowerBI. The right answer for your environment will vary.

The first step is to define a database structure. This is easy since we can query the metadata of our service by adding **/$metadata/** to the end of the service URL. Like this...

```
https://[YOUR_SAP_HOST_NAME]/sap/opu/odata/sap/ZGMF_SALES_SRV/$metadata/
```

The <entitytype> tag will have all the data definitions necessary for us to create the SQL database:

```
<edmx:Edmx xmlns:edmx="http://schemas.microsoft.com/ado/2007/06/edmx"
xmlns:m="http://schemas.microsoft.com/ado/2007/08/dataservices/metadata"
  xmlns:sap="http://www.sap.com/Pro
tocols/SAPData" Version="1.0">
 <edmx:DataServices m:DataServiceVersion="2.0">
 <Schema xmlns="http://schemas.microsoft.com/ado/2008/09/edm"
   Namespace="YGMF_SALES_SRV" xml:lang="en"
sap:schema-version="0">
 <EntityType Name="SalesOrder" sap:content-version="1">
 <Key>
 <PropertyRef Name="Vbeln"/>
 <PropertyRef Name="Posnr"/>
 </Key>
 <Property Name="Vbeln" Type="Edm.String" Nullable="false" MaxLength="10"
   sap:label="Sales Document" sap:creatable="false" sap:updatable="false"
   sap:sortable="false"sap:filterable="false"/>
 <Property Name="Erdat" Type="Edm.DateTime" Precision="7" sap:label="Created on"
   sap:creatable="false"
sap:updatable="false" sap:sortable="false"sap:filterable="false"/>
 <Property Name="Posnr" Type="Edm.String" Nullable="false" MaxLength="6"
   sap:label="Item" sap:creatable="false" sap:updatable="false"
   sap:sortable="false"sap:filterable="false"/>
 <Property Name="Matnr" Type="Edm.String" MaxLength="18"
sap:label="Material" sap:creatable="false"
sap:updatable="false" sap:sortable="false" sap:filterable="false"/>
 <Property Name="Kwmeng" Type="Edm.Decimal" Precision="13" Scale="3"
   sap:label="Quantity" sap:creatable="false" sap:updatable="false"
   sap:sortable="false"sap:filterable="false"/>
 <Property Name="Kunnr" Type="Edm.String" MaxLength="10" sap:label="Customer"
   sap:creatable="false" sap:updatable="false" sap:sortable="false"
   sap:filterable="false"/>
 </EntityType>
 <EntityContainer Name="YGMF_SALES1_SRV_Entities"
   m:IsDefaultEntityContainer="true" sap:supported-formats="atom json">
 <EntitySet Name="SalesOrderSet" EntityType="YGMF_SALES_SRV.SalesOrder"
   sap:creatable="false" sap:updatable="false" sap:deletable="false"
   sap:pageable="false"sap:content-version="1"/>
 </EntityContainer>
 <atom:link xmlns:atom="http://www.w3.org/2005/Atom" rel="self"
href="http://<host>:<port>/sap/opu/odata/sap/YGMF_SALES1_SRV/$metadata"/>
 <atom:link xmlns:atom="http://www.w3.org/2005/Atom" rel="latest-version"
href="http://scsecccid.sces1.net:8001/sap/opu/odata/sap/
     YGMF_SALES1_SRV/$metadata"/>
```

```
</Schema>
</edmx:DataServices>
</edmx:Edmx>
```

 To do the next steps you will need SQL, SQL Server Management Studio, and Microsoft Visual Studio Community. If you don't currently have a SQL Server we recommend playing with SQL Express[4] first. There are many good tutorials on the installation process.[5] If you haven't had fun with SQL Server Management Studio, you're about to. Install SQL Server Management Studio[6] and connect it to your SQL Express.[7] Finally, if you have not used Visual Studio Community, we envy you. It's like telling a friend about a wonderful movie that you wish you could watch again for the first time. Download Visual Studio Community[8] and install it. If you haven't used any of these tools it may seem at first daunting, but trust us, these are powerful and fun tools that will change how you look at data and analytics. Dive in, don't look back, have fun.

SQL Server

Before we build our database, let's talk about what we intend to do. We want to load from our backend system in the simplest and easiest way possible. To do this we will load all data first into a Repository table. The data types of this repository will be simple Unicode strings. Then the data moves to a staging table where the data definitions are more precise. Upon successful completion of this, the data will be then loaded into the final mart table using an Upsert command. This will insert any new records and overwrite any existing records based on the keys we define (which will be Sales Order and Line Item).

---

4 Download SQL Server Express here (*https://www.microsoft.com/en-us/sql-server/sql-server-editions-express*).

5 Installation tutorial for SQL Express at *https://www.sqlshack.com/install-microsoft-sql-server-express-localdb/*.

6 Download SQL Server Management Studio at *https://docs.microsoft.com/en-us/sql/ssms/download-sql-server-management-studio-ssms?view=sql-server-2017*.

7 Connect SSMS to SQL at *https://docs.microsoft.com/en-us/sql/relational-databases/lesson-1-connecting-to-the-database-engine?view=sql-server-2017*.

8 Visual Studio Community at *https://visualstudio.microsoft.com/downloads/*.

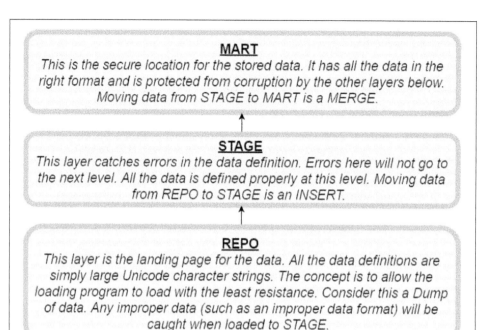

Figure 5-35. Data flow for storing data in SQL

Open SQL Server Management Studio, enter your Server Name and your credentials, and click on the Connect button (Figure 5-36).

Figure 5-36. Connecting to your server

Right-click on the Databases folder (Figure 5-37) and select New Database (Figure 5-38).

Figure 5-37. SQL hierarchy

Figure 5-38. Creating a new database

Enter a Database name and click on the OK button (Figure 5-39).

Figure 5-39. Entering a SQL database name

Click on the newly created database and then right-click on the Tables folder. Select New → Table (Figure 5-40).

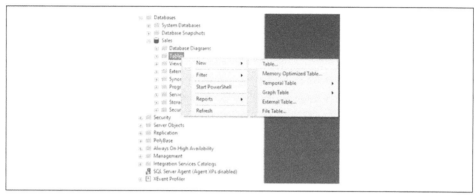

Figure 5-40. Creating a new SQL table

Enter the details of the table using Unicode Data Types with an ample length (Figure 5-41).

Figure 5-41. Entering the SQL table variables

Click on the Save button.

Enter the name of the table denoting in some way that it is the repository table. Click on the OK button (Figure 5-42).

Figure 5-42. Naming the SQL table for repo

Repeat the process and create another table but this time with the types accurately defined, as shown in Figure 5-43.

Column Name	Data Type	Allow Nulls
Sales_Order	nvarchar(10)	☐
Create_Date	date	☐
Sales_Item	nvarchar(6)	☐
Material	nvarchar(18)	☐
Quantity	decimal(13, 3)	☐
Customer	nvarchar(10)	☑

Figure 5-43. Identifying the SQL variables for stage

Click on the Save button.

Enter the name of the table denoting in some way that it is the stage table. Click on the OK button (Figure 5-44).

Figure 5-44. Naming the SQL table for stage

Repeat the process again exactly as was done for the stage table but denote this one as the mart table (Figure 5-45). This will be the location from which we read into PowerBI.

Figure 5-45. Entering the SQL table name for mart

Now that our database is ready, we need to create the operation that will load the data from SAP into it.

SQL Server Integration Services (SSIS)

First, let's open Visual Studio Community.

Follow the menu path File → New → Project (Figure 5-46).

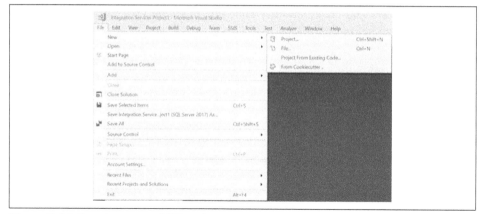

Figure 5-46. Creating a new SSIS project

Here are the steps you'll need to follow (Figure 5-47):

1. Open the folder Business Intelligence.
2. Click on Integration Services.
3. In the righthand panel, right-click on Integration Services Project.
4. Enter a Name for the project.
5. Click on the OK button.

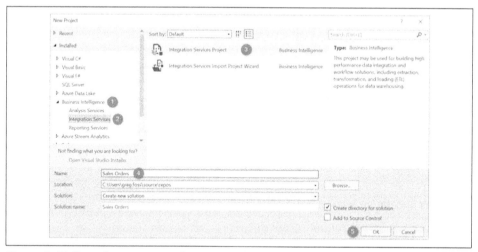

Figure 5-47. Steps for starting an Integration Services project

In the Solution Manager panel, right-click on Connection Manager and select New Connection. This is where we will define our connection to the OData model we have from SAP. The connection manager has by default an OData option (Figure 5-48).

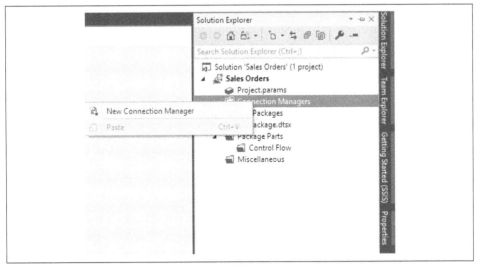

Figure 5-48. Adding a new connection in SSIS

Select the type of connection we will be reading from the NWG (NetWeaver Gateway). This is an OData connection; therefore, click on ODATA and then click the Add button. Then follow these steps (Figure 5-49):

1. Enter a meaningful Connection manager name.

2. Enter the Service document location, which is the URL to our NWG data feed. Make sure to use the service and not the collection.

3. Change the Authentication Type to Basic Authentication.

4. Enter an authorized User name.

5. Enter the Password.

Figure 5-49. Connection settings in SSIS for SAP Gateway service

Click on the Test Connection button to make sure the settings are all correct. You should then see the dialog box shown in Figure 5-50.

Figure 5-50. Testing the connection from SSIS to SAP

Click on the OK button and then click on OK again to save the connection. Next we need to define the workflow for the reading process. Click on the Data Flow Task in the SSIS Toolbox and drag it to the Control Flow panel (Figure 5-51).

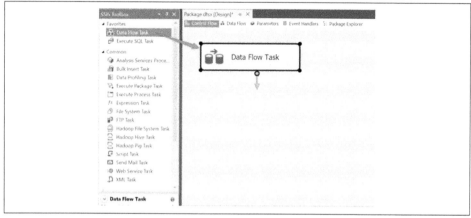

Figure 5-51. Creating a data flow task

Rename the data flow task (Figure 5-52).

Figure 5-52. Rename the data flow task

Double-click on the data flow task to navigate to the Control Flow or click on the Control Flow tab. Drag a OData Source component from the Common section. Rename it something meaningful (Figure 5-53).

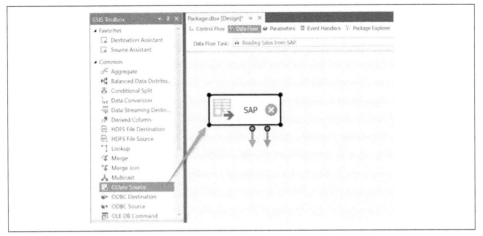

Figure 5-53. Creating an OData source connection within the data flow

1. Double-click on the OData Component.

2. Select the connection created earlier.

3. The collections or entity sets from the NWG service will display.

4. Click on the Preview button (Figure 5-54).

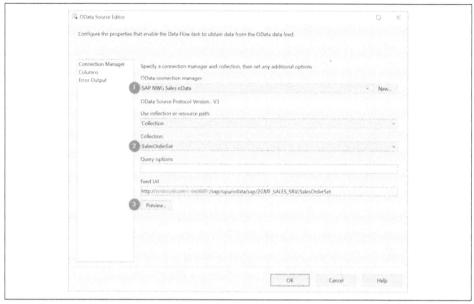

Figure 5-54. OData source settings for the SAP connection

A small preview will display (Figure 5-55). If things look good, close the preview window and click on the OK button.

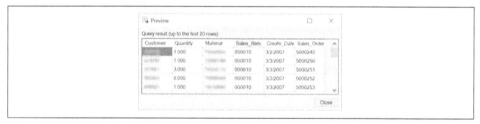

Figure 5-55. Previewing the data coming from SAP in SSIS

We can read the data from SAP, and now we need to put it in the SQL database we created earlier.

In the Solution Manager panel, right-click on Connection Managers and select New Connection Manager (Figure 5-56). This is where we will define our connection to SQL Database.

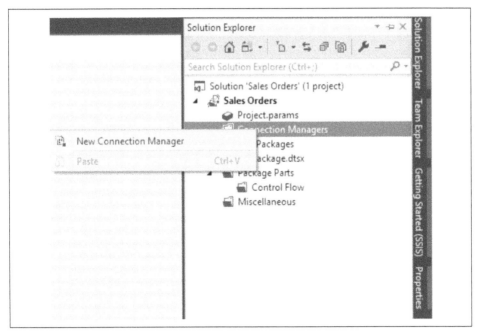

Figure 5-56. Adding a connection to SQL from SSIS

Select OLEDB from the list and then click the Add button (Figure 5-57).

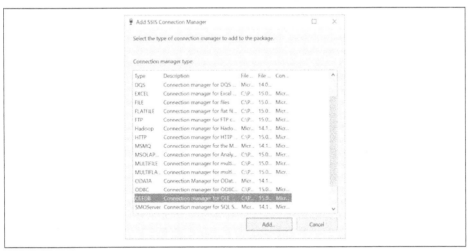

Figure 5-57. Selecting the OLEDB connection type for SQL

Click on the New button. Enter the SQL Server name, Authentication, and Database name. Then click on the Test Connection button (Figure 5-58).

Figure 5-58. SQL database connection settings in SSIS

If all is successful a positive test will result (Figure 5-59).

Figure 5-59. Testing the connection to SQL

Click on the OK button three times to save.

The Connection Managers pane now shows both of the connections we created (Figure 5-60).

Figure 5-60. The connections to the different systems in SSIS

The next step is to connect the SAP connection to the SQL connection. Select the OLE DB Destination component and drag it into the Data Flow tab. Give it a meaningful name (Figure 5-61).

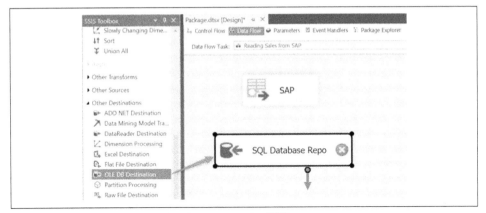

Figure 5-61. Creating a OLE DB Destination in SSIS

Connect the SAP component to the SQL component with the blue arrow (Figure 5-62). The red arrow is for errors.

Figure 5-62. Connecting SAP and SQL in SSIS

Double-click on the SQL component. It will automatically connect to the SQL connection as there is only one. If there is more than one option select the appropriate one from the OLE DB connection manager. Select the repository table from the SQL database (Figure 5-63).

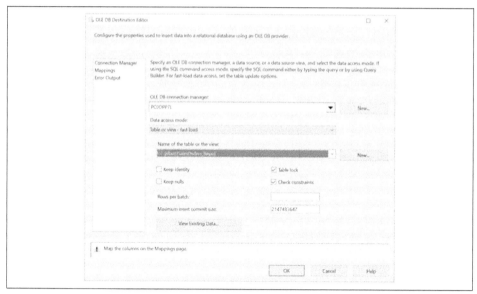

Figure 5-63. Connecting to a specific SQL database table

Click on the Mappings option on the left. If the names are the same in the database as they are in the SAP feed then the entries will map automatically. If they are not, map them manually. Then click on the OK button (Figure 5-64).

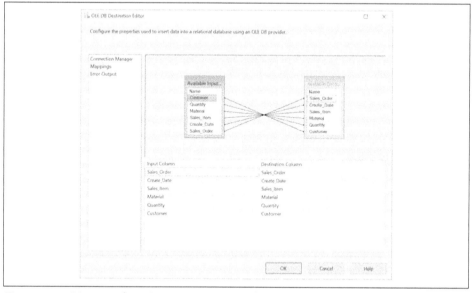

Figure 5-64. Mapping from SAP source to SQL database destination

The data flow should now show no errors (Figure 5-65).

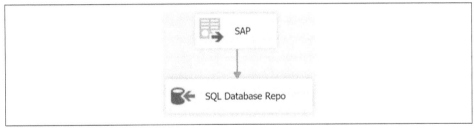

Figure 5-65. No errors present in current mapping

Click on the Save button and then click on the Start button to test the process. When it is complete there will be two green checkmarks (one for the successful reading from SAP and one for the successful writing to the SQL repository table), as shown in Figure 5-66.

Figure 5-66. Executing the SAP to SQL Database flow in SSIS

Let's make sure that the data is in our database. Open SQL Server Management Studio and navigate to the repository table. Right-click on the table and select Select Top 1000 Rows from the context menu (Figure 5-67).

Figure 5-67. Checking SQL Database

The results from SAP are now in the database repository table (Figure 5-68).

	Sales_Order	Create_Date	Sales_Item	Material	Quantity	Customer
1	5000240	2007-03-02	000010		1.000	
2	5000250	2007-03-03	000010		1.000	
3	5000251	2007-03-03	000010		3.000	
4	5000252	2007-03-03	000010		8.000	
5	5000253	2007-03-03	000010		1.000	
6	5000254	2007-03-03	000010		3.000	
7	5000255	2007-03-03	000010		1.000	
8	5000258	2007-03-03	000010		1.000	
9	5000259	2007-03-03	000010		1.000	
10	5000259	2007-03-03	000020		1.000	

Figure 5-68. SAP data is now in SQL via SSIS

Why did we create two more tables? Well, we load simply without rules to the repository table. What that means is we will not check if integers are integers, dates are dates, or any other validation. Remember our flow from Figure 5-35. If there are data errors, they will be caught when we move to Stage. There is little risk of error because we are using large Unicode character strings. Now we will move the data from the repository to the stage table.

In Visual Studio, click on the Stop button to end the test. In the SSIS Toolbox drag the Execute SQL Task to the Control Flow tab and give it a meaningful name (Figure 5-69).

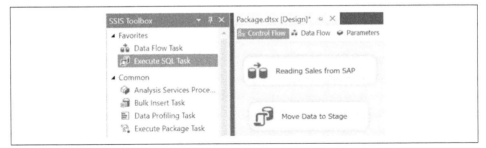

Figure 5-69. Creating an Execute SQL Task in SSIS

Double-click on the SQL task to bring up the properties. Ensure that the Connection is pointed at the SQL Server. Click on the ellipsis button to bring up the SQL editor (Figure 5-70).

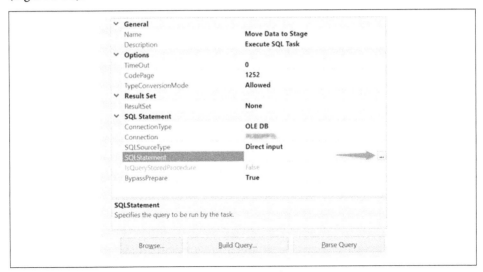

Figure 5-70. Opening the SQL editor in an SSIS task

Enter the SQL statement to move all data from the repository table into the stage table. Then click on the OK button twice (Figure 5-71).

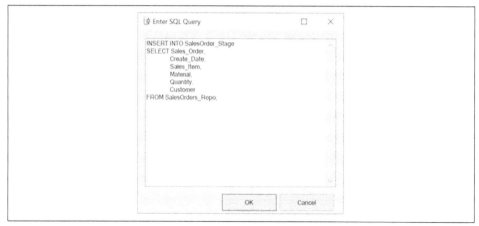

Figure 5-71. SQL code to move data from the repo table to the stage table

Right-click on Execute SQL Task and select Execute Task to test. Upon successful completion of this task there will be data in the stage table in the SQL database (Figure 5-72).

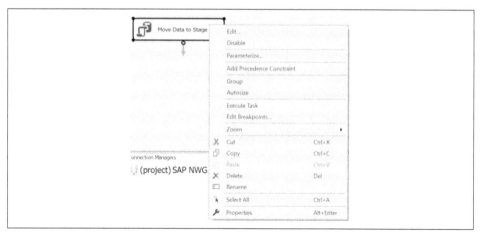

Figure 5-72. Executing the single task in SSIS

Finally, we will move the data from stage to mart. Drag another Execute SQL Task to the Control Flow tab. Give it a meaningful name (Figure 5-73).

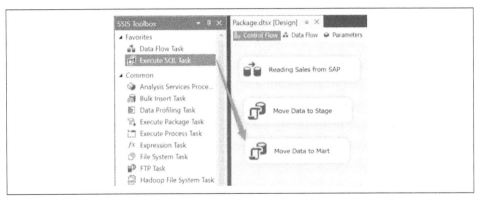

Figure 5-73. Adding another Execute SQL Task to the workflow

As we had done for the move from the repository to stage, double-click on the SQL task to bring up the properties. Ensure that the Connection is pointed at the SQL Server. Click on the ellipsis button to bring up the SQL editor.

The SQL code here is a bit different. It uses a MERGE statement based on the sales order and item. If the mart table already has this sales order and item it will update it, otherwise it will insert it. Once finished, click on the OK button twice (Figure 5-74).

Figure 5-74. SQL code to move data from the stage table to the mart table

As we had done before, right-click on the Execute SQL Task and select Execute Task to test. Upon successful completion of this task there will be data in the mart table in the SQL database.

The concept here is to dump to the repository table, insert to the stage table, and merge to the mart table. For this flow to work, we must clean up the repo table upon successful completion of the load to stage and clean up the stage table upon successful load to the mart table. By not writing directly to the mart table we have a safe process and reduce the risk of accidentally corrupting our mart table.

Copy two new Execute SQL Tasks to the Control Flow panel. Give them names indicating what they are going to do. We are going to *truncate* or drop the repo and stage tables once the data has successfully moved on (Figure 5-75).

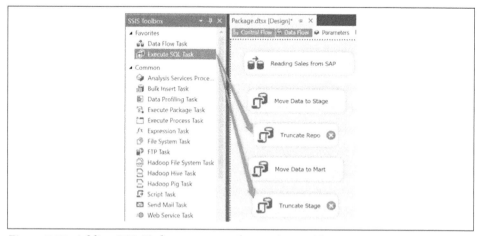

Figure 5-75. Adding SQL Tasks to truncate the previous tables

As we had done earlier, assign the proper connection to the SQL database and open the SQL editor. For the Truncate Repo task, put in the simple code:

```
TRUNCATE TABLE SalesOrders_Repo;
```

For the Truncate Stage task put in:

```
TRUNCATE TABLE SalesOrder_Stage;
```

Test them and then check in SQL Server Management Studio to ensure that the repo and stage tables are empty.

Each of these components are standalone, for the moment. Connect them to create a workflow Figure 5-76. If any of these steps fail, the process will stop there and not continue—which is what we want! Refer back to Figure 5-35 again. We want to protect our MART such that errors anywhere in the process will stop the overall process before data is moved to mart.

Some may assume that the whole repo → stage → mart process adds an unnecessary level of complexity. If you wisely monitor your data and are cautious on data loads you can directly load to mart. However, recently when updating a more than 70 million row database for pharmaceutical analytics our process failed at the INSERT to stage. The source data structure had unknowingly changed. The repo → stage → mart design saved us a major rebuild, tons of time, and perhaps most importantly, avoided any system downtime.

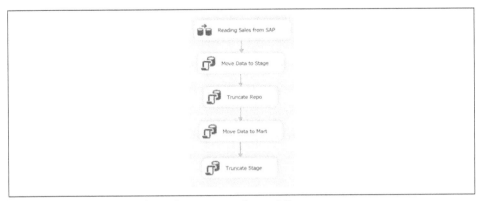

Figure 5-76. Connecting the tasks into a single workflow

Click on the Save button and then click on the Start button to test the process. All the components will show a green check if they have successfully completed (Figure 5-77).

Figure 5-77. Executing the entire workflow and checking the status

We have completed the process of extracting the data from SAP via the NetWeaver Gateway. We have used an extraction tool SSIS to automate the process and pull the data into a SQL Database. Now the data is available for advanced analytics and machine learning!

Finding Anomalies

For the advanced analytics and machine learning work, we will use PowerBI and R with the `anomalize` package introduced earlier. For nerdy fun, we'll also do the same thing with PowerBI and Python—illustrating some key capabilities of both languages and the PowerBI tool itself. Greg's an R addict, while Paul hacks around in Python. PowerBI is the perfect place to meld those preferences.

PowerBI and R

Let's learn about yet another powerful tool in our data scientist's toolbox...PowerBI. What exactly is PowerBI? In technical terms, PowerBI is an abstraction layer between the data and the presentation. You can model and transform your data before presenting it to the user. Furthermore, you can merge and modify disparate data sources into one report using PowerBI. How about an example for our SAP users. You know that ALV (ABAP List Viewer) report that is so ubiquitous? That is an abstraction between the data and the reporting. PowerBI is hundreds of times more powerful than that. For those familiar with Business Intelligence models, PowerBI provides an ETL (Extract-Transform-Load) layer before the actual reporting.[9]

First, download and install PowerBI.[10] To use R together with PowerBI, we need to set up the connection to our SQL mart. Open up PowerBI and click on the Get Data button. Then select the Database option and highlight SQL Server database. Click on the Connect button (Figure 5-78).

---

9 In our humble opinion, tools like PowerBI and Tableau with their ETL layers are the death knell of traditional data warehouse models.

10 PowerBI can be downloaded from *https://powerbi.microsoft.com/en-us/downloads/*.

Figure 5-78. Connecting PowerBI to a SQL database

Enter the Server and the Database name and click the OK button (Figure 5-79).

Figure 5-79. Naming the SQL database connection in PowerBI

Accept the authorization settings or change them if not using Windows credentials. Click on the Connect button (Figure 5-80).

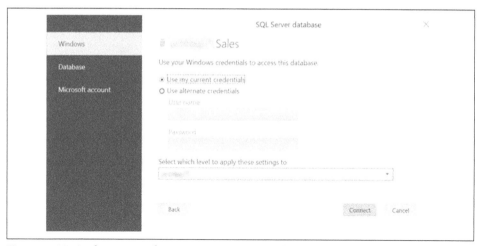

Figure 5-80. Authorization for connecting to a SQL database in PowerBI

PowerBI will notify you that it tried an encrypted connection first unsuccessfully and now it is going to use an unencrypted connection. Click on the OK button (Figure 5-81).

Figure 5-81. Warning message in PowerBI for encryption support

Select the mart table from the SQL database. A preview will show in the right panel. Click on the Load button (Figure 5-82).

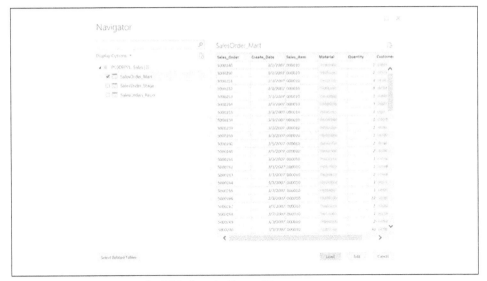

Figure 5-82. Previewing the SQL data in PowerBI

While PowerBI loads the data, it will display the dialog box shown in Figure 5-83.

Figure 5-83. PowerBI loading indicator

Once the data is finished loading PowerBI will display a blank canvas with tools for visualizations and the fields from our SQL database. Click on the Slicer button first (Figure 5-84). This allows us to filter our data dynamically in the PowerBI report.

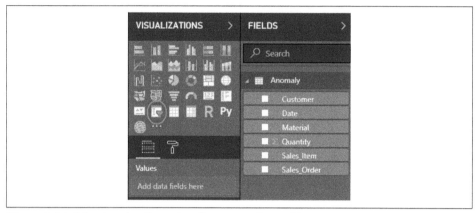

Figure 5-84. Selecting the slicer visualization in PowerBI

Then click on the field for Customer to assign it to the slicer. The slicer on the canvas shows the assignment. If you want there to be a "searchable" capability in the slicer, click on the ellipsis in the upper-right corner and select Search, as in Figures 5-85 and 5-86.

Figure 5-85. Using the searchable option for the slicer visual in PowerBI

Figure 5-86. The searchable option in the slicer visual

Repeat the process for Material and Date (Figure 5-87).

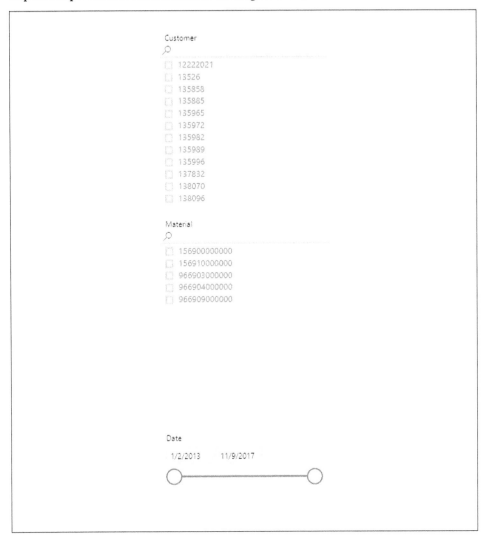

Figure 5-87. Adding other slicer visuals in PowerBI

Our first visualization is a simple line chart showing sales of material by date. Click on the Line chart button and place it on the canvas. As shown in Figure 5-88, assign Date to the axis, Quantity to the values, and Material to the legend. Then add whatever tooltips you'd like.

Figure 5-88. Adding variables to the line chart visual in PowerBI

The line chart is very busy because it has not been filtered yet. We've created a slicer for the report, but we haven't put any filter criteria into it yet (Figure 5-89).

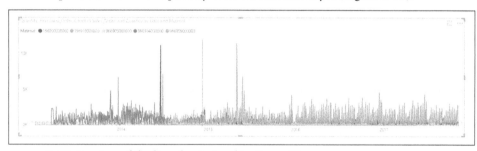

Figure 5-89. Preview of the line chart visual in PowerBI

The next step is to add an R visualization. Click on the R button and place it on the canvas under the line chart. Drag the variables we are going to use to the R visualization. These are Date and Quantity (Figure 5-90).

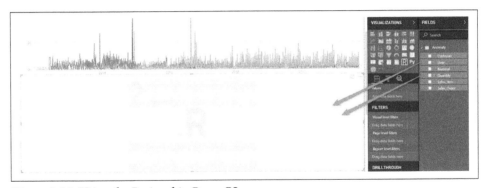

Figure 5-90. Using the R visual in PowerBI

In the script editor the fields selected will be shown as part of the dataset (Figure 5-91).

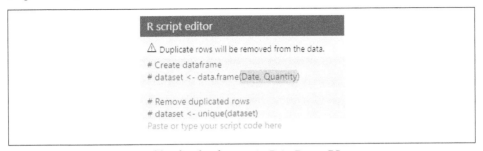

Figure 5-91. Selecting variables for the dataset in R in PowerBI

Place the following R code in the script editor (the comments in the code are preceded by a hash mark (#) and will describe what the next line of code is doing):

```
#anomalize package by Matt Dancho and Davis Vaughan @business-science.io
library(anomalize)
#tidyverse package by Hadley Wickham @ RStudio.com
library(tidyverse)
#tibble time package by Matt Dancho and Davis Vaughan @business-science.io
library(tibbletime)

#make sure that R sees the Date as a date variable
dataset$Date <- as.Date(dataset$Date)

#convert the dataframe to a tibble, which is still a dataframe but
#with tweaks to old behavior to make life easier
dataset <- as_tbl_time(dataset, index = Date)

#identify the dataset to be used
#Reference
#https://cran.r-project.org/web/packages/magrittr/vignettes/magrittr.html
dataset %>%
```

```
as_period("weekly") %>%        #set the period to daily
time_decompose(Quantity) %>%   #generate a time series decomposition
anomalize(remainder) %>%       #detect outliers in a distribution
time_recompose() %>%           #generate bands around the normal levels
plot_anomalies(time_recomposed = TRUE) +
  ggtitle("Anomalies")         #plot the findings with the time_recompose
```

Then press the Play button to see it work.

It doesn't make a lot of sense at first since it is evaluating anomalies across all available materials for all customers. It hasn't been filtered yet (Figure 5-92).

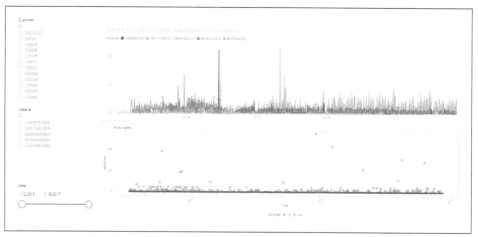

Figure 5-92. Unfiltered view of R and line visual in PowerBI

Select one material to see anomalies across all customers for that particular material (Figure 5-93).

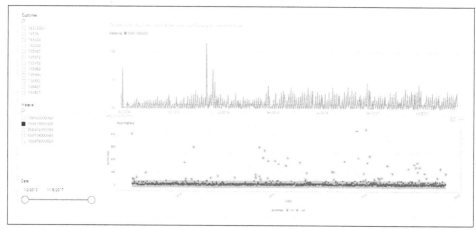

Figure 5-93. Filtering the line and R visual via the slicer

The first thing to notice is that the line chart does not intuitively show anomalies. One would guess that spikes are anomalies, but the `anomalize` package did not always classify them as such. Now click on a customer to subset the values further to display anomalies for a particular customer and material combination (Figures 5-94 and 5-95).

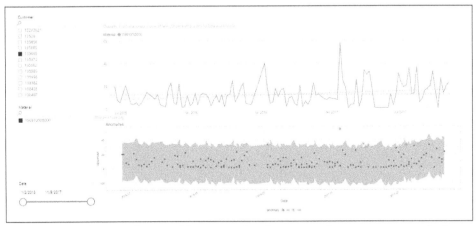

Figure 5-94. Subsetting the visual by material and customer for accurate anomaly detection

Anomalies are now more in line with the line chart and large spikes do show as anomalies, but not all of them.

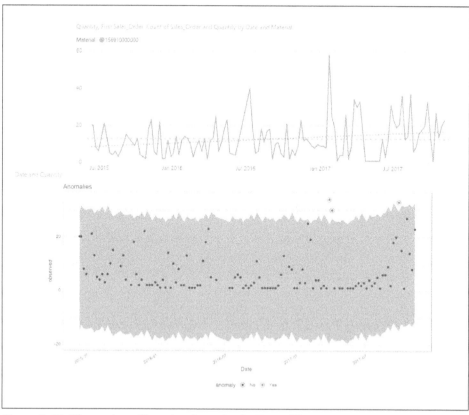

Figure 5-95. Closer view of just the charts in the PowerBI report

PowerBI and Python

Whether you're a SAP analyst or a data scientist, everyone who wrangles code has their own preferences for language, syntax, style, and platform. Microsoft took this to heart when designing PowerBI. The preceding section set up and analyzed sales order data looking for anomalies in R—but let's make the jump to Python. A couple of packages help us make this an efficient process:

luminol

A package designed for time series data analysis. It's open sourced from the folks at LinkedIn. Considering the sheer amount of data being handled at LinkedIn, as well as its relative worth in the value of that product, it's easy to imagine that their data science team is top-notch. And this package proves it, by providing an easy-to-use API for detecting anomalies as well as fine-tuning how the detection works.

Matplotlib

A package designed for 2D plotting. Very powerful, feature-packed, and common across the Python world. We'll visualize our results using this library.

We can even keep our language preference in the same tool, because PowerBI has built-in support for using Python to output charts and graphs, allowing us to use these libraries. This support is currently available in preview, so let's set it up. After all, a huge part of data science is daring to try something new!

To make sure your computer can run the new Python feature, install the latest version of Python and then use the following three `pip` commands to install the packages we'll use:[11]

```
$ pip install pandas
$ pip install luminol
$ pip install matplotlib
```

Next, open PowerBI and use the same file we created earlier for R analysis. Navigate to the settings menu, and in the Global section, the Preview Features menu allows you to add upcoming features that are not part of the full current release (Figure 5-96).

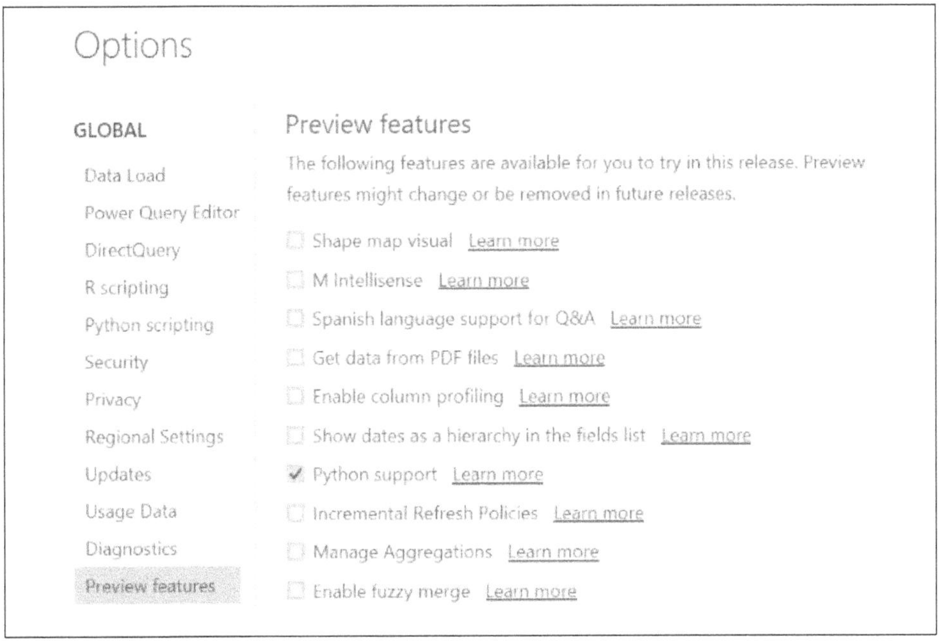

Figure 5-96. Turning on the Python support in PowerBI

---

11 There are many ways to install new packages in Python. In our example, we are using a basic command line.

Check the box next to Python support and close the options menu. You're set to use Python in this document. We'll add a Python graph right below the R graph we created. In the Visualizations menu, choose Py to add another analysis section to the dashboard (Figure 5-97).

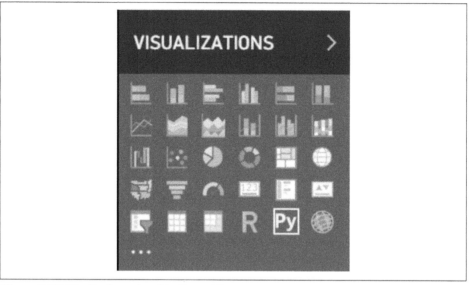

Figure 5-97. The Python visual in PowerBI

For the last bit of PowerBI setup, make sure the Fields properties for this visualization match the properties of the R visualization we set up earlier (Figure 5-98).

Figure 5-98. Selection fields for the Python visual in PowerBI

With PowerBI set up and packages installed, we're ready. Click on the Python analysis section and enter the following code:

```python
from luminol.anomaly_detector import AnomalyDetector
import matplotlib.pylab as plt
import matplotlib.ticker as pltickerr
# Helper function to make the raw dates into numbers for
# luminol to interpret
def make_date_int(date):
    date_parts = date.split('-')
    year = int(date_parts[0]) * 10000
    month = int(date_parts[1]) * 100
    day = int(date_parts[2][:2])
    return year + month + day
# PowerBI sends the dataset as a dataframe with the field values
# as individual lists.
dataset_parts = dataset.to_dict('list')
# Create a list of integer-ified dates, then make a dictionary with
# keys as those integer-ified dates and values as the Quantity
dates_to_int = list(map(make_date_int, dataset_parts['Date']))
data_for_detection = dict(zip(dates_to_int, dataset_parts['Quantity']))
# Keep a copy of the data with original dates on hand, zipped up nice
```

```
base_preserved_dates = dict(zip(dataset_parts['Date'],
                                dataset_parts['Quantity']))
anomalies = AnomalyDetector(time_series=data_for_detection,
                            score_threshold=2,
                            algorithm_name='exp_avg_detector'
                           ).get_anomalies()
# Extract out the dates that the AnomalyDetector found.
# (List comprehensions are the best)
anomaly_dates = [int(x.start_timestamp) for x in anomalies]
# Here's where we set up a plot.
ordered_data = sorted(base_preserved_dates.items())
xaxis, yaxis = zip(*ordered_data)
fig, ax = plt.subplots()
# Plot all the data, and then loop on the anomaly data to add
# markers to the graph.
plt.plot(xaxis, yaxis)
for date in anomaly_dates:
    highlight = data_for_detection[date]
    timestamp_str = str(date)
    timestamp = timestamp_str[:4] + '-' + timestamp_str[4:6] +
    '-' + timestamp_str[6:8] + 'T00:00:00.0000000'
    plt.plot(timestamp, highlight, 'ro')
# Showing the plot with x-axes ticks every 25 data points,
# and makes the data nicely readable in '2018-09-12' date format.
loc = plticker.MultipleLocator(base=25.0)
ax.xaxis.set_major_locator(loc)
ax.get_xaxis().set_major_formatter(
    plticker.FuncFormatter(lambda x, p: xaxis[int(x)][:10] if int(x) <
                           len(xaxis) else ""))
plt.show()
```

Click the Play button in the code console, and watch as the graph is generated (Figure 5-99).

If you compare this graph to the one generated from the R code, you'll see that the two packages agree on the late January 2017 spike as an anomaly, as well as a July 2016 spike. The R graph captured a couple of other points later in 2017 as suspect that weren't flagged by the luminol library.

There are two great things about running your questions through two analyses. First, you get the chance to learn new approaches and tools. SAP analysts and data scientists alike can surely see the value in expanding their toolsets. Today's technology professionals can't afford not to do that.

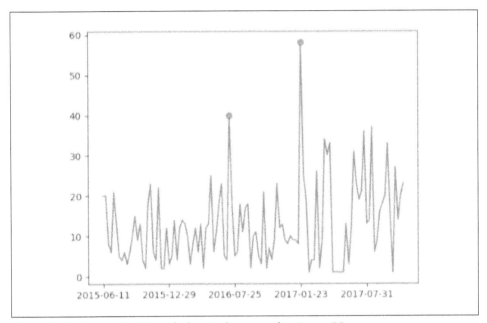

Figure 5-99. Anomalies identified in Python visual in PowerBI

Second, and most important for our data analysis purposes, is that you get to use multiple approaches to fine-tune your answers to the questions you ask of the data. For example, note that in the Python code the `AnomalyDetector` constructor takes a `score_threshold` parameter. By using a `score_threshold` value of 2, we set the algorithm to only unpack certain anomalies. While experimenting with that parameter, note that in this case setting the parameter to a lower or higher number will start to uncover anomalies that exist in the lower bounds of the data as well.

Janine in the regulatory department and Duane the SAP analyst need to ask themselves: for the purposes of the analysis and meeting the regulatory requirements, are suspiciously low orders something to watch out for? Conversely for high number thresholds, what do I know about this customer? Are they ordering more product than they can fit in their warehouse? Is that suspicious? Many ERP and EDI systems can store information about customer facilities.

Summary

In this chapter the data science team completed a process of extracting sales data from SAP, storing it in SQL, and displaying the results in a PowerBI dashboard with the help of either R or Python. It may have seemed like a lot of steps to get this to work, but one could follow these steps and in a single day create a sales order anomaly dashboard from SAP. With large data warehouse teams trying to stay ahead of hundreds of similar requests from departments all over the business, the same process would take weeks if not months. We have been able to prototype an anomaly detection system for SAP sales orders in a single day. This is illustrative of the speed and power of data science when applied to business data with modern tools.

We discovered through readily available libraries in R (`anomalize`) and Python (`luminol`) that we can quickly and easily detect anomalies in our data. We have only scratched the surface of anomaly detection, but we've exposed ourselves to the possibility of doing this with business data from SAP. The processes we've learned in this chapter encompass much more than just anomaly detection. Extracting data from SAP through NetWeaver Gateway and storing it in SQL via SSIS is a common useful process for all types of data science endeavors. In our example, it is not truly necessary to store the data outside of SAP; however, if you find yourself working with financials in SAP this technique will likely help. Financial data in SAP is nearly always voluminous and often requires extraction before analysis.

Despite our good start, this is likely not the end of our journey in detecting sales order anomalies. We have provided the business with a proof-of-concept and a prototype. Janine from the regulatory department has always known what the regulations state about remaining compliant. Now, however, she understands what type of analytics and data science the IT department can provide. This prototype will go through some iterations and refinement before being the robust dashboard that will protect Janine and her company from noncompliance with government standards. This project would have served other companies well—companies that came under government scrutiny and ended up with hefty fines.

## CHAPTER 6

Predictive Analytics in R and Python

The team at Big Bonanza Warehouse is running into some problems with sales forecasting, and the VP of Sales has turned to Duane, who works as a Sales and Distribution Analyst, for some help. About once per quarter they gather their data and send it to an outside company that performs some magic on it. The result is a forecast of all their products for the upcoming quarters, but they've found that the forecast being generated for them is too generic (based on quarters) and often woefully inaccurate. Couldn't they get something that would help them understand what sales might be next week? To put it succinctly, they want a forecast of sales of their top-selling products by week.

Duane has some ideas. Having worked with his company's data scientists Greg and Paul, he knows a little bit about data science. Sales of a product over a period is a time-series[1] problem. They have enough historical data to attempt to look for patterns. This is not pure forecasting, but pattern detection. It is something that the sales team could use, rather than their gut feelings. Duane decides to use a bit of *predictive analytics*. With the right set of R or Python tools and some up-front knowledge of predictive analytics, Duane won't need to spend months of time paying expensive consultants to build massive data lakes. He can get his hands dirty and find answers.

There are many slippery terms in data science (including *data science* itself!), but *predictive analytics* owns a special share of un-graspability. You may have heard of the now infamous "prediction" tale. Retail giant Target predicted a teenager's pregnancy before her father even knew. In case you haven't heard the story... Target started sending baby coupons to a teenage girl. Her father complained that they were encouraging her daughter to get pregnant. The reality was, the girl was already pregnant. Did

---

1 Time series: a series of data points indexed over time.

Target *predict* this teenager's pregnancy? The answer is no. This is not a prediction; this is inference or classification. The features they use are the shopping behaviors of their customers. The buying habits of the teenage girl led the classification algorithm to put her in the category "pregnant."

The point of this story is to highlight two common uses of the word *prediction*. One of those predictions is statistical inference and the other is forecasting. Let's be honest here, you can debate these definitions ad nauseum. For our purposes, we will draw a line in the sand between forecasting and inference. Prediction for us will be forecasting.[2] Let's make sure we have a common understanding of the term: *prediction is the act of predicting the future.*

The litmus test for determining if the analysis falls into prediction is to ask, "Has the event occurred?" If it has, then, from our definition, it is likely something other than prediction.

Below are some examples of common topics and exercises in data science learning materials that are often mislabeled as predictions:

Predicting Boston housing value
> This is a classification/inference problem based on the features of a given property such as location, square footage, number of bedrooms, etc.

Predicting the survival rate on the Titanic
> This is another classification/inference problem based on features such as sex, cabin number (location), number of family members, embarking point, and others.

Predicting fraudulent credit card behavior
> This is an anomaly detection problem determining if the behavior of the card holder falls within tolerance. It'd be more descriptive to call it "detecting fraudulent credit card behavior."

Predicting why and when a patient will readmit
> This sounds very close to prediction. It is another classification/inference problem based on patients that have already readmitted. If their features match the features of a patients not yet readmitted, there is a likelihood they will readmit.

Some examples of topics and exercises that are properly labeled as predictions:

---

2 You may disagree with this sharp distinction between inference and forecasting and our use of the term prediction. This is a very slippery semantic slope. However, you should understand the need to make the definition clear for the purposes of teaching.

Predicting Boston housing value next year

Next year's house values is a classification of the current value of the home based on certain features. This classification merges with other salient data such as GDP to make a future prediction.

Predicting future stock value

You figure this one out...let us know. Many different sources of data contribute to predicting a stock's performance. A company's quarterly performance reports in EDGAR[3] is a good starting point.

Predicting Sales in R

In this chapter, we will walk through Duane's exercise in predictive analytics and try to do sales order predictions. We will follow the process in Figure 6-1 for this mission.

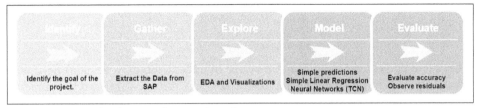

Figure 6-1. Flow for data analysis and prediction

Step 1: Identify Data

Not ready to completely fly on his own, Duane approached the data science team to obtain better metrics for predicting sales in the near and semi-near future—the upcoming weeks, months, quarters, and as far out as one year. Prediction accuracy becomes more volatile the further out we get. Quite simply, it is much easier to predict tomorrow's sales because we know yesterday's. However, it is not the same to say we can predict next year's sales because we knew last year's. What we do know is that we will have sales data for a list of products over time.

Step 2: Gather Data

Our source of data is SAP. We will extract the data using the same method used in Chapter 4. Using an ABAP QuickViewer Query, we gather simple sales data from the

---

3 EDGAR: The government's open source Electronic Data Gathering, Analysis, and Retrieval system. It uses XBRL (eXtensible Business Reporting Language). Trust us, it's a fun rabbit hole. *https://www.codeproject.com/Articles/1227765/Parsing-XBRL-with-Python.*

VBAP and VBAK tables. We will take only the created date ERDAT from VBAK. We will take MATNR (material) and KWMENG (quantity sold) from table VBAP.

Step 3: Explore Data

Once we have exported the data as a CSV file from SAP we will read it into R to take a look at it:

```
sales <- read.csv('D:/DataScience/Data/Sales.csv')
```

Let's take a look at the first 10 rows:

```
head(sales)
```

```
    X DailySales Material      ReqDeliveryDate
1  0   48964.75      1234 /Date(1420416000000)/
2  1   30853.88      1234 /Date(1420502400000)/
3  2   65791.00      1234 /Date(1420588800000)/
4  3   17651.20      1234 /Date(1420675200000)/
5  4   36552.90      1234 /Date(1420761600000)/
6  5    5061.00      1234 /Date(1420848000000)/
```

We see two things right away. The rows came in under column X, we don't need that. Also, the date field came in oddly, it looks like UNIX time and we need to convert it. When we look into it further we see it is indeed UNIX, but it is padded on the end with three unnecessary zeros. Let's correct these before moving on:

```
#Remove the X column
sales$X <- NULL
#Remove all nonnumeric from the date column
sales$ReqDeliveryDate <- gsub("[^0-9]", "", sales$ReqDeliveryDate)
#Convert the unix time to a regular date time using the anytime library
library(anytime)
#First trim the whitespace
sales$ReqDeliveryDate <- trimws(sales$ReqDeliveryDate)
#Remove the final three numbers
sales$ReqDeliveryDate <- gsub('.{3}$', '', sales$ReqDeliveryDate)
#Convert the field to numeric
sales$ReqDeliveryDate <- as.numeric(sales$ReqDeliveryDate)
#Convert the unix time to a readable time
sales$ReqDeliveryDate <- anydate(sales$ReqDeliveryDate)
```

Now that we've done some manipulation let's take a look at the structure of our data. Use the function str() to view the structure of the data:

```
str(sales)
 'data.frame': 2359 obs. of 3 variables:
  $ DailySales   : num 48965 30854 65791 17651 36553 ...
  $ Material     : int 1234 1234 1234 1234 1234 1234 1234 1234 1234 1234 ...
  $ ReqDeliveryDate: Date, format: "2015-01-04" "2015-01-05" "2015-01-06"  ...
```

We see that we have a dataframe with 2,359 observations of three variables. Let's find the distribution of the materials in the dataframe. Use the following command from the ggplot2 library (this renders in Figure 6-2).

```
ggplot(sales, aes(Material)) + geom_bar()
```

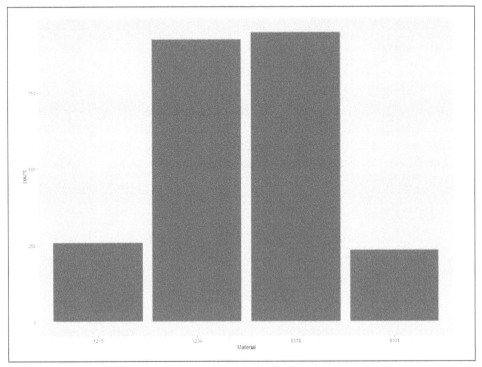

Figure 6-2. The distribution of materials in our sales data

We have the data in a format we'd like. Now it is time to plot and explore the data.

Step 4: Model Data

We will use the ggplot2 (*https://ggplot2.tidyverse.org/*), dplyr (*http://bit.ly/2lRCudc*), and scales (*http://bit.ly/2lRCudc*) libraries from R to model our data. These are some of the most useful and versatile packages in the R ecosystem:

```
library(ggplot2)
library(dplyr)
require(scales)
```

First let's do some up-front work. We want our chart to have nice numbers, so we use the format_format function from scales to define this for us. The effect of this function is to simply format our numbers such that the decimal is a period, the thousands break is a comma, and scientific notation is not used.

```
point <- format_format(big.mark = ",", decimal.mark = ".", scientific = FALSE)
```
Let's simply plot the sales of the materials over time:
```
sales %>%
  ggplot(aes(x=ReqDeliveryDate, y=DailySales)) +
  geom_point(color = "darkorchid4") +
  scale_y_continuous(labels = point) +
  labs(title = "Sales over time",
       subtitle = "sales for all materials",
       y = "Sales Quantities",
       x = "Date") +
  theme_bw(base_size = 15)
```
In human-speak this R code says, "Take the sales dataframe and send it ("%>%") to ggplot. Make the x-axis the ReqDeliveryDate and the y-axis the DailySales. Use points with a color palette of darchorchid4. Then scale the y to have the point format. Finally, label everything nicely and give it a basic theme and size." The results are shown in Figure 6-3.

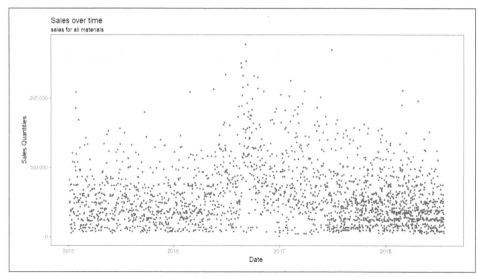

Figure 6-3. Sales for all materials over time

This gives us an idea of the distribution of sales over time, but it mixes the materials and points aren't the best for plotting a time series. Let's break out the materials and choose line instead of point. We see the results in Figure 6-4.

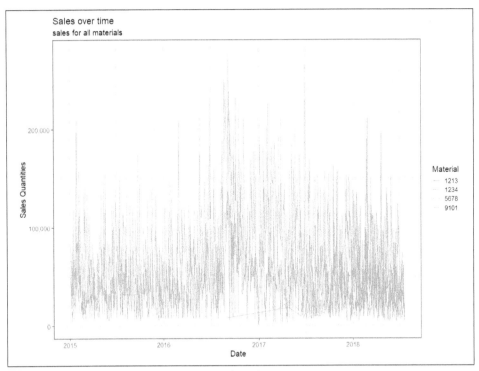

Figure 6-4. Sales for materials broken out by color over time

This is better, but the materials are still too mixed to be clear. Perhaps we need to break them out completely. ggplot2's `facet_wrap` does this nicely. The following code produces the chart in Figure 6-5:

```
sales %>%
  ggplot(aes(x=ReqDeliveryDate, y=DailySales, color)) +
  geom_line(color = "darkorchid4") +
  facet_wrap( ~ Material) +
  scale_y_continuous(labels = point) +
  labs(title = "Sales over time",
       subtitle = "sales for all materials",
       y = "Sales Quantities",
       x = "Date") +
  theme_bw(base_size = 15)
```

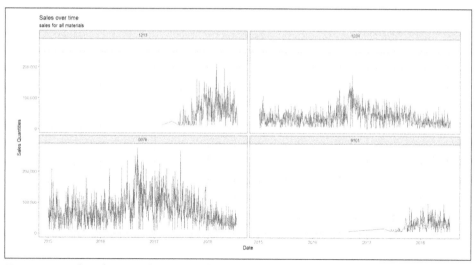

Figure 6-5. Sales of material over time broken up so we can see each plot separately

We can more easily see now the distributions of each of the materials. We can quickly spot that two of these materials only recently began to sell.

Let's focus on just one material, 1234. We will add a simple linear model using the `geom_smooth` function. We only have one material here, but we leave in `facet_wrap` because it makes such a nice header (the results are shown in Figure 6-6).

```
sales %>%
  subset(Material == '1234') %>%
  ggplot(aes(x=ReqDeliveryDate, y=DailySales, color)) +
  geom_line(color = "darkorchid4") +
  facet_wrap( ~ Material ) +
  geom_smooth(method = "lm") +
  scale_y_continuous(labels = point) +
  labs(title = "Sales over time",
    subtitle = "sales for all materials",
    y = "Sales Quantities",
    x = "Date") +
  theme_bw(base_size = 15)
```

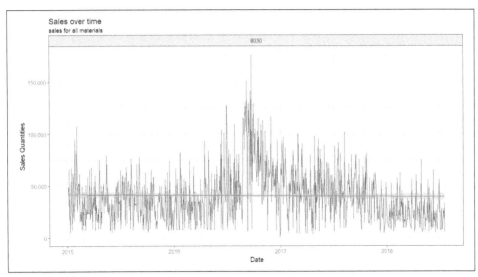

Figure 6-6. Sales over time with a simple linear mapping

We are curious about how these sales by year match up against one another. The line chart makes it difficult to see if overall sales by week are greater in 2015 than they are in 2018.

Let's sit back and approach this in an intuitive way. There are many important concepts in R programming, but two of the most influential are *Tidy Data* and *Split-Apply-Combine*.

Simple Data Analysis Strategies

Hadley Wickham described these two influential data analysis software concepts in the *Journal of Statistical Software*. Follow these and you can't go wrong.

Tidy Data (from https://vita.had.co.nz/papers/tidy-data.pdf).
- "Each variable forms a column."
- "Each observation forms a row."
- "Each type of observational unit forms a table."
- The `tidyverse` package applies all the tidy data concepts.

      library(tidyverse)

Split-Apply-Combine (from https://vita.had.co.nz/papers/plyr.pdf)
- "Break up a big problem into manageable pieces."
- "Operate on each piece independently."

- "Put all the pieces back together."

The library most applicable for this, dplyr, will be put to use later in this chapter.

Understanding these concepts will help you think through problems more easily. We will simply split our `sales` dataframe into one that we can more easily plot with. First we will copy our sales data into a subsetted dataframe for just our material:

```
sales_week <- sales %>% subset(Material == '1234')
```

Secondly, we need to make a week variable and a year variable from our date variable. This is easy in R with the base function `strftime`:

```
sales_week$week <- strftime(sales_week$ReqDeliveryDate, format = '%V')
sales_week$year <- strftime(sales_week$ReqDeliveryDate, format = '%Y')
```

We no longer need the `ReqDeliveryDate` or the `Material`:

```
sales_week$ReqDeliveryDate <- NULL
sales_week$Material <- NULL
```

We also want to aggregate our weeks into one bucket. We may have had multiple sales for a given week in our `sales` dataframe, which we want in only one week in our sales_week dataframe:

```
sales_week <- sales_week %>% group_by(year, week) %>% summarise_all(sum)
```

If we look at our dataframe now it has these columns:

```
head(sales_week)
# A tibble: 6 x 3
# Groups:   year [1]
  year week DailySales
  <chr> <chr>    <dbl>
1 2015 01      48965.
2 2015 02     173920.
3 2015 03     213616.
4 2015 04     243433.
5 2015 05     304793.
6 2015 06     265335.
```

Now we can use `ggplot2` again to see what the sales year over year look like when the weeks are compared (the results are in Figure 6-7):

```
sales_week %>%
  ggplot(aes(x = week, y = DailySales, group = year)) +
  geom_area(aes(fill = year), position = "stack") +
  labs(title = "Quantity Sold: Week Plot", x = "", y = "Sales") +
  scale_y_continuous() +
  theme_bw(base_size = 15)
```

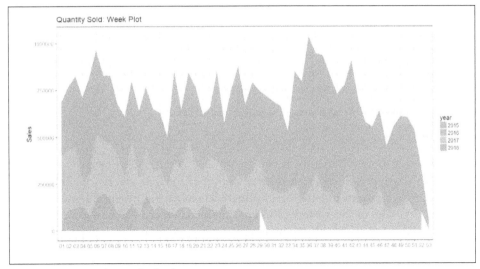

Figure 6-7. Area chart of sales by year

This chart shows us something that we couldn't see clearly before. The spikes and valleys of each year's sales are strongly correlated. Such a strong correlation between the years would lead us to believe we can model based on that pattern. 2018 did not have a full recorded year of sales so that chart stops on week 29. We also see a distinct uptick in sales between weeks 35 and 40 and 4 and 9.

To move further in our exploration we need to visit a base object in R, the `ts` (time-series) object. It is an array of values over time periods. What we have been working with thus far is a dataframe. It is easy to convert a `data.frame` to a `ts` object in R. This function takes the data itself as its first argument and then has a series of other arguments we will cover now. Type **args(ts)** into the console to see a list of arguments for the base `ts` function:

```
args(ts)
function (data = NA, start = 1, end = numeric(), frequency = 1,
    deltat = 1, ts.eps = getOption("ts.eps"), class = if (nseries >
        1) c("mts", "ts", "matrix") else "ts",
        names = if (!is.null(dimnames(data)))
        colnames(data) else paste("Series",
        seq(nseries)))
```

The arguments that we will use are:

- The `start` and `end` arguments define the starting date and ending date of the `ts` object.

- The `frequency` argument specifies the number of observations per unit of time.

In order to do this more easily and clearly we need to reformat our dataframe. This will lead to a nice clean `ts` object.

This time we will do an analysis by month. Just like we did with the week-by-week analysis, we will subset the `sales` dataframe. However, this time we will rename the columns so they are easier to use and remember:

```
sales_month <- sales %>% subset(Material == '1234')
  sales_month$Material <- NULL
  colnames(sales_month) <- c('sales', 'date')
```

Also, `ts` objects do not like gaps. If you are going to analyze data by days, `ts` objects want every day represented...even if there is no data for that day. If you are going to analyze data by minutes, likewise every minute has to have a presence. For instance, if there were no sales of this material for a particular day there will be a gap in the date sequence. We want to fill all of these gaps with 0 because that is how much was actually sold on that day. First we create a new dataframe with all the possible dates starting at our first day of our `sales_month` and ending with the last:

```
all_dates = seq(as.Date(min(sales_month$date)),
                as.Date(max(sales_month$date)),
                by="day")
```

Then we want to merge this dataframe with `sales_month`:

```
sales_month <- merge(data.frame(date = all_dates),
                     sales_month,
                     all.x=T,
                     all.y=T)
```

Let's take a look at our data:

```
head(sales_month, n=10)
        date    sales
1  2015-01-04 48964.75
2  2015-01-05 30853.88
3  2015-01-06 65791.00
4  2015-01-07 17651.20
5  2015-01-08 36552.90
6  2015-01-09 5061.00
7  2015-01-10       NA
8  2015-01-11 18010.00
9  2015-01-12 24015.00
10 2015-01-13 39174.25
```

We notice right away that we have NAs in our data. This is for the days when there were no sales. Let's replace that with zeros:

```
sales_month$sales[is.na(sales_month$sales)] = 0
```

Now it is easy to create a `ts` object. Frankly, `ts` objects in R have always been a bit of a quandary. Follow our advice—take the time to nicely and simply format your dataframe and you'll breeze through the `ts` object part:

```
require(xts)
sales_ts <- xts(sales_month$sales, order.by = as.Date(sales_month$date))
```

Now that we have a nicely formatted `ts` object, we can do some simple charting on it:

```
plot(sales_ts)
```

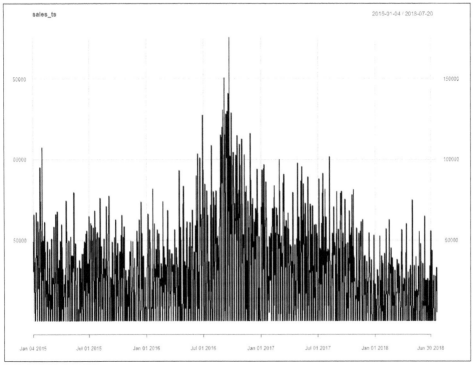

Figure 6-8. Simple plot of ts object

We can also see monthly sales and averages easily. Looking at the average sales across months in Figure 6-9 we can see that the overall sales amount is relatively equal despite the peaks and valleys:

```
monthplot(sales_ts)
```

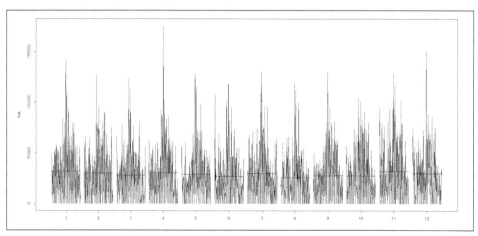

Figure 6-9. Month plot of ts object

Plots for prediction

There are three types of simple plots that we typically want to use in predictive analytics: mean, naive, and drift. Let's examine each of these.

The first plot is a simple prediction of the mean into the future. This prediction assumes that the average of past sales will continue to be the average. To make these charts we will need the forecast[4] library. We see the results of the mean forecast in Figure 6-10:

```
library(forecast)
sales_ts <- ts(sales_month$sales)
sales_ts_mean = meanf(sales_ts,h=35,level=c(90,90),
                      fan=FALSE, lambda = NULL)
plot(sales_ts_mean)
```

You may wonder what the gray rectangular area of the chart (at far right) is telling you. The gray area is the confidence interval, which by default is 95%. The line in the middle of the gray area indicates where the prediction should fall, the gray area says, "I am 95% confident that the value, if not on the line, is within the grey area." As may be assumed, a 95% confidence interval is pretty high so the area must therefore be large enough to ensure this.

---

4 The forecast library *https://cran.r-project.org/web/packages/forecast/forecast.pdf* is written by Rob J. Hyndaman and contains methods for displaying and analyzing univariate time series.

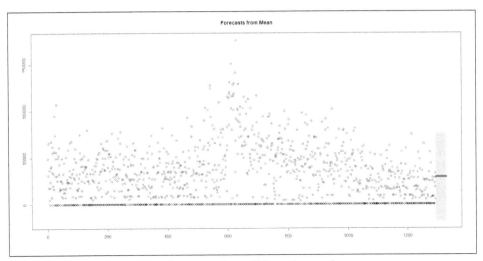

Figure 6-10. Simple mean prediction with confidence intervals

The naive assumption is that the sales will be the same as the last observation as seen in Figure 6-11:

```
sales_ts_naive <- naive(sales_ts,h=35,level=c(90,90),
                        fan=FALSE,lambda=NULL)
plot(sales_ts_naive)
```

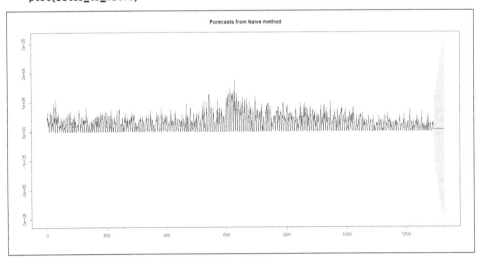

Figure 6-11. Simple naive prediction with confidence intervals

Finally, we can view the drift of the chart easily with the forecast library. Drift starts with the naive beginning, but then is adjusted positively or negatively based on the average overall change in the data. We see the results in Figure 6-12. Notice the ever so slight downward trend:

```
sales_ts_drift <- rwf(sales_ts,h=35,drift=T,level=c(90,90),
                      fan=FALSE,lambda=NULL)
plot(sales_ts_drift)
```

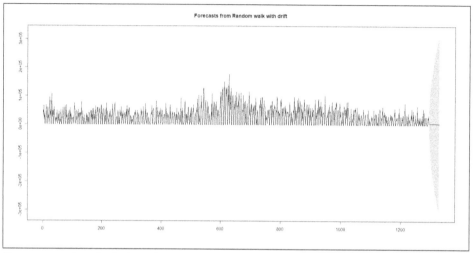

Figure 6-12. Simple drift prediction with confidence intervals

Clearly these plots are not going to be satisfying to the VP of sales, but it is the start of our prediction process and we will refine this process until we have results we like.

Step 5: Evaluate Model

First, let's analyze the accuracy of the three plots that we just created. With the `fore cast` package this is easy, but before we do that we need to discuss how accuracy can be measured. There are six ways we will analyze accuracy, and Table 6-1 illustrates the most commonly used measurements.

Table 6-1. Measures of acccuracy

Measurement	Description	Notation
ME	Mean error: the average of the total number of errors in predictions. The positive errors have the potential of wiping out the negatives.	mean(e_i)
MAE	Mean absolute error: measurement of the mean of the errors in predictions. This does not take into consideration whether it is over or under…just the magnitude of the error.	mean($|e_i|$)
RMSE	Root mean squared error: same as the MAE but errors are squared before the square root of the total is taken. This results in large errors having more value than small errors. Consider this an improvement over MAE if you want to strongly penalize large errors.	SQRT(mean(e^2_i))

Measurement	Description	Notation
MPE	Mean percentage error: the mean of the percentage of the errors.	$mean((e_i / actual_i) *100)$
MAPE	Mean absolute percentage error: the mean of the absolute percentage of the errors.	$mean((|e_i / actual_i| *100|)$
MASE	Mean absolute scaled error: the mean of the absolute values of the *scaled*[a] *(q)* errors. Scaling is an alternative to percentage errors. A MASE of > 1 indicates the prediction is worse than the naive prediction. If it is < 1 it is better.	$mean(|q_i|)$

[a] MASE was proposed in 2005 by statistician Rob Hyndman (*http://bit.ly/2ZKRo7z*) and is used for determining comparative accuracy of forecasts.

We can view these values easily with the `forecast` package (see Table 6-2):

```
accuracy(sales_ts_mean)
accuracy(sales_ts_naive)
accuracy(sales_ts_drift)
```

Table 6-2. Measures of accuracy for mean, naive, and drift forecasts

	ME	RMSE	MAE	MPE	MAPE	MASE
Mean	-2.46E-13	28535.31	23019.78	-Inf	Inf	1
Naïve	-33.81419	31653.02	23017.03	-Inf	Inf	1
Drift	1.25E-12	31653	23021.87	NaN	Inf	1.00021

What are good values for these evaluations? Consider that every set of data is different and has different scales. Data in one experiment might have a range of 1 to 1,000,000 and the RMSE is 10, which seems pretty good. However, the same RMSE value if the data has a range of 1 to 20 is terrible. Because of this, consider using your evaluation methods as a comparison between different plots and tests; avoid the pitfall of blindly seeing small evaluation results as good. In the simple methods we just looked at, the mean seems to pull ahead. Our results also shows us some of the dangers of using percentages. There is a risk of division by zero or near zero, which leads to infinite values.

Another thing we can look for in our data is seasonality. This is a different way to explore the data that is made much easier using the `tseries`[5] library. Is there some kind of pattern based on a recurring event? An example of seasonality in a time series would be the sales of mittens. Clearly sales of mittens increase in the winter and decrease in the summer. Another way of stating this is to say that the data is either stationary or not stationary. Stationary data is independent of the actual time series. We can test for stationarity or nonstationarity with the `tseries` package by using the `adf.test` method:

---

[5] *https://cran.r-project.org/web/packages/tseries/tseries.pdf*

```
library(tseries)
sales_ts_adf <- adf.test(sales_ts)
sales_ts_adf
```

The result we get indicates clearly that the data is stationary (has no seasonality):

```
Augmented Dickey-Fuller Test
data: sales_ts[, 1]
Dickey-Fuller = -5.8711, Lag order = 10, p-value = 0.01
alternative hypothesis: stationary
```

Now it is time to do some predictions that are better than mean, naive, or drift. We will use the ARIMA model to start with. ARIMA[6] stands for Autoregressive Integrated Moving Average. ARIMA is a prediction (forecasting) technique that projects the future values of a series depending on its previous data points. Like the name says, it uses a moving average. First we create the future values with the following command:

```
sales_future <- forecast(auto.arima(sales_ts))
```

To better understand the results, let's take a look at the structure of the time series object we are working with. Use the str() command:

```
> str(sales_ts)
An 'xts' object on 2015-01-04/2018-07-20 containing:
  Data: num [1:1294, 1] 48965 30854 65791 17651 36553 ...
  Indexed by objects of class: [Date] TZ: UTC
  xts Attributes: NULL
```

This tells us that we have 1,294 objects in our time series. Our forecast function will plot out another 10 values into the future. This gives us the following sales values with confidence intervals of 80 and 95. Let's look at time series object 1300 as an example. This tells us that the forecast is 20892.628 with a *Lo 80* of -8393.256 and a *Hi 80* of 50178.51. This means that we are 80% confident sales will be between $-8,393.256 and $50,178.51. A confidence interval of 95 is obviously wider to account for a higher degree of confidence and therefore has a higher range of $-23,896.27 to $65,681.52:

```
     Point Forecast      Lo 80     Hi 80      Lo 95     Hi 95
1295        907.887 -26883.351  28699.12  -41595.14  43410.92
1296      11811.826 -16743.171  40366.82  -31859.27  55482.93
1297      21790.271  -6768.050  50348.59  -21885.91  65466.45
1298      23937.037  -5022.613  52896.69  -20352.92  68227.00
1299      25546.677  -3730.630  54823.98  -19229.10  70322.46
1300      20892.628  -8393.256  50178.51  -23896.27  65681.52
1301      10542.993 -19636.125  40722.11  -35611.98  56697.97
1302       5537.931 -27502.193  38578.06  -44992.58  56068.44
1303      10655.408 -24005.266  45316.08  -42353.52  63664.34
1304      19295.901 -15714.125  54305.93  -34247.31  72839.12
```

---

6 Fitting an ARIMA model is sometimes referred to as the Box–Jenkins method.

Now let's plot this chart. This time we will have a starting point that is later than the beginning of the chart so we don't have such a small prediction interval. We will only plot the time series from point 750 to 1304. The results in Figure 6-13 show the point value in a dark line, the 80% confidence interval in a light shading, and the 90% confidence interval in an even lighter shading:

```
plot(sales_futue, xlim = c(750,1304))
```

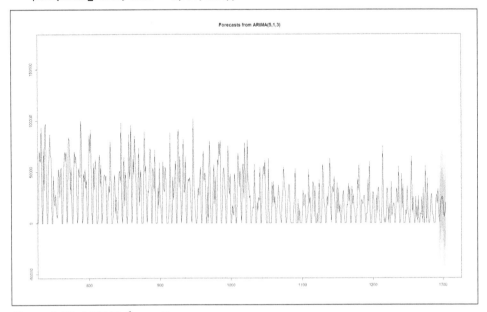

Figure 6-13. ARIMA forecasting

We've done a bit of prediction so far and learned a lot along the way. Perhaps we should sit back and look at our data and wonder if this ARIMA is good enough as it is? Should we try something new? What comes to mind when you look at Figure 6-13? When we look at it we see those flat lines on the bottom. That is where we put in missing dates, those dates when the material has zero sales. Should that be included in the model that does the prediction? In many cases the answer would be no. However, there is a good argument here that sales of zero are important. Any day of sale is a data point as well as any day of nonsales.

Next we will shift to a different language and a different model. We will take the same series of data that we explored in R and perform the same five-step analysis in Python.

Predicting Sales in Python

There are many ways to analyze data using different tools such as Python and R. In this section we will approach the same data from a Python perspective.

Step 1: Identify Data

This time we will use a quick OData utility class that could speed up future identify-gather phases. We will use OData and Python to help predict future sales for upcoming weeks, months, and up to a year. This identification phase is the same as what we did for R earlier.

Step 2: Gather Data

Remember Chapter 3 when we created an example OData service for listing plants out of the SAP backend? We're going to do exactly the same thing here—only with some adjusted structures, fields, and a little bit of ABAP code to make the pull easy. Most importantly, defining a process in this way will allow you to programmatically gather different sets of materials and date ranges with ease! We'll highlight the major differences here versus the approach as laid out in Chapter 3.

First, create a structure in transaction SE11 and choose the fields from Figure 6-14 to populate it. We're going to give this the same basic shape as the R example from before.

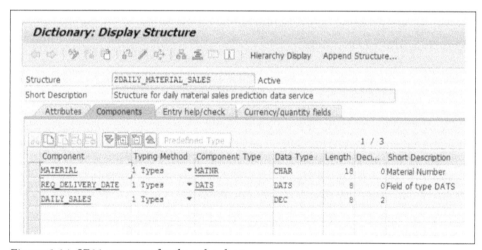

Figure 6-14. SE11 structure for the sales data

Next, go to transaction SEGW to create a new OData service and enter project details as noted in Figure 6-15.

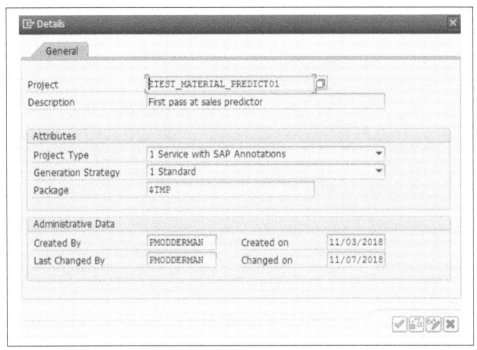

Figure 6-15. OData service details from SEGW

Remember to import the structure we created, just like in Chapter 3. See Figures 6-16, 6-17, and 6-18 for settings to use.

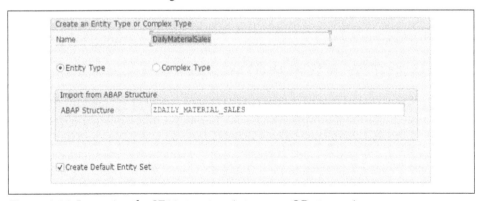

Figure 6-16. Importing the SE11 structure into a new OData service

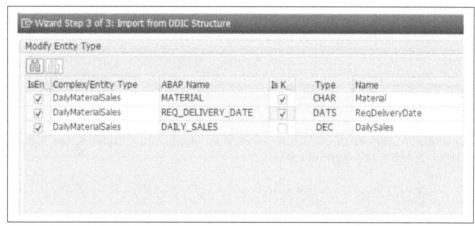

Figure 6-17. Choose all the available fields to import

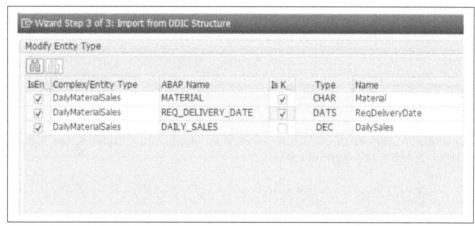

Figure 6-18. MATERIAL and REQ_DELIVERY_DATE are the key fields

Again just like Chapter 3, redefine the `GetEntitySet` (`Query`) method for the entity we just created. Use the following ABAP code to set up a quick filtering operation on sales order item data. Remember, as discussed before: we won't dive deep into explanations of ABAP code in this book. If you're a data scientist who really wants SAP data and you don't have a SAP team to help you, then you might wish to supplement this material with some of the ABAP basics available on SAP's free training site, *https://open.sap.com*:

```
"This code will return a list of sales dollars by date per material.
"The filtering mechanism for OData allows us to limit this to a subset
"of materials, and the below Python code incorporates this feature.

"If you named your entity set differently than our example screenshots,
"this method will be named differently.
```

```
METHOD dailymaterialsal_get_entityset.
  DATA lr_matnr TYPE RANGE OF matnr.
  DATA ls_matnr LIKE LINE OF lr_matnr.
  DATA lr_vdatu TYPE RANGE OF edatu_vbak.
  DATA ls_vdatu LIKE LINE OF lr_vdatu.

  "Here we extract the filters that our Python code will insert.
  LOOP AT it_filter_select_options INTO DATA(ls_select).
    IF ls_select-property EQ 'Material'.
      LOOP AT ls_select-select_options INTO DATA(ls_option).
        MOVE-CORRESPONDING ls_option TO ls_matnr.
        ls_matnr-low = |{ ls_option-low ALPHA = IN }|.
        APPEND ls_matnr TO lr_matnr.
      ENDLOOP.
    ELSEIF ls_select-property EQ 'ReqDeliveryDate'.
      LOOP AT ls_select-select_options INTO ls_option.
        MOVE-CORRESPONDING ls_option TO ls_vdatu.
        ls_vdatu-low = |{ ls_option-low ALPHA = IN }|.
        APPEND ls_vdatu TO lr_vdatu.
      ENDLOOP.
    ENDIF.
  ENDLOOP.

  "This SELECT statement incorporates the filters that are sent by the
  "Python code below into the SQL logic. For example, if the programmer
  "enters 3 materials to filter, then the variable 'lr_matnr' contains
  "a reference to those 3 materials to pass to the database engine.
  SELECT item~matnr AS material
         head~vdatu AS req_delivery_date
         SUM( item~netpr ) AS daily_sales
    FROM vbak AS head
      INNER JOIN vbap AS item ON head~vbeln = item~vbeln
      INNER JOIN knvv AS cust ON head~kunnr = cust~kunnr
        AND head~vkorg = cust~vkorg
        AND head~vtweg = cust~vtweg
        AND head~spart = cust~spart
      INNER JOIN mara AS mtrl ON item~matnr = mtrl~matnr
    INTO CORRESPONDING FIELDS OF TABLE et_entityset
      WHERE head~vdatu IN lr_vdatu
        AND item~matnr IN lr_matnr
      GROUP BY item~matnr vdatu
      HAVING SUM( item~netpr ) > 0
      ORDER BY item~matnr vdatu.
ENDMETHOD.
```

Once the SAP Gateway code is completed and activated, you have a service that can send the required sales data to any client that can make OData requests. Naturally, you'd love to use your own laptop as one of those clients, so we came up with a little utility class that can do some basic OData filtering, requesting, and creating of CSV files on your local computer. This may be useful in many SAP data retrieval scenarios, since any basic OData service should work:

```python
# Utility is exposed as a class to be instantiated per request run
class GatewayRequest(object):
    def __init__(self, gateway_url='', service_name='', entity_set_name='',
                 user='', password=''):
        self.gateway_url = gateway_url.strip('/')
        self.service_name = service_name.strip('/')
        self.entity_set_name = entity_set_name.strip('/')
        self.filters = []

        # Basic authentication: a username and password base64 encoded
        # and sent with the OData request. There are many flavors of
        # authentication for available for OData - which is just a RESTful
        # web service - but basic authentication is common inside corporate
        # firewalls.
        self.set_basic_auth(user, password)

    # Adds a filter to the main set of filters, which means our OData
    # utility can support multiple filters in one request.
    def add_filter(self, filter_field, filter_option, filter_value):
        # OData supports logical operators like 'eq' for equals,
        # 'ne' for does not equal, 'gt' for greater than, 'lt' for less
        # than, 'le' for less than or equal, and 'ge' for greater than or
        # equal. 'eq' is the most common, so if the logical operator is
        # omitted we assume 'eq'
        if not filter_option:
            filter_option = 'eq'

        new_filter = [filter_field, filter_option, filter_value]
        self.filters.append(new_filter)

    # Encode the basic authentication parameters to send with the request.
    def set_basic_auth(self, user, password):
        self.user = user
        self.password = password
        string_to_encode = user + ':' + password
        self.basic_auth = \
            base64.b64encode(string_to_encode.encode()).decode()

    # OData works through sending HTTP requests with particular query
    # strings attached to the URL. This method sets them up properly.
    def build_request_url(self):
        self.request_url = self.gateway_url + '/' + self.service_name
        self.request_url += '/' + self.entity_set_name

        filter_string = ''

        if len(self.filters) > 0:
            filter_string = '?$filter='
            for filter in self.filters:
                filter_string += filter[0] + ' ' + filter[1]
                filter_string += ' \'' + filter[2] + '\' and '
```

```python
        filter_string = filter_string.rstrip(' and ')

    if not filter_string:
        self.request_url += '?$format=json'
    else:
        self.request_url += filter_string + '&$format=json'

# Perform the actual request, by adding the authentication header and
# the filtering options to the URL.
def perform_request(self):
    try:
        self.build_request_url()
        if self.basic_auth:
            headers = {'Authorization':'Basic ' + self.basic_auth}
            self.result = requests.get(self.request_url,
                                       headers=headers)
        else:
            self.result = requests.get(self.request_url)
    except Exception as e:
        raise Exception(e)

# Utility function to return a pandas dataframe from the results of
# the OData request.
 def get_result_dataframe(self):
    try:
        self.perform_request()
        json_obj = json.loads(self.result.text)
        json_results = json.dumps(json_obj['d']['results'])
        return pandas.read_json(json_results).drop('__metadata',axis=1)
    except Exception as e:
        raise Exception(e)

# Utility function to return a basic JSON object as the results of
# the query.
 def get_result_json(self):
    self.perform_request()
    return json.loads(self.result.text)

# The utility function we use, to save the results to a local .csv
def save_result_to_csv(self, file_name):
    self.get_result_dataframe().to_csv(file_name)

# A utility to properly parse the dates that are returned in a json
# request.
@staticmethod
def odata_date_to_python(date_string):
    date_string = date_string.replace('/Date(', '').replace(')/', '')
    date_string = date_string[:-3]
    new_date = datetime.datetime.utcfromtimestamp(int(date_string))
    return new_date
```

With the utility class defined, we are ready to perform the request. You'll need to replace the code set in italics with your own values.

```
sales_request = GatewayRequest(gateway_url='http://YOUR_SAP_HOST/sap/opu/
                                           odata/sap/',
                entity_set_name='DailyMaterialSalesSet',
                service_name='ZTEST_MATERIAL_PREDICT01_SRV',
                user='YOUR_USER', password='YOUR_PASS')

# We added three materials here, but you could add as many as you like in this
# syntax
sales_request.add_filter('Material', 'eq', 'YOUR_MATERIAL1')
sales_request.add_filter('Material', 'eq', 'YOUR_MATERIAL2')
sales_request.add_filter('Material', 'eq', 'AS_MANY_AS_YOU_WANT')

# Note for dates OData requires the below filtering syntax
# Yes - dates are a little weird
sales_request.add_filter('ReqDeliveryDate', 'gt',
                         "datetime'2015-01-01T00:00:00'")

sales_request.save_result_to_csv('D:/Data/Sales.csv')
```

Step 3: Explore Data

Now that we have our data we can easily read it into Python. We will need some standard libraries to start with. These are very common, oft-used libraries:

```
import pandas as pd
import numpy as np
import matplotlib.pyplot as plt
from datetime import datetime
```

We will use the `pandas` library to read in the data:

```
df = pd.read_csv('D:/Data/Sales.csv')
```

Let's view our data by taking a look at the first few rows:

```
df.head()
```

It should be of no surprise that the data has the same problems we experienced when reading it into R. In Figure 6-19 we see that there are columns to be removed, and a date column to be adjusted.

	Unnamed: 0	DailySales	Material	ReqDeliveryDate
0	0	48964.75	8939	/Date(1420416000000)/
1	1	30853.88	8939	/Date(1420502400000)/
2	2	65791.00	8939	/Date(1420588800000)/
3	3	17651.20	8939	/Date(1420675200000)/
4	4	36552.90	8939	/Date(1420761600000)/

Figure 6-19. Unconverted sales dataframe in Python

We will perform the same functions we did in R but this time in Python. Those basic steps are:

1. Drop a column
2. Convert the date column to a true date
3. Subset the dataframe by a single material
4. Drop the material column
5. Make the date the index of the dataframe

```
#Drop the column 'Unnamed'
df = df.drop(['Unnamed: 0'], axis = 1)
#Convert the date column to numeric and take out any nonnumeric chars.
df.ReqDeliveryDate = pd.to_numeric(df.ReqDeliveryDate.str.replace('[^0-9]', ''))
#Convert the date column to a proper date using to_datetime
df['ReqDeliveryDate'] = pd.to_datetime(df['ReqDeliveryDate'], unit='ms')
#Subset the dataframe by the single material 8939
df_8939 = df['Material']==8939
df = df[df_8939]
#Drop the material column
df = df.drop(columns=['Material'])
#make the date column the index
df = df.set_index(['ReqDeliveryDate'])
```

Let's take a look at our dataframe again, but this time by doing a quick plot (which is shown in Figure 6-20):

```
plt.plot(df)
```

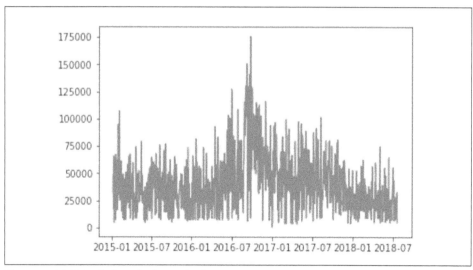

Figure 6-20. Initial plot of sales in Python

We will then use the `statsmodels` package in Python to perform a decomposition of the time series. This is a statistical task that deconstructs the time series object into several categories or patterns. These patterns are observed, trend, seasonal, and residual. Residuals can also be referred to as errors. We will decompose our time series and plot it (the results are in Figure 6-21):

```
from statsmodels.tsa.seasonal import seasonal_decompose
result = seasonal_decompose(df, model='multiplicative', freq = 52)
result.plot()
```

This gives us a general view of our time-series data. The *Observed* chart gives us an exact representation of what is observed in the data. The *Trend* chart shows us what the overall trend of the observations. Think of this as the smoothing of the observations. The *Seasonal* chart highlights if there are any seasonal aspects to the data. If you observe repeating patterns here there could be seasonality in your data. Finally, the *Residual* chart shows the errors between the observed value and a predicted value.

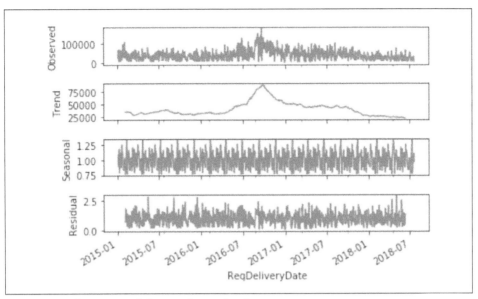

Figure 6-21. Decomposed charts of our sales data

Step 4: Model Data

Like we did in R, we are now going to create an ARIMA prediction. This is made easy in Python with the `pyramid.arima`[7] package. Explore the package to understand all the settings that can be made:

```
from pyramid.arima import auto_arima
step_model = auto_arima(df, start_p=1, start_q=1,
                        max_p=3, max_q=3, m=12,
                        start_P=0, seasonal=True,
                        d=1, D=1, trace=True,
                        error_action='ignore',
                        suppress_warnings=True,
                        stepwise=True)
print(step_model.aic())
```

The log will print as it is running:

```
Fit ARIMA: order=(1, 1, 1) seasonal_order=(0, 1, 1, 12); AIC=21114.204,
  BIC=21138.271, Fit time=2.342 seconds
  .
  .
  .
Fit ARIMA: order=(1, 1, 2) seasonal_order=(0, 1, 1, 12); AIC=21076.593,
```

---

7 *https://pypi.org/project/pyramid-arima/*

```
BIC=21105.474, Fit time=4.335 seconds
Total fit time: 35.598 seconds
```

The next step is to break our time series into two sets. One for training and one for testing. We want to train on the majority of our data and test on the remaining. For our dataset, we have a time series from 2015-01-05 to 2018-07-21. Therefore, we've decided to take the range from 2015-01-05 to 2018-04-01 to train against and the remaining dates to validate against:

```
train = df.loc['2015-01-05':'2018-04-01']
test = df.loc['2018-04-02':]
```

The next step is to fit the model to the training data:

```
step_model.fit(train)
```

Let's predict what will come after 2018-04-01 for the number of time steps in the test set. The number of time steps in the test series is seen with:

```
len(test)
73
```

The command to make the prediction is easy:

```
future = step_model.predict(n_periods=73)
```

To see the results of our prediction you can simply type **future**. Our `future` object is an array of predictions made from our training data. We used 73 periods because we want the length of the prediction to be exactly as long as the length of our `test` array. This way, as you will see later, we can plot them on top of one another and visualize the accuracy:

```
array([26912.93298004, 31499.53327771, 31600.12890142, 25459.90672847,
       30282.82366396, 27135.66098529, 28756.53431911, 31096.66619926,
    … ])
```

Step 5: Evaluate Model

While this all looks fine now, what does our prediction look like when charted against the real results of our test dataframe? First we need to convert our future to a proper dataframe with a column title "Prediction."

```
future = pd.DataFrame(future,index = test.index,columns=['Prediction'])
```

Next, we simply concatenate the test and the future together and plot them, which is made easy using Pandas (the results are shown in Figure 6-22):

```
pd.concat([test,future],axis=1).plot()
```

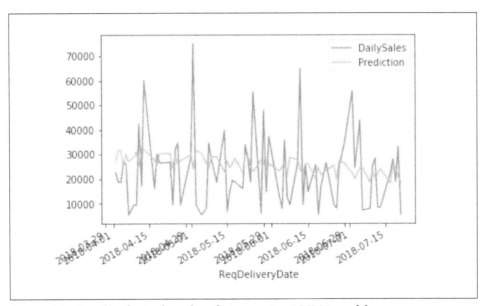

Figure 6-22. Results of actuals and predictions using ARIMA model

The results of the ARIMA model look like they are somewhat close to the mean of the sales for the time period. Looking at the combination of peaks and valleys of the prediction compared to the actuals shows that the direction of the prediction is in line with the actuals, just not to the same degree. This means that when the actuals go up, often the prediction goes up on or near that time period.

To see how the prediction looks against the entirety of the data is just as simple (the results are in Figure 6-23):

```
pd.concat([df,future],axis=1).plot()
```

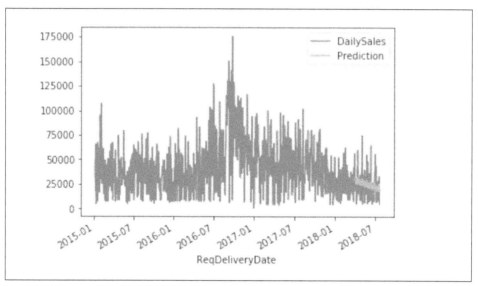

Figure 6-23. Results of prediction when compared to the original data

The results of our visualization make something clear that was not previously apparent. When looking at the daily sales over time we cannot really tell if sales are declining or increasing from 2015 to 2018. The prediction that is plotted here makes it clear that sales overall are declining. We can see that by the distinct downward trend of the prediction line.

Summary

In this chapter we have completed the process of identifying a business need for prediction, extracting data from SAP, exploring the data, modeling that data, and evaluating the accuracy of that model. Time-series predictions are a fascinating and multifaceted area of data science. In our model we simply had univariate time series data; that is, simply a date and a value. With that we looked for patterns in the data that might help us make future predictions using standard ARIMA models in both R and Python. Multivariate time-series analysis is when there are multiple factors influencing the target variable. This is often more robust and can take into account features that affect a target variable (such as sales) across time.

Univariate time-series data is simply a single value over time. Think of the closing price of a stock over time. You could easily employ the techniques here for stock data and get some interesting results. However, it would not be very robust and would not take into account countless other factors that affect the stock price.

Multivariate time-series data is multiple features over time. Let's use our closing stock price again. We have the value of stock over time, but we also have the quarterly company's earnings from EDGAR (see footnote 2) and social sentiment analysis from Twitter.[8] Making stock predictions based on these multiple features would be more robust, but significantly more difficult. As an introduction to making predictions, we felt inclined not to go with multivariate analysis.

Back to our univariate times series data. What if you just have sales and date and nothing more, like we have here? Are we stuck with just univariate analysis? Maybe not. Think of what else in that data could influence sales. Perhaps day of the week? Week of the year? There could be value within the date variable itself. With R and Python, it is easy to extract those values. In Python for instance, these commands give you all the help you need from a date variable:

```
df['year'] = df['date'].dt.year
df['month'] = df['date'].dt.month
df['week_of_year'] = df['date'].dt.week
df['day_of_week'] = df['date'].dt.weekofyear
df['day_of_year'] = df['date'].dt.dayofyear
df['day_of_month'] = df['date'].dt.day
```

In an afternoon's work, the data scientists made some basic predictions using SAP data and common tools. They return to Duane from the SAP team and show him that Big Bonanza can indeed do predictions on sales data. It is up to him and the business to decide if the current ARIMA model, either in R or Python, is good enough or if they need something more accurate and robust. If business leaders want more accuracy, then a multivariate time-series analysis is likely in order and perhaps a recursive neural network or a temporal convolutional network.

8 For example, see *https://ieeexplore.ieee.org/document/7955659* and *https://www.tandfonline.com/doi/full/10.1080/23322039.2017.1367147*.

Clustering and Segmentation in R

Big Bonanza Warehouse is at the beginning of a big change: they're going to upgrade their current SAP system to S/4HANA. Furthermore, they've decided they will not migrate all of their old data unless necessary. Each department has been tasked with identifying its own crucial data. Rod works as a national account rep and his responsibility is to identify which customers in their system should be migrated. They have decades of customer data, much of which is obsolete.

Rod has long wanted to understand his customers better so this process will be rewarding for him. Which customers are the highest value? Does this exercise entail a simple calculation of the top N sales by customer? Is it the frequency of a customer purchase? Maybe it is a combination of factors. He turns to Duane, his SAP Sales and Distribution Analyst, for suggestions on how to approach this. Duane, having read this book, thinks immediately, "This is a task for clustering and segmentation!"

Clustering is any one of several algorithmic approaches to dividing a dataset into smaller, meaningful groups. There's no predetermined notion of what dimension (or dimensions) best allow that grouping. Practically speaking, you'll almost always have some idea what dimension (or features) you want to analyze. For example, we have sales data and you want to know customer value. Well, clearly overall purchase history and dollar value is important. What about the frequency of a customer purchase? What about how recent they purchased? Perhaps they moved away? We will use all three of these features to demonstrate clustering in this chapter.

Segmentation applies the clustering to business strategies. Its most common use comes in researching markets. If you can identify groups of customers (or potential customers, or opportunities), you can identify efficient ways to approach them based on their cluster position. For example, you could cluster customers based on what time of the week they are likely to respond to ads, then fine-tune your advertising from that information.

Clustering and segmentation are often used interchangeably. However, there is a technical distinction. Clustering is considered the act of using machine learning to bunch the customers together. Segmentation is used to *apply the results of clustering*. It absolutely looks like nit-picky semantics, but it's more than that. It also reminds us of a coworker who had a fit when someone used the term *on-premise* incorrectly...calm yourself.

In this chapter we will walk through the process of clustering and segmenting customer data using a variety of techniques. This is a one-time report to be delivered to Rod. We've decided to use R Markdown[1] as it is an easy way to report our results. There is no need to build a dynamic dashboard such as PowerBI as we did in Chapter 5 since the data is not going to change. R Markdown can become quite complex; however, in our example we're going to use the basic features. Figure 7-1 shows the process we will follow. We have seen this flow before, but this time we've added a "Report" as the final step. Remember, Rod is a national account representative; sales people don't want to see code.

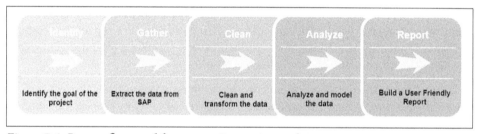

Figure 7-1. Process flow used for segmenting customer data

Understanding Clustering and Segmentation

Before we can segment our customers, we need to understand a few different types of clustering and segmentation techniques. There are many different clustering techniques, but we will focus on:

- The recency, frequency, and monetary value (RFM) approach
- *k*-means clustering
- *k*-medoid or partitioning around medoids (PAM) clustering
- Hierarchical clustering
- Time-series clustering

---

1 A nice introduction with a great cheat sheet can be found on the R Studio website (*http://bit.ly/2lSzWLO*).

RFM

RFM is a clustering method that evaluates customers based solely on their purchase history. The scenario is pretty straightforward. The customer is evaluated based on the following three factors:

Recency
> When was the last purchase?

Frequency
> How many purchases did they make in a given time period?

Monetary value
> What is the total dollar value of the purchases in this time period?

Once these questions are answered the customer is assigned a value for each factor, typically 5 for the top 20%, 4 for the next 20%, and so on. Once they are given values in each category, we can cluster the customers based on those values. These are individual RFM *values*. These values are combined (concatenated) into the RFM *score*. For instance, if a customer has a recency of 5, a frequency of 4, and a monetary value of 3, their RFM score would be 543.

These customers are then placed into a category from which actions can be taken (i.e., during segmentation), as shown in Table 7-1. This can be a very granular or more generic approach; there is a detailed list of options on the Putler website (*https://www.putler.com/rfm-analysis*).

Table 7-1. RFM customer segment characteristics

Customer Segment	Factor	Characteristics
Champions	R - High	Bought recently
	F - High	Buy often
	M - High	Spend the most
Potential Champions	R - High	Bought recently
	F - Medium	Not often
	M - High	Spent a lot
Middle of the Road	R - Medium to High	Bought fairly recently
	F - Medium to High	Have some frequency
	M - Medium	Spend a medium amount
Almost Inactive	R - Low to Medium	Haven't bought in a while
	F - Medium	Had some frequency
	M - Low to Medium	Spent a medium to low amount
Inactive	R - Low	No recent activity
	F - Low	Not much if any frequency
	M - Low	Not spending much

Customer Segment	Factor	Characteristics
One-Timers	R - Anything	Any time frame recently
	F - Low	Not much if any frequency
	M - Anything	Any monetary value
Penny Pinchers	R - Anything	Any time frame recently
	F - Anything	Any type of frequency
	M - Low	Low monetary value

Businesses will have different definitions of what they consider *High*, *Medium*, and *Low*. For our purposes, we will say High is 4 to 5, Medium is 2 to 3, and Low is 1.

Pareto Principle

Many clustering and evaluation techniques that are ultimately used for customer segmentation are based on the *Pareto principle*, which is summed up in Figure 7-2.

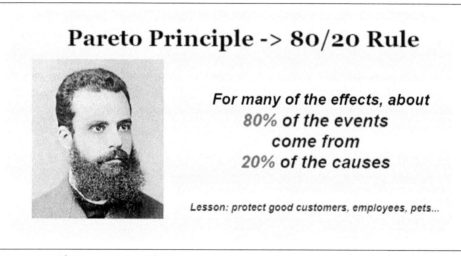

Figure 7-2. The Pareto principle

This principle indicates that 80% of the sales for Big Bonanza Warehouse is driven by only 20% of the customers. For our conversion task, that means we want to make sure that these key customers are converted into the new system.

k-Means

k-means is an algorithm that clusters values around a geometric center. When using *k*-means you need to define the number of clusters you'd like to use. The process of choosing the number of clusters is both intuitive (in the respect that you may know your data and have an idea of how many clusters or groups you will need) and experimental. We will also explore automatically finding the optimal clusters later in this chapter. For now, let's choose three. The algorithm randomly initializes three points called centroids. Then it goes through each of the data points (our customers' RFM score perhaps) and assigns them to the closest centroid. Then the algorithm focuses back on the centroids and moves them to the average distance from all points that were assigned to it. This process repeats until the centroids stop moving. If there are few centroids, *k*-means is computationally fast. An example process might look something like Figures 7-3 through 7-6.

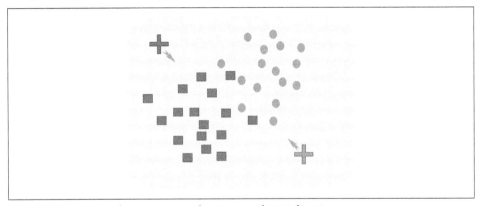

Figure 7-3. Step 1 in k-means—random centroid initialization

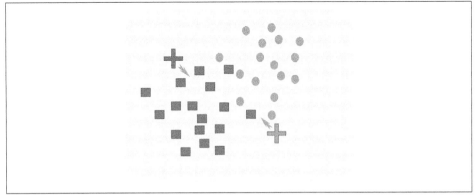

Figure 7-4. Step 2 in k-means—moving centroids via average distance

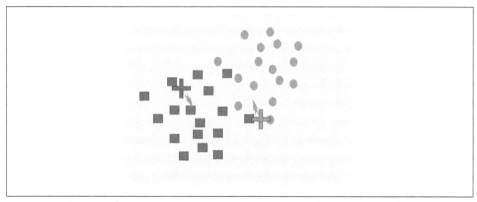

Figure 7-5. Step 3 in k-means—continuing to move centroids via average distance

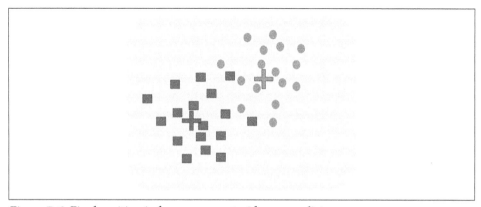

Figure 7-6. Final position in k-means - centroid average distance convergence

k-Medoid

k-medoid is a data partitioning algorithm like *k*-means, except where *k*-means minimizes the total squared error of centroid distance *k*-medoid minimizes the sum of the dissimilarities. This can make it more robust to noise and outliers when compared to *k*-means. The most common implementation of *k*-m is the PAM algorithm. The steps would look similar to the ones shown above for *k*-means.

Simply put, *k*-means uses the mean and *k*-m uses the median.

Hierarchical Clustering

Hierarchical clustering uses a technique to build a hierarchy from the ground up. It does not require the number of clusters to be specified beforehand. There are two types of hierarchical clustering: agglomerative and divisive. We introduced these concepts in Chapter 2. To quickly recap, agglomerative clustering works by first putting each point into its own cluster. For our example, every customer would be a cluster. Then it identifies the closest two clusters and combines them into one. It repeats this process until every data point is in one cluster. Divisive clustering works in reverse. All of our customers are put into a cluster. That cluster is split recursively until all the customers are in their own individual cluster.

There are different linkage types that can be used to determine the pairing of the data points into clusters. The two most common are complete and mean:

Complete linkage
: Finds the maximum possible distance between two points belonging to two clusters.

Mean linkage
: Finds all possible pairwise distances for points belonging to two different clusters and then takes the mean.

These cluster regions become wider and more discernible as the categories move upward as shown in Figure 7-7. Diagrams of hierarchical clustering are referred to as *dendrograms*.

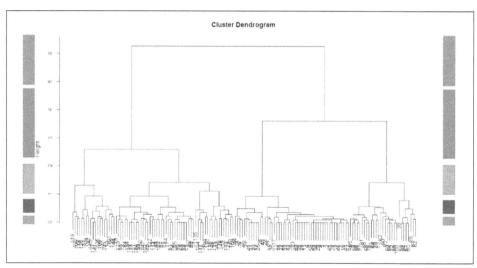

Figure 7-7. Cluster dendrogram (the colored bars on the y-axis represent the levels of clustering)

What Are Distances?

You may be wondering what these *distances* actually are. Here is a simple method to help you understand it more intuitively. The distances calculated in this diagram are the pairwise distances between all the values for an observation in a cluster. Let's take a look at some illustrative code.

Create a matrix of five observations and with one variable by using this R code in your RStudio console; the results are shown after the code.

```
x <- matrix(rnorm(5), ncol=1)
```

```
1    0.8486870
2   -1.7190450
3   -0.2461595
4    0.5916308
5   -0.6591891
```

Create a distance matrix with the dist function. Format it in as a normal matrix using the as.matrix function. The results are shown after the code.

```
as.matrix(dist(x))
```

```
               1         2         3         4         5
1  0.0000000  2.567732  1.0948465  0.2570562  1.5078761
2  2.5677320  0.000000  1.4728855  2.3106758  1.0598560
3  1.0948465  1.472885  0.0000000  0.8377903  0.4130295
4  0.2570562  2.310676  0.8377903  0.0000000  1.2508199
5  1.5078761  1.059856  0.4130295  1.2508199  0.0000000
```

Notice all the distances along the diagonal are zero. These are the distances of each observation to themselves. The other distances are simply the difference between each of the points. For instance, the difference between point 1 (0.8486870) and 5 (-0.6591891) is 1.5078761. It can get much more complex than this, but we think this is a good illustration of hierarchical clustering basics.

Time-Series Clustering

Time-series clustering is not something we are going to do with our customer segmentation, as it requires much more computational power and data than regular clustering. However, it is a fascinating type of clustering and something we want to mention. Time-series clustering creates clusters from the data based on their behavior over time. For instance, considering our scenario, we may have customers that exhibit a particular behavior right before going inactive. They had a high frequency of purchases in the past, slowed gradually, and the monetary value decreased. Perhaps we have additional data and we can see that these customers had an increased number of returns (and therefore frustration). By clustering this pattern over time we can see when a current customer, exhibiting the same pattern and belonging to the same cluster, has not yet gone inactive. Marketing, in particular, would be interested in knowing about these customers to prevent churn.

 There is a very robust and wonderful R package *TSclust* (*http://www.jstatsoft.org/v62/i01/paper*) made specifically for time-series clustering. Time-series hierarchical clustering is not only useful—it's also a lot of fun.

Step 1: Collecting the Data

We have explored a number of ways to extract data from SAP. This time we are going to use a Core Data Service (CDS) view. In Chapter 3 we detail the process for defining a CDS view for sales data. That is the exact CDS view we will use here, so make sure to brush up on Chapter 3!

Step 2: Cleaning the Data

Once we have downloaded the data from SAP, we need to clean it. We have done this so far for every chapter, and you may recall in the introduction that SAP data is clean! Here's some perspective: if you are a data scientist, you will agree that this data is as clean as it gets. Data scientists are often dealing with wildly unclean data. For instance, data we recently worked with from the FDA's Orange Book (*http://bit.ly/2lSCKZm*) has a particularly interesting "therapeutic class" column. These classes can be of multiple categories. If there is more than one class it is just added to the field. You never know how many classes of which group are going to be in that one field. There may be one class, there may be a dozen. To get the data out of this column you have to split it, stack it, shape it, do some regular expression (regex) work on it, and then it still isn't quite there. We use this as an example of what a dirty column might look like, and this is not a very complex example of the daily toils of cleaning data. From that perspective, SAP's data is sparkling clean.

Nonetheless, our sparkling data still needs a little shine. First let's load the libraries that we are going to need for our next steps:

```
library(tidyverse)
library(cluster)
library(factoextra)
library(DT)
library(ggplot2)
library(car)
library(rgl)
library(httr)
```

The `httr` library in R (*http://bit.ly/2k0DsTW*) makes it easy to extract data directly from our CDS view. The first step is to identify the URL (refer back to "Core Data Services" on page 80 for a refresher on this).

```
url <- 'http:/<host>:<port>/sap/opu/odata/sap/ZBD_DD_SALES_CDS/ZBD_DD_SALES'
```

The next step is to simply call the service and authenticate with your SAP credentials:

```
r <- GET(url, authenticate("[YOUR_USER_ID]", "[PASSWORD]", "basic"))
```

The r object is a *response* object. It contains details on the HTTP response including the content. Access the content with the following command:

```
customers <- content(r)
```

The `customers` object is a large list. We need to get that into a friendlier format before we move on. First we will extract the results of the list in this way:

```
customers <- customers$d$results
```

We still have a list, but it is only a list of the results of our call and not the HTTP details. We can turn that list into a dataframe using a `do.call` command (*http://bit.ly/2lxahIr*) and binding all the rows of the list together:

```
customers <- do.call(rbind, customers)
```

 Take some time to get to know `do.call` (*https://www.rdocumentation.org/packages/base/versions/3.6.0/topics/do.call*). This simple and unassuming command will become a well-used tool in your data scientist's toolbox.

Finally, we convert our object into a dataframe:

```
customers <- as.data.frame(customers)
```

Let's take a look at it. This time instead of using the messy `head` function by itself, we will leverage the `DT` library (*https://rstudio.github.io/DT/*). Here's the command we'll need to run (the results are shown in Figure 7-8):

```
datatable(head(customers))
```

Show 10 ▾ entries

	__metadata	SalesDocument	UoM	CustomerMaterial	ItemCategory	NetPrice	SalesDocumentLine	CreateDate
1	[object Object]		PC		ZAN	11.00000	000010	Date(1528934400000)
2	[object Object]		EA		ZAN	22.62000	000010	Date(1529366400000)
3	[object Object]		EA		ZAN	14.17000	000020	Date(1529366400000)
4	[object Object]		EA		ZAN	14.17000	000010	Date(1529366400000)
5	[object Object]		EA		ZAN	19.40000	000010	Date(1529539200000)
6	[object Object]		EA		ZAN	131.88000	000010	Date(1543190400000)

Figure 7-8. Datatables view (datatables are a nicely formatted and sortable dataframe from the DT library)

As we have done a few times already, there are some quick and easy cleanups to do—get rid of a couple extra columns, some whitespace, and a few columns that we don't want. We also drop the __metadata, CreateTime, CustomerMaterial, ItemCategory, DocumentType, and DocumentCategory columns as they are not needed for our analysis:

```
customers$__metadata <- NULL
customers$CreateTime <- NULL
customers$Material <- trimws(tab$Material)
customers$DocumentType <- NULL
customers$CustomerMaterial <- NULL
```

```
customers$ItemCategory <- NULL
customers$DocumentCategory <- NULL
```

We notice that the date comes over in Unix format. We will fix this the same way we fixed it in Chapter 6:

```
#Remove all nonnumeric from the date column
customers$CreateDate <- gsub("[^0-9]", "", customers$CreateDate)

#Convert the unix time to a regular date time using the anytime library
library(anytime)

#First trim the whitespace
customers$CreateDate <- trimws(customers$CreateDate)

#Remove the final three numbers
customers$CreateDate <- gsub('.{3}$', '', customers$CreateDate)


#Convert the field to numeric
customers$CreateDate <- as.numeric(customers$CreateDate)

#Convert the unix time to a readable time
customers$CreateDate <- anydate(customers$CreateDate)

detach(package:anytime)
```

We also noticed when previewing our data that some units of measure (UoM) were blank. Units of measure are an important and complex master data concept in SAP. If our transactional data is missing the UoM, this indicates we do not know the actual quantity. For example, if we have a quantity of 10 but no UoM do we have 10 each or 10 boxes of 12 each? In the event the UoM is missing, we should exclude those entries:

```
customers <- customers[customers$UoM != '',]
```

Let's also make sure that the fields are appropriately typed: dates are dates, integers are integers, and so on. We will also clear up whitespace that appears in some of the columns:

```
#The price has commas - remove 'em
customers$NetPrice <- gsub(',', '', customers$NetPrice)

#The price should be converted to a numeric
customers$NetPrice <- as.numeric(customers$NetPrice)

#There are commas in the quantity, take them out.
customers$Quantity <- gsub(',', '', customers$Quantity)

#The quantity should also be numeric
customers$Quantity <- as.numeric(customers$Quantity)
```

```
#The date should be in a standard date format. It is currently MM/DD/YYYY.
customers$CreateDate<- as.Date(customers$Created.on, '%m/%d/%Y')

#trim the whitespace out of the unit of measure.
customers$UoM <- trimws(customers$UoM)
```

Now we have a dataframe of customers and their sales. Let's think for a moment about our mission. We want to identify characteristics per *customer*, so our dataframe should have unique rows per customer. Currently, we have all sales for each customer. Our key therefore is not *customer;* it is *order*. Let's change that and create a dataframe of RFM values for each customer as the basis for all other analysis.

First we will work on recency. To do this, create a new entry in the dataframe that indicates the number of days since the sale:

```
#get the number of days since the last purchase
customers$last_purchase <- Sys.Date() - customers$CreateDate
```

Remember that important statistical paper titled "The Split-Apply-Combine Strategy for Data Analysis" (*http://bit.ly/2lvfPTO*) referenced in Chapter 6? We will use those same techniques here. We want a dataframe of the most recent purchase by customers. We do this using the aggregate function and taking the minimum value. We are *splitting* data off of our main dataframe by aggregating it and *applying* the minimum function to it:

```
#create a dataframe of most recent orders by customer.
recent <- aggregate(last_purchase ~ Customer, data=customers, FUN=min, na.rm=TRUE)
```

In true *combine* fashion we put them back together again, which will create a column of the most recent purchase by customer:

```
#Merge the recent back to the original
customers <- merge(customers, recent, by='Customer', all=TRUE, sort=TRUE)
names(customers)[names(customers)=="last_purchase.y"] <- "most_recent_order_days"
#What we have now is the most_recent_order_days in our original dataframe
```

Next we will work on frequency, following the same theory as we did for recency. Create a dataframe for the count of orders by customer by aggregating the data by sales document and customer. The way you count in R is by asking "what is the length?" Because we have multiple lines on an individual order and we want to count orders not lines we say, "what is the *unique* length?" or "how many lines are on the order?"

```
#create a seperate dataframe of the count of orders for a customer
order_count <- aggregate(SalesDocument ~ Customer, data=customers,
    function(x) length(unique(x)))
```

Again, add the newly split dataframe back into the original to leave a column of order count assigned to the customer:

```
#Merge the order_count back
customers <- merge(customers, order_count, by='Customer', all=TRUE, sort=TRUE)

#Rename the field to be nice
names(customers)[names(customers)=='SalesDocument.y'] <- 'count_total_orders'
```

Finally, we will deal with the monetary value of a customer. We have in our dataframe columns for price and quantity. Multiply these together to get the value per line:

```
#calculate order values. Get per line then aggregate.
customers$order_value <- customers$Quantity * customers$NetPrice
```

Again, in true *Split-Apply-Combine* fashion, aggregate the values of all lines per customer:

```
#Split off the aggregated value per customer.
total_value <- aggregate(order_value ~ Customer, data=customers, FUN=sum,
                         na.rm = TRUE)
```

Repeat the process to merge the newly split dataframe back to the original.

```
#Merge the total_value back
customers <- merge(customers, total_value, by='Customer', all=TRUE)

#nicify  the name
names(customers)[names(customers)=='order_value.y'] <- 'total_purchase_value'
```

 All those split-off dataframes are no longer of use. To keep your workspace clean and free up some memory, remove them with this simple command:

```
    rm(recent, order_count, total_value)
```

A little cleanup of our main dataframe is in order after all that splitting and combining. We want to make sure that each row is unique. There should be no duplicate rows when comparing all fields. After all, no order number and line number should be the same for multiple rows:

```
customers <- customers[!duplicated(customers), ]
```

We also want to ensure that there are no customer values that are blank. We are identifying customers and their RFM values so obviously a blank customer is of no use. There should be none, but it is good practice to double-check this:

```
customers <- na.omit(customers)
```

What we want is a dataframe of our four key values: customer number, most_recent_order_days, count_total_orders, and total_purchase_value. View the column names and position with the colnames function.

```
colnames(customers)
 [1] "Sold.To.Pt"      "Sales.Doc..x"     "Created.on"      "Name.1"
 [5] "City"            "Rg"               "PostalCode"      "Material"
```

```
 [9] "Matl.Group"            "Order.Quantity"       "SU"                    "Net.Price"
[13] "Material.description"   "last_purchase.x"      "most_recent_order_days" "count_total_orders"
[17] "order_value.x"         "total_purchase_value"
```

We want only the columns 1, 15, 16, and 18. All the other columns are no longer necessary, they were just needed to create the RFM values. We want a dataframe of these RFM values by customer only. This is simple, as we just slice off all other columns:

```
#slice off the required columns
customer <- customers[, c(1, 15, 16, 18)]
```

Now when we look at the dataframe we see just the columns we want. However, we also notice at this point that we have duplicate rows:

```
> head(customer)
  Sold.To.Pt most_recent_order_days count_total_orders total_purchase_value
1     1018              153                   1                 37734.08
2     1035              138                   1                    89.85
3     1082              143                   1                 36181.46
4     1082              143                   1                 36181.46
5     1082              143                   1                 36181.46
6     1082              143                   1                 36181.46
```

Remove the duplicate rows with the !duplicated command:

```
#remove customer duplicates
customer <- customer[!duplicated(customer$Customer),]
```

How in the world are we going to rank them the way we need them? This seems like a big task. Not with R! We simply create a new dataframe from customer. Make a column titled R that is a mutation of most_recent_order_days. The mutation is to create a percentage ranking based on 5. That is, put the top 20% in 5, the next 20% in 4, and so on. Repeat this process for count_total_orders and total_purchase_value.

```
#Now that we have a value for each of our customers, we can create an RFM
customer_rfm <- customer %>%
  mutate(R = ntile(desc(most_recent_order_days), 5),
         F = ntile(count_total_orders, 5),
         M = ntile(total_purchase_value, 5))
```

Now that we have our R, F, and M values, we can turn the column for customer into an index and clean up our workspace:

```
#make the customer the row names
row.names(customer_rfm) <- customer$Customer

#ditch customer because it is an index
customer_rfm$Customer <- NULL

#clean up the workspace and free memory
rm(customer, customers)
```

Ever worked with someone who complained they lost all their work because their computer crashed? "I was working on that for four hours and now it's lost!" Well, that can happen to us too, so let's create a little output that can be read in easily if we want to pick up from this point:

```
#We now have a clean file with customers and their RFM values.
#(recency, frequency, monetary value)
#To save time in the future, we will write this to a csv.
write.csv(customer_rfm, 'D:/Data/customer_rfm.csv')
```

Step 3: Analyzing the Data

After those simple steps the data is ready to analyze. We have six different techniques we are going to employ in analysis. It is redundant, but illustrative of the different ways you can analyze data. These methods are:

- Pareto principle
- *k*-means clustering
- *k*-medoid clustering
- Hierarchical clustering
- Manual clustering

Revisiting the Pareto Principle

Remember the Pareto principle suggests that 80% of our sales is dictated by 20% of our customers. How close is our data to that principle? For that matter, how would we tell which customers contribute to 80% of the sales? Let's break the concept into small components:

1. Calculate what the cutoff is for 80% of the sales.
2. Order our dataframe from largest monetary value to smallest.
3. Create a column that has the cumulative sum of the monetary value. That is, it will add row by row.
4. Label each customer as "Top 20" if the cumulative sum is less than the cutoff and "Bottom 80" if it is greater than the cutoff.
5. Calculate the percentage of customers in each group.
6. Interpret the findings.

Calculating 80% of the sales is simple:

```
#first question is what is 80% of the total sales?
p_80 <- 0.8 * sum(customer_rfm$total_purchase_value)
```

Then we sort the dataframe from largest to smallest monetary value:

```
#First step is to order the dataframe by monetary value.
customer_rfm <- customer_rfm[order(-customer_rfm$total_purchase_value),]
```

Add a column to the dataframe that is the rolling sum of the monetary values:

```
customer_rfm$pareto <- cumsum(customer_rfm$total_purchase_value)
```

Label the customers before and after the cutoff:

```
customer_rfm$pareto_text <- ifelse(customer_rfm$pareto <= p_80,
                                   'Top 20', 'Bottom 80')
```

Calculate the percentages using prop.table (*http://bit.ly/2ksaXhY*).

```
prop.table(table(customer_rfm$pareto_text))*100
Bottom 80  Top 20
94.090016  5.909984
```

By our calculations, roughly the top 6% of the customers contribute to 80% of the sales. This sounds quite far off of the Pareto principle until you consider that Big Bonanza Warehouse has a lot of customers. However, they also have distributors and resellers. It is the distributors and the resellers that are driving the vast majority of the sales. At first glance, this feature in the data may not seem very useful. Until you think about it. Big Bonanza Warehouse has stores and distribution centers all over the United States. Distributors and resellers get their product from distribution centers and not the stores. If it comes to making a decision whether to close a distribution center or a store, the choice is clear: close the store.

Finding Optimal Clusters

For *k*-means and *k*-medoid clustering we need to manually choose the optimal number of clusters. This process is as much an art as it is a science. However, there are some tools we can employ to choose the optimal number of clusters. The R library factoextra (*http://bit.ly/2lzUTuM*) has a method fviz_nbclust that will help to find and visualize the optimal cluster number. We want to do this before we start our *k*-means and *k*-medoid clustering. There are three possible options in this method:

Elbow method
> Minimizes the within-cluster sum of squares (wss). The total of the wss measures how compact a cluster is. Theoretically, this should be as small as possible. It is referred to as the Elbow method because the chart has an elbow in it where increasing the number of clusters no longer contributes much to minimizing the wss.

Average Silhouette method

Measures how well each point falls within a cluster. A high value indicates good clustering. It performs this by measuring the average distance between the clusters.

Gap Statistic method

Measures the total within intra-cluster variation. The gap statistic is optimal when it is maximized and further clusters do not contribute much if any to the value.

We will use each of these methods and then decide which one or combination to use. Our dataframe has over a quarter million rows, which is too much for these statistical methods. We can deal with this by taking a representative sample of the data with enough points to ensure a similar distribution. Because we want reproducibility in our sampling, we need to set a seed. Otherwise, every time this step is run the randomness could lead to slightly different results. We also only want the RFM values for which we are clustering:

```
#Set a seed for reproducibility
set.seed(12345)
#Take only the R, F and M values from the dataframe, in columns 4,5,6
customer_rfm_sample <- customer_rfm[, c(4,5,6)]
#Take a sample using sample_n from dplyr library (in tidyverse)
customer_rfm_sample <- sample_n(customer_rfm_sample, 1000)
```

These clustering algorithms run better when the data is normalized. We will log transform the data for each of our features:

```
#Log transform the data
customer_rfm_sample$R <- log(customer_rfm_sample$R)
customer_rfm_sample$F <- log(customer_rfm_sample$F)
customer_rfm_sample$M <- log(customer_rfm_sample$M)
```

Now we use `fviz_nbclust` to optimize and visualize our different methods. The first will be the Elbow method shown in Figure 7-9:

```
#Finding the optimal number of clusters
 fviz_nbclust(customer_rfm_sample, kmeans, method="wss")
```

Second is the visualization of the optimal number of clusters using the Silhouette method (the results are shown in Figure 7-10):

```
fviz_nbclust(customer_rfm_sample, kmeans, method="silhouette")
```

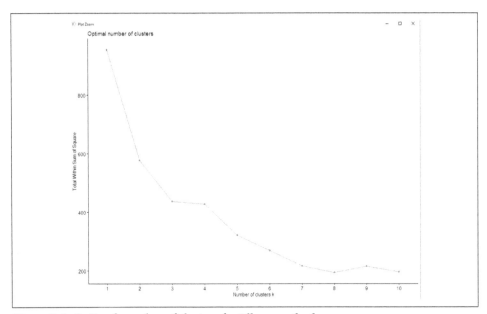

Figure 7-9. Optimal number of clusters for Elbow method

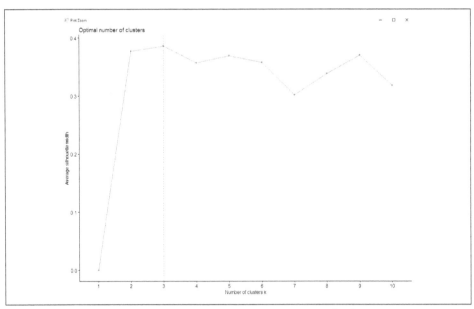

Figure 7-10. Optimal number of clusters for the Silhouette method

Finally, we will use the Gap Statistic method (the results are shown in Figure 7-11):

```
fviz_nbclust(customer_rfm_sample, kmeans, method="gap_stat")
```

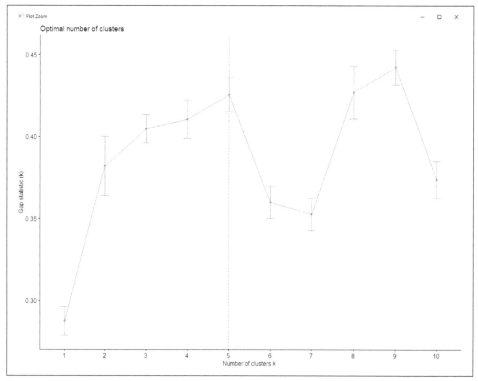

Figure 7-11. Optimal number of clusters using the Gap Statistic method

Each method had different results. The Elbow method left a chart that did not have a distinct "elbow" in it. When we look at it, it seems the elbow could be at point 5, 6, or 7. The silhouette method distinctly shows the average distance between the clusters peaking at 3. The Gap Statistic method also clearly shows the optimal number to be at 5. We know our data and we feel comfortable with five clusters. Three we feel is too small. Five clusters would be in agreement with two of the three methods we have charted.

k-Means Clustering

Once the data is formatted and the number of clusters is identified, executing *k*-means is easy. The first step is to set the number of clusters:

```
#Identify the number of clusters
  number_of_clusters <- 5
```

Then we create a dataframe of our original values (not the RFM values, but the actual values from the customer):

```
cust <- customer_rfm[, c(1,2,3)]
```

Because we do not have a normal distribution we want to normalize these values. If we do not, the charting we do will be squashed and not be very legible. There are many different methods for normalizing data (previously we've used min-max scaling). In this example, we will use a log transformation (*http://bit.ly/2lxpPMj*):

```
cust$most_recent_order_days <- log(cust$most_recent_order_days)
cust$count_total_orders <- log(cust$count_total_orders)
cust$total_purchase_value <- log(cust$total_purchase_value)
```

Now we simply use the k-means (*http://bit.ly/2lszdkl*) method. We put in the dataframe we created, the number of clusters, and the number of times the process should run. By default, k-means initializes its starting point (or initial position) randomly. Because of this, there are occasions when it starts so poorly it fails to cluster well. There is a simple way to overcome this. Simply run k-means numerous times. It's extremely unlikely to start poorly every time. The nstart parameter can be used to specify the number of run times:

```
#Perform the kmeans calculation on our
km <- kmeans(cust, centers = number_of_clusters, nstart = 20)
```

km is a structure with clusters and other attributes related to clustering as is shown in Figure 7-12. For our purposes, we are only interested in the cluster attribute.

```
◎ km                          Large kmeans (9 elements, 16.5 Mb)
    cluster : Named int [1:248867] 5 4 4 4 4 5 5 5 2 3 ...
    ..- attr(*, "names")= chr [1:248867] "2747975" "1943352" "10039640" "10044628" ...
    centers : num [1:5, 1:3] 87.6 86.5 70.5 54.7 39.8 ...
    ..- attr(*, "dimnames")=List of 2
    .. ..$ : chr [1:5] "1" "2" "3" "4" ...
    .. ..$ : chr [1:3] "most_recent_order_days" "count_total_orders" "total_purchase_value"
    totss : num 79192919
    withinss : num [1:5] 699109 626244 608279 695992 816050
    tot.withinss: num 3445675
    betweenss : num 75747244
    size : int [1:5] 99262 71595 21308 24728 31974
    iter : int 4
    ifault : int 0
    attr(*, "class")= chr "kmeans"
```

Figure 7-12. Large k-means structure

We want to create a new dataframe with our customer details and the clusters from km. The clusters need to be factors:

```
viz <- data.frame(cust, cluster=factor(km$cluster))
```

Now we are ready to chart. Our first chart will be a simple `ggplot` of the monetary value and recency (the result is shown in Figure 7-13):

```
ggplot(viz, aes(x=most_recent
_order_days, y=total_purchase_value,
color=cluster)) + geom_point()
```

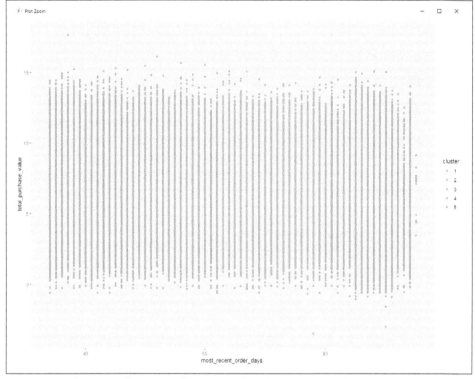

Figure 7-13. k-means clustering of customer data by recency and monetary value

This is not a very satisfying representation of our clusters. While we can see the values of recency and monetary value clearly clustered by color, we do not see how they relate to frequency. What if we try a change to this and plot recency by frequency and then size the points by order value. We will apply an alpha to the points because there are so many of them and this allows us to see when they are blending together (the results are shown in Figure 7-14):

```
ggplot(viz, aes(x=most_recent_order_days,
               y=count_total_orders,
               size=total_purchase_value,
               color=cluster)) +
geom_point(alpha=.05)
```

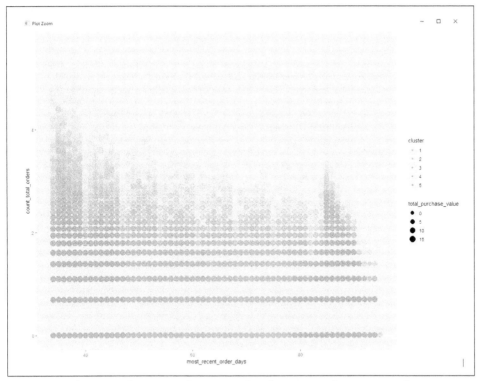

Figure 7-14. k-means clustering of customer data by recency, frequency, and monetary value

Again, not very satisfying. When we chart more than two variables on a two-dimensional plane the results can be rather disappointing. Fortunately in R there are ways to create three-dimensional plots. We will use the car (*http://bit.ly/2kg2ChA*) and the rgl (*http://bit.ly/2lRH6zT*) libraries to do this (the results are shown in Figure 7-15):

```
#create a color scheme for our chart
 colors <- c('red', 'blue', 'orange', 'darkorchid4', 'pink1')

scatter3d(x = viz$count_total_orders,
          y = viz$total_purchase_value,
          z = viz$most_recent_order_days,
          groups = viz$cluster,
          xlab = "Log of Frequency",
          ylab = "Log of Monetary Value",
          zlab = "Log of Recency",
          surface.col = colors,
          axis.scales = FALSE,
          surface = TRUE,
          fit = "smooth",
```

```
ellipsoid = TRUE,
grid = TRUE,
axis.col = c("black", "black", "black"))
```

 You may need to change the recency values from a difftime attribute to numeric. To do this execute the following command:

```
viz$most_recent_order_days <- as.numeric(viz$most_recent
_order_days)
```

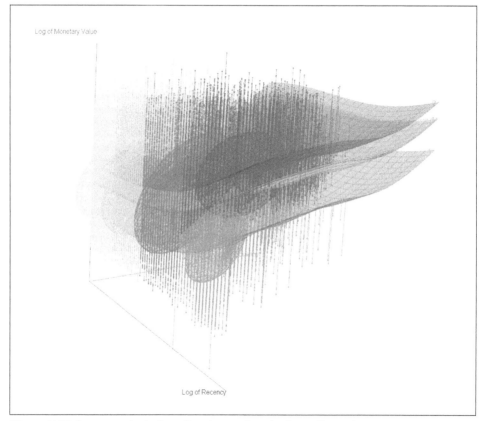

Figure 7-15. k-means clustering of customer data in three dimensions

This is a much more satisfying representation of our clusters in *k*-means and gives us a good idea of how our customers group into five clusters. You can see one group of clusters in the upper right that represents our most recent, most frequent, and highest monetary valued customers. Likewise, in the lower left of the chart we see the least frequent, least recent, and least monetary valued.

Next, we will use *k*-medoid to get a different view of these clusters.

k-Medoid Clustering

k-medoid is similar to *k*-means except that *k*-means uses the mean distance to create clusters, while *k*-medoid uses the median. This makes *k*-medoid less sensitive to noise and outliers. As we discussed earlier, the most common *k*-medoid clustering method is the PAM algorithm.

From our work on *k*-means we have a dataframe titled `cust` with a scaled (log) value of `most_recent_order_days`, `count_total_orders`, and `total_purchase_value`. This is also the format needed for PAM. The `pam` function itself is limited to 65,536 observations so sampling is needed first (we've already done this when estimating the number of clusters):

```
cust_sample <- sample_n(cust, 10000)
```

Execute the PAM clustering algorithm with the following command:

```
#First identify the number of clusters
number_of_clusters <- 5
#Execute PAM with euclidean distance and stand set to
#false as we've already standardized our observations
pam <- pam(cust_sample,
           number_of_clusters,
           metric = "euclidean",
           stand = FALSE)
```

The PAM object consists of the components `medoids` and `clustering`. To view these results use the following commands:

```
head(pam$medoids)
          most_recent_order_days count_total_orders total_purchase_value
2126695                 4.406719          0.6931472             7.799405
10041958                4.442651          0.0000000             2.618125
10040360                4.454347          0.0000000             4.245634
10043047                4.330733          0.6931472             6.116488
2911968                 4.174387          1.0986123            10.480677

head(pam$clustering)
 2382503 3048698 2843476 10055962 10079604   490487
       1       2       1        1        3        4
```

Visualizing the clusters is also easy using the `fviz_cluster` method (the results are shown in Figure 7-16):

```
fviz_cluster(pam, geom='point',
             show.clust.cent = TRUE,
             ellipse = TRUE)
```

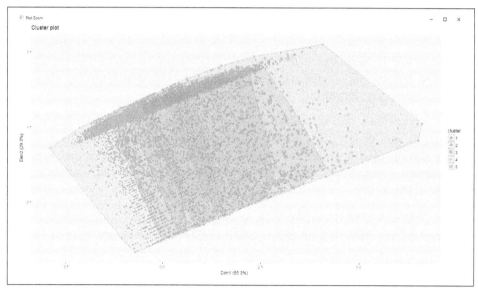

Figure 7-16. k-medoid PAM clustering

pamk() in the fpc library is a wrapper for pam. It prints the suggested number of clusters based on the optimum average silhouette width.

The *k*-medoid visualization of the five clusters gives us a new view of our observations. There appears to be a lot of overlap in this type of clustering, leading us to believe the optimal number of clusters for using this technique is less than what we chose. As an investigation, we will try the pamk function, which determines the number of clusters for us:[2]

```
library(fpc)
pamk <- pamk(cust_sample,
        metric = "euclidean",
        stand = FALSE)
```

Next we will again use the three-dimensional visualization to see how many clusters pamk thinks are optimal (the results are shown in Figure 7-17):

```
colors <- c('red',
        'blue',
        'orange',
```

---

[2] If you are wondering, "why not use pamk simply to determine the optimal number of clusters?" This process can be computationally expensive and run a long time.

```
                    'darkorchid4',
                    'pink1')

    viz <- data.frame(cust_sample,
                      cluster=factor(pamk$pamobject$cluster))

    scatter3d(x = viz$count_total_orders,
              y = viz$total_purchase_value,
              z = viz$most_recent_order_days,
              groups = viz$cluster,
              xlab = "Log of Frequency",
              ylab = "Log of Monetary Value",
              zlab = "Log of Recency",
              surface.col = colors,
              axis.scales = FALSE,
              surface = TRUE,
              fit = "smooth",
              ellipsoid = TRUE,
              grid = TRUE,
              axis.col = c("black", "black", "black"))
```

 Remember that the pamk function uses the Silhouette method for determining the optimal number of clusters.

These results are interesting and should be cause for pause. Using the optimal Average Silhouette method yields two clusters. Why? Remember that there are distributors and resellers in our customer base. Earlier when we applied the Pareto principle we saw that a very small number of our customers contributed to the majority of sales. We surmised that these were our distributors and resellers. In the preceding chart, the upper cluster likely represents our distributors and resellers. The lower cluster likely represents regular customers. The SAP business analyst and data scientist should be questioning these results. What is this visualization telling us? We think this visualization is telling us that the distributors and resellers are skewing the clustering results. We may want to start this process over again but this time exclude the distributors and resellers.

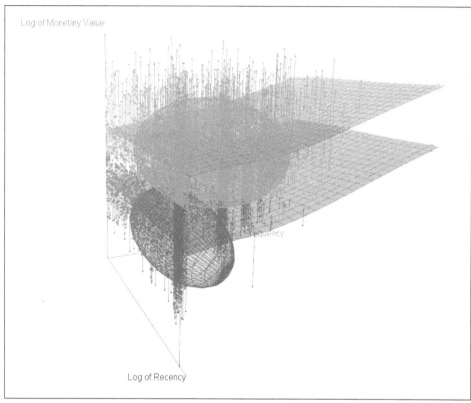

Figure 7-17. Visual results for pamk clustering

What if your SAP system does not discriminate between distributors and resellers and regular customers? How would we exclude distributors and resellers, then? The clustering process we've used with pamk seems to have done that pretty nicely. Save the customers from the lower cluster and restart the clustering process again on that subset.

Next, we will use hierarchical clustering to get another perspective.

Hierarchical Clustering

Hierarchical clustering, as we've discussed, is another approach for identifying segments among observations. Unlike *k*-means and *k*-medoids, it does not require that the number of clusters be identified.[3]

We will perform one of each type of hierarchical clustering. Both of them have five fundamental steps:

- The observations are put in a dataframe, where each column is a value by which to cluster.
- The data is scaled (we will use log).
- A dissimilarity matrix is calculated (distance).
- Clustering is performed.
- Results are displayed.

Our first step is to create a new RFM dataframe. We have done this process a few times now:

```
cust <- customer_rfm[, c(4,5,6)]
```

Now we'll apply logarithm to our values:

```
cust$R <- log(cust$R)
cust$F <- log(cust$F)
cust$M <- log(cust$M)
```

Like our other machine learning clustering techniques, we are limited to a particular maximum number of observations so we must again sample our data:

```
cust_sample <- sample_n(cust, 10000)
```

Now we are ready to create a dissimilarity matrix. We will apply it with the standard default values. The dist() function returns the computed distances between the rows of a data matrix.

```
d <- dist(cust)
```

 To view the parameters and details of the dist function put ?dist into the console and press Enter. Documentation will appear in the right panel of RStudio. If this isn't enough, try ??dist for even more.

---

3 In Chapter 2 we discussed the two types of hierarchical clustering: divisive and agglomerative. Take note that hierarchical clustering is sensitive to outliers.

Agglomerative hierarchical clustering is performed with `hclust()`. Alternatively, divisive hierarchical clustering can be performed with `agnes()`. We will perform both of them here:

```
#Agglomerative Hierarchical Clustering
hcl_a <- hclust(d)
#Divisive Hierarchical Clustering
hcl_d <- agnes(d)
```

Visualizing our findings is easy with the `plot` command (the results of agglomerative hierarchical clustering are shown in Figure 7-18):

```
#Plot Aggplomerative HC - hang the results a bit
#to line them up.
plot(hcl_a, cex = 0.6, hang = -1)
```

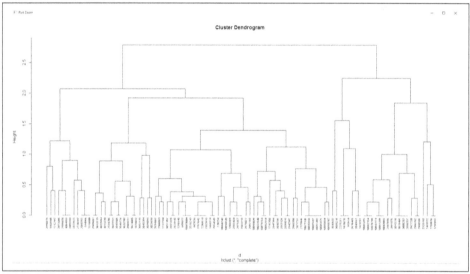

Figure 7-18. Agglomerative hierarchical clustering plot

We can do the same for divisive hierarchical clustering (the results are shown in Figure 7-19):

```
plot(hcl_d, hang = -1)
```

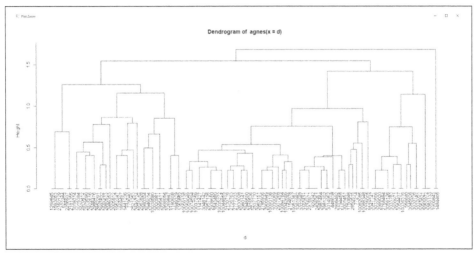

Figure 7-19. Divisive hierarchical clustering plot

Both of these dendrograms are showing the same thing—the clustering of customers based on their recency, frequency, and monetary value. They come to slightly different clusters because their techniques differ.

Personally, we don't think that our observations (customers) worked well as dendrograms. For one thing, to get accurate and readable visualizations we had to sample down quite a bit, probably too much actually to maintain integrity in our observations' relationships. However, the purpose here was to demonstrate another type of clustering.[4]

Manual RFM

For our final technique, we will define manual buckets into which our RFM scores fall. It is a method of manual clustering of the customers. It may seem cheap, but it works and fulfills the requirements for many types of analyses.

---

4 There are a number of ways to display dendrograms—do a simple internet search for "beautiful dendrograms" for some options. Some of our favorite techniques can be done using the ape# package. You can get pretty creative with colors and shapes in dendrograms. This is more than simply aesthetics. Visualizations bring out the data in ways that our minds more easily interpret. *The Functional Art: An Introduction* by Alberto Cairo is a wonderful, insightful must for anyone wanting to get more from their visualizations.

Sometimes the simplest tool is the best. The range of neural networks and machine learning algorithms is wide and robust. It is tempting to grab the shiniest one and try to make that fit your data. We are guilty of that, especially when it comes to nature-inspired algorithms. Read the fantastic book *Clever Algorithms* (*http://bit.ly/ 2kpe2Q8*) and you'll try to apply ant colony optimization to everything. We make this comment now because in this exercise we just use "if" statements...about the least flashy technique there is.

The hardest part of performing manual RFM is defining the categories. What constitutes a *champion* customer as opposed to a *potential champion*? Big Bonanza Warehouse moves a large number of products to individual customers, but they also have distributors. The distributors are going to always look like champions compared to customers. Their definitions for the RFM model will vary drastically from the definitions for a company that does not have distributors. This business process requires you to work closely with marketing and sales teams to define the RFM categories. For our purposes, we will define them exactly as Table 7-1 above defines them. The code is a simple nest of `ifelse` statements:

```
#What about manual clustering? Why not? Don't overlook the simple for the #shiny.
customer_rfm$segment <- ifelse(customer_rfm$R >= 4 &
                               customer_rfm$F >= 4 &
                               customer_rfm$M >= 4,
                               'Champion', '')
customer_rfm$segment <- ifelse(customer_rfm$segment == '',
                               ifelse(customer_rfm$R >= 4 &
                                      customer_rfm$F >= 2 &
                                      customer_rfm$F <= 3 &
                                      customer_rfm$M >= 4,
                                      'Potential Champion', ''),
                               customer_rfm$segment)
customer_rfm$segment <- ifelse(customer_rfm$segment == '',
                               ifelse(customer_rfm$R >= 2 &
                                      customer_rfm$R <= 5 &
                                      customer_rfm$F >= 2 &
                                      customer_rfm$F <= 5 &
                                      customer_rfm$M >= 2 &
                                      customer_rfm$M <= 3,
                                      'Middle Of The Road', ''),
                               customer_rfm$segment)
customer_rfm$segment <- ifelse(customer_rfm$segment == '',
                               ifelse(customer_rfm$R >= 1 &
                                      customer_rfm$R <= 3 &
                                      customer_rfm$F >= 2 &
                                      customer_rfm$F <= 3 &
                                      customer_rfm$M >= 1 &
                                      customer_rfm$M <= 3,
                                      'Almost Inactive', ''),
                               customer_rfm$segment)
```

```
customer_rfm$segment <- ifelse(customer_rfm$segment == '',
                        ifelse(customer_rfm$R == 1 &
                               customer_rfm$F == 1 &
                               customer_rfm$M == 1,
                               'Inactive', ''),
                        customer_rfm$segment)
customer_rfm$segment <- ifelse(customer_rfm$segment == '',
                        ifelse(customer_rfm$F == 1,
                               'One Timers', ''),
                        customer_rfm$segment)
customer_rfm$segment <- ifelse(customer_rfm$segment == '',
                        ifelse(customer_rfm$M == 1,
                               'Penny Pinchers', ''),
                        customer_rfm$segment)
customer_rfm$segment <- ifelse(customer_rfm$segment == '',
                        'Unclassified', customer_rfm$segment)
```

Once the code is done we can see the results with a `table` statement:

```
table(customer_rfm$segment)
Almost Inactive        Champion          Inactive
          28933           34264              5134
Middle Of The Road     One Timers     Penny Pinchers
          61326           44640             13839
Potential Champion   Unclassified
          11907           48824
```

The `ggplot2` package (*https://ggplot2.tidyverse.org/*) can quickly show us a visual distribution of the classes (the results are shown in Figure 7-20):

```
ggplot(customer_rfm, aes(segment)) + geom_bar().
```

This chart shows us some interesting findings. In particular, there is a high number of customers who did not get classified at all (unclassified). Most of the customers, not surprisingly, fall into the *Middle of the Road* category. Our initial goal was to identify customers who should be converted to the new system. Clearly *Champion* and *Potential Champion* should make the cut. However, it is up to the business to decide if *Middle of the Road* and *Unclassified* should make it. Our recommendation would be to err on the side of caution and keep them. However, even if we keep those large groups we've reduced our conversion task substantially by not including the *Almost Inactive, Inactive, One-Timers,* and *Penny Pinchers*.

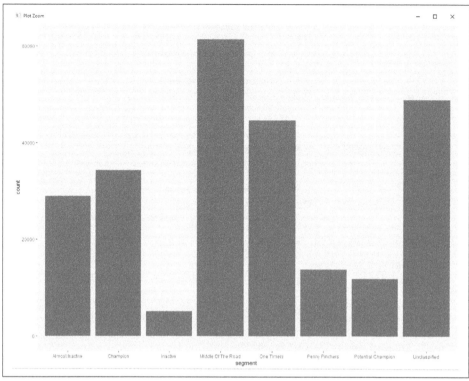

Figure 7-20. Distribution of manually segmented customers

Step 4: Report the Findings

We've done the analysis and have some interesting findings. Now, however, we want to report these findings to others. Presenting lines of code will not go over well in meetings. We will use R Markdown to generate a unique report. First we will code the R Markdown document. Then we will *knit* (*http://bit.ly/2lScRcc*) the document to make it presentable to end users. *Knitting* in R studio is similar to publishing.

To begin, start a new R Markdown document by following the menu path File → R Markdown in RStudio, as shown in Figure 7-21.

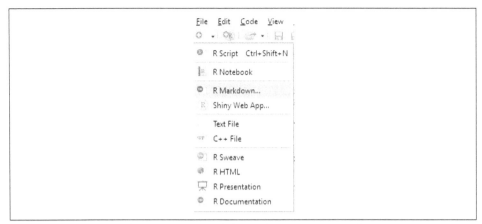

Figure 7-21. Menu path to create a Markdown document in RStudio

Create a title for the presentation and add your name as the author (Figure 7-22).

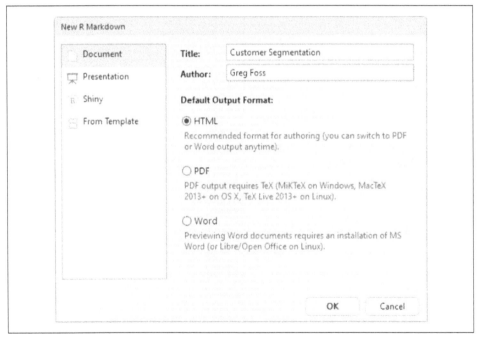

Figure 7-22. Create R Markdown document

Let's take a look at the basic structure of an R Markdown document, as shown in Figure 7-23.

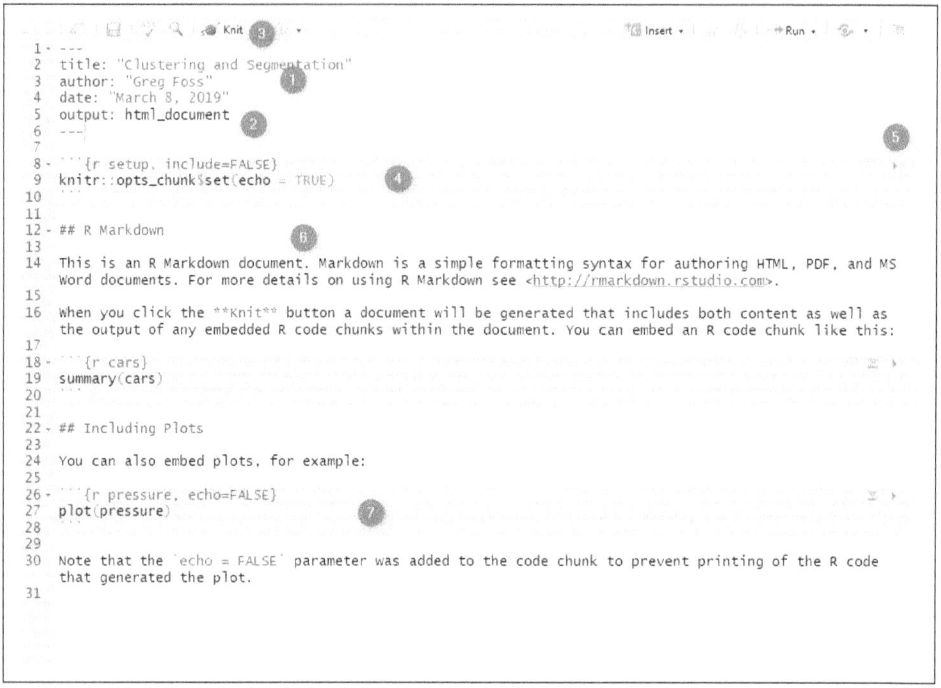

Figure 7-23. Basic structure of Markdown document

The basic information of your document:

1. The type of document you are creating. HTML is default but you could have PDFs, Word or RTF documents, GitHub files, and others.

2. Click the Knit button to create/render the report.

3. Write code between ```{ } and ``` sections.

4. Test code for specific sections using the run button.

5. Use text to describe and document your code and findings.

6. Put plots in your document and hide the code that runs them with the echo=FALSE command.

There is much more to R Markdown than this! Refer to this cheat sheet—one of many—at R Studio (*http://bit.ly/2jXi8i1*).

R Markdown Code

We have already done our analysis so to be concise we will create a very simple report in R Markdown for illustrative purposes. This is the code created in RStudio:

```
---
title: "Customer Segmentation"
author: "Greg Foss"
date: "March 5, 2019"
output: html_document
---


```{r setup, include=FALSE}
knitr::opts_chunk$set(echo = TRUE)
knitr::opts_chunk$set(message = FALSE)
library(tidyverse)
library(ggplot2)
library(knitr)
library(kableExtra)
customer_rfm <- read.csv('D:/DataScience/Oreily/customer_rfm.csv',
                    stringsAsFactors = FALSE)
row.names(customer_rfm) <- customer_rfm$X
customer_rfm$X <- NULL

#RMarkedown is a rich and rewarding way to display your findings. Refer to
https://rmarkdown.rstudio.com/index.html for a wealth of information.
```
Simple Customer Segmentation

Our customers are important to us. Therefore we want to know as much about them as
possible. We collected sales data from our SAP system to analyze and investigate.
In this document we will explore a small range of our customer data. If our findings
prove fruitful, we may want to continue this adventure. One of the first things we
should explain is the number of customers in our dataset.

<b>Number of Customers</b>
```{r range_of_order_dates, echo=FALSE}
count(customer_rfm)
```

Customers display a recency, a frequency and a monetary value. Below is displayed
the distribution of these values for our customers and the overall average.
```{r median_recency, echo=FALSE, fig.height = 7, fig.width = 14}
#use the mutate function to limit the number. Outliers will be binned in one value.
In this case 100.
customer_rfm %>%
  mutate(mrod = ifelse(most_recent_order_days > 100, 100, most_recent_order_days))
  %>% ggplot(aes(mrod)) +
  geom_histogram(binwidth = .7,
                 col = "black",
                 fill = "blue") +
  ylab('Count') +
  xlab('Most Recent Order Days') +
```
```

```
    ggtitle('Histogram of Most Recent Orders')
```

```{r median_recency_number, echo=FALSE}
wd <- mean(customer_rfm$most_recent_order_days)
print(paste0("Average Rececnt Order: ", wd))
```

```{r median_frequency, echo=FALSE, fig.height = 7, fig.width = 14}
customer_rfm %>%
  mutate(cto = ifelse(count_total_orders > 20, 20, count_total_orders)) %>%
  ggplot(aes(cto)) +
  geom_histogram(binwidth = .7,
                 col = "black",
                 fill = "green") +
  ylab('Count') +
  xlab('Order Count or Frequency') +
  ggtitle('Histogram of Frequency of Orders')
```

```{r median_frequency_number, echo=FALSE}
wd <- mean(customer_rfm$count_total_orders)
print(paste0("Average Order Frequency: ", wd))
```

```{r median_monetary_large, echo=FALSE, fig.height = 7, fig.width = 14}
#We need to break the monetary value into two because of potential great
#differences between distributors and regular customers
customer_rfm_big_players <-
  customer_rfm[customer_rfm$total_purchase_value >= 100000 &
customer_rfm$total_purchase_value < 1000000,]
customer_rfm_big_players %>%
  mutate(tpv = ifelse(total_purchase_value > 1000000,
    1000000, total_purchase_value)) %>%
  ggplot(aes(tpv)) +
  geom_histogram(binwidth = .7,
                 col = "black",
                 fill = "orange") +
  ylab('Count') +
  xlab('Total Monetary Value') +
  ggtitle('Histogram of Customer Monetary Value ( > 100,000 )')
```

This is just a very small example of reporting with R Markdown. This is just the tip of the iceberg and hopefully it inspires you to dive deeper into the world of R Markdown. We will end with this simple example because, quite frankly, we could write an entire book on this wonderful tool alone.

R Markdown Knit

Obviously you will not report your data science findings using lines of code. R Markdown allows you to *knit* your findings into a report to be distributed to the business. Click on the Knit button in RStudio to display the report in Figures 7-24 and 7-25.

Customer Segmentation

Greg Foss

March 5, 2019

Simple Customer Segmentation

Our customers are important to us. Therefore we want to know as much about them as possible. We've collected sales data from our SAP system to analyze and investigate. In this document we will explore a small range of our customer data. If our findings prove fruitful, we may want to continue this adventure. One of the first things we should explain is the number of customers in our dataset.

Number of Customers

```
## # A tibble: 1 x 1
##        n
##    <int>
## 1 248867
```

Customers display a recency, a frequency and a monetary value. Below is displayed the distribution of these values for our customers and the overall average.

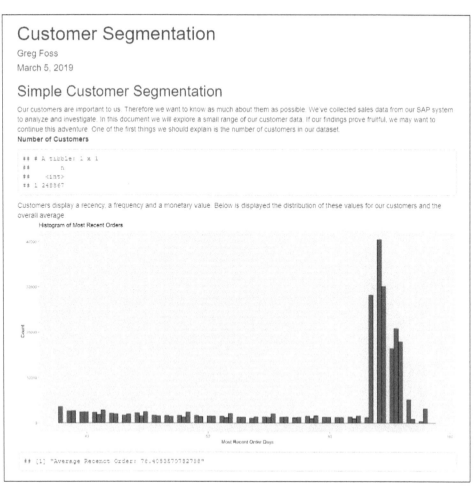

```
## [1] "Average Recenct Order: 78.4093670732738"
```

Figure 7-24. R Markdown document rendered

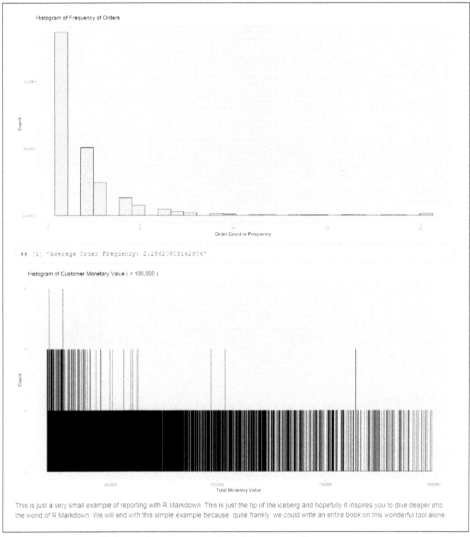

Figure 7-25. R Markdown document rendered (continued)

Summary

We've completed quite a journey in clustering and segmentation, starting with the concepts and ending with a report to display to the business. Remember that our original requirement came from Rod at Big Bonanza Warehouse. He wanted to know which customers should be migrated to the new system and which should be left behind. We've gained insight into that question and much more in our data exploration. For the migration to the new system we will keep the *Champion, Potential Champion, Middle of the Road,* and *Unclassified* customers. This will reduce conversion time, validation, and cost by not converting tens of thousands of unnecessary customer records. Duane takes the findings to the Master Data team in preparation for their work in the S/4HANA conversion.

Furthermore, the results helped us understand the importance of distributors in our customer base as well as the key evaluation parameters of recency, frequency, and monetary value. In addition to Rod's project, surely the marketing team would like to see this evaluation to guide or validate their efforts.

Like all of our previous exploration, this is just the beginning. Knowing your customers is a valuable and often underappreciated aspect of business. Techniques we have touched upon in this chapter will help you gain insight into your SAP business data and raise questions the business may not have thought to ask.

Association Rule Mining

Amir is the VP of Sales at Big Bonanza Warehouse. The other evening while shopping for cookies on Amazon he got a little message. "People who ordered cookies also ordered cookie-holders." "Cookie-holders? That's ridiculous." He thought. But he clicked on the item anyway. "Cookie-holders are only a buck, I'll try one." A moment later he realized, "I bought something I didn't intend to buy. I'm happy with the purchase and the recommendation. How can I do this for my own sales and customers?"

The next day in the office he called in Duane, the SAP business analyst for Sales. He explained what he was thinking and wanted to know how they could do it. "I want to provide sales recommendations for all my retail locations. When a customer buys a product, I want the system to provide recommendations for related products." Duane's first thought was, "SAP doesn't do that."

Upon talking to Greg and Paul, Duane learns that what Amir wants can be achieved by using a technique called association rule mining. We intend to take sales orders from SAP and create associations, or discover the general rules of patterns in item purchases. We want to know what products are most often purchased together. Consider groceries: if a customer buys bread and eggs, what is the likelihood they will buy milk?

However, if you understand that association rule mining employs the rules of probability, you start to see many more applications:

Laboratory studies

What is the probability of a result based on previous study results? If X and Y happen in a study, what is the likelihood of Z? In the pharmaceutical industry, ending a study at the right time can have significant financial impacts.

Medical diagnoses

Diagnosing a patient is not always an easy process. Understanding the co-occurrences of symptoms helps healthcare providers make more accurate diagnoses.

Class schedules

Understanding what classes a student may take can help an organization accurately use resources and avoid scheduling bottlenecks.

Equipment maintenance

Predicting a malfunction on the manufacturing line can greatly assist in productivity. What is the probability that a piece of equipment will malfunction if it has gone through maintenance A, B, and C?

Customer order assistance: as a distinct subset of straight upselling, take into account that certain products are often bought together for a reason. If a customer buys hundreds of perfectly square tiles, it is likely they need some corner or oddly shaped tiles to complete their project. Use association rule mining to create ways for customer service to guide customers to ensuring their interactions meet their needs the first time around.

In this chapter, our goal is to create an application that will create a sales order in SAP and provide the user with product recommendations. To do this we use SAPUI5, a standard SAP frontend technology.

By now the basic order of operations should be familiar. We will follow much the same course of action we have with the other chapters, except this time we will operationalize the results (Figure 8-1). Operationalization of data science is an important and often overlooked step, which is dependent on your company's infrastructure. Perhaps your company uses Azure or Amazon Web Services heavily. Perhaps they only use on-premise machines. In this chapter, we will create a locally accessible webservice in R, but the deployment options will vary depending on you and your company's infrastructure and preference.

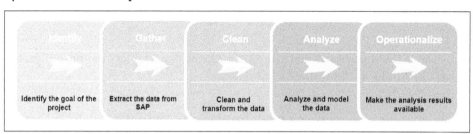

Figure 8-1. Process flow used for finding associations in sales data

Understanding Association Rule Mining

The techniques in association rule mining (ARM) are all about associating observations with rules—for example, we can associate the observation in our data X with the rule Y. Unlike sequence mining,[1] ARM does not care about the order of the observations. ARM only cares that they occur together. ARM is a mature and well-known method of discovering associations in large datasets and it works well with categorical data. There are four main concepts in ARM. These are support, confidence, lift, and the apriori algorithm.

Support

Support is how frequently the set appears in the data. For example, Figure 8-2 shows that whiskey *and* beer purchases occur in 10 out of 100 total purchases. This means a support of 10/100 or 10%.

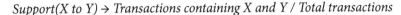

Support(X to Y) → Transactions containing X and Y / Total transactions

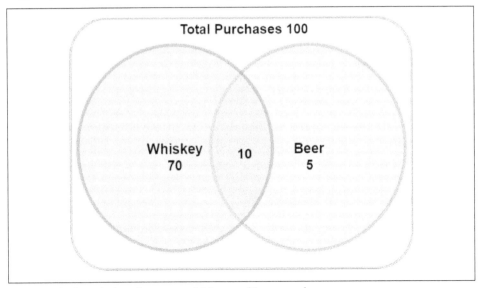

Figure 8-2. Associations between whiskey and beer purchases

Confidence

Confidence indicates how often a rule is true. Using the same example as before, out of all the orders, 10 contain whiskey and beer, 15 contain at least beer, and 80 contain at least whiskey. So 10 / 10 + 5 is a confidence value of .67. That is a pretty high confi-

---

1 Sequence mining is a type of association rule mining but is not included here. Some things just can't make it.

dence value indicating these two items are bought together. However, confidence can be misleading; items that are simply frequent will naturally have higher confidence values. Limitations such as this are overcome by using support, confidence, and lift together.

Confidence(X to Y) → Transactions containing X and Y / Transactions containing X

Lift

Lift is an indication of how likely something is to be purchased with the presence of another item, as opposed to how often it is likely to be purchased independently. In other words, how much does product A *lift* the likelihood of product B? Using our example with the lift formula: lift = (10 / 10 + 5) / (80/100). The result is .84. A lift value of near one indicates there is no effect of one item on the other. A lift value of less than one indicates there could be a replacement (negative lift) happening. Despite our high confidence from earlier, there is no lift to the relationship between whiskey and beer. In fact, the lift is less than one, indicating whiskey might be a replacement for beer or visa versa:

Lift(X to Y) → Confidence(X to Y) / ((Probability of Y without X) / Total transactions)

Apriori Algorithm

The apriori algorithm was presented by R. Agrawal and R. Srikant in 1994. It is a method of finding frequent itemsets in a dataset. It uses prior knowledge of frequent itemset properties to do this. It is this algorithm in the R `arules` (*http://bit.ly/2ltQ3iX*) library that creates the association rules. We will use this library later in the chapter, when we analyze the data.

Operationalization Overview

Before we begin creating our application, we need to clearly define our programming goals. The architecture of our process is not complex, but it is important to understand the pieces of the process that will bring our vision to life. Figure 8-3 shows a basic flow of the extraction and transformation, going from extracting the data through to display in an SAP Fiori (SAPUI5) application.

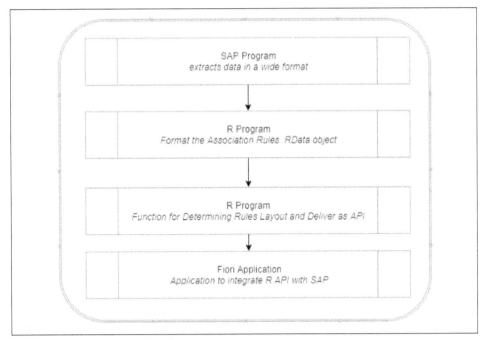

Figure 8-3. Programs and applications overview

SAP developed SAPUI5 as an HTML5/JavaScript-based web application development framework. SAP also created a set of design standards called Fiori that SAPUI5 strives to help developers meet. The reason? The standard SAP user interface, the decades-old SAP GUI, stinks. Nobody likes to use it.

SAPUI5 helps developers to create applications that responsively scale all the way from desktop-sized monitor screens to mobile handheld screens. SAPUI5 with Fiori design principles has become commonplace for SAP end users, and this includes the sales staff at Big Bonanza. We'll detail one way to use SAPUI5 to enhance the sales experience and display the recommendations that we generate from our data science adventure. Data scientist and SAP analyst readers please note: just like our other brief forays into ABAP, this book is not intended as an SAPUI5 primer.

Collecting the Data

This business problem requires a process that ultimately creates association rules around purchases. This is something that would not be done too frequently, perhaps on a quarterly basis. Our plan is to create a process that we can update once a quarter and will be the foundation of an API to an SAP application.

Sales data is easily found in SAP in the VBAK and VBAP tables. All we want to know is what products are purchased together. In the end, we want something like

Table 8-1, where each record has separate columns for the individual items sold. The first row represents an order where two items were sold, the second row an order where four were sold, and so on.

Table 8-1. Flattened product-to-order mapping

item1	item2	item3	item4	item5
ProductA	ProductB			
ProductC	ProductB	ProductE	ProductG	
ProductA	ProductC			

However, when we select data from the tables in SAP, we end up with Table 8-2.

Table 8-2. Product-to-order mapping before flattening

Sales Document (VBAK)	Sales Material
10001	ProductA
10001	ProductB
10002	ProductC
10002	ProductB
10002	ProductE
10002	ProductG
10003	ProductZ

There are a few things that we need to take into consideration here:

- We don't care about orders with only one item; there is no association there.
- We want our data wide and not long. Recall that we're aiming for records that have columns identifying individual items on the order, not separate records for each item in the order.
- We don't care about the sales order number; it is just used to group materials.
- Flipping back to anomaly detection concepts in Chapter 5, we determine that any order with more than 25 lines is an anomaly and simply cut off the table at 25 items.

 Finding that 25-line cutoff simplifies this step. If we allowed for any number of lines we would need to dynamically build the internal table in ABAP thereby adding complexity.

We created the simple ABAP program that follows to fulfill our needs. It reads all sales order items for a specified date range and creates a local CSV file in the format we want. This will make our code for doing the association rules super-simple and intuitive. This is a good example of merging various technologies. We can format and extract from SAP using ABAP, then the process for R and Python is simplified. By simplifying and designing the extract from SAP in a thoughtful manner, we turned the R process into three lines of code:

```
REPORT zgmf_sales_wide.
**************************************************************************
*Data Declarations
**************************************************************************
TABLES: vbak, vbap.
* ty_items is our limited-to-25-items column-per-record structure.
TYPES: BEGIN OF ty_items,
         item1 TYPE matnr,
         item2 TYPE matnr,
         item3 TYPE matnr,
         item4 TYPE matnr,
         item5 TYPE matnr,
         item6 TYPE matnr,
         item7 TYPE matnr,
         item8 TYPE matnr,
         item9 TYPE matnr,
         item10 TYPE matnr,
         item11 TYPE matnr,
         item12 TYPE matnr,
         item13 TYPE matnr,
         item14 TYPE matnr,
         item15 TYPE matnr,
         item16 TYPE matnr,
         item17 TYPE matnr,
         item18 TYPE matnr,
         item19 TYPE matnr,
         item20 TYPE matnr,
         item21 TYPE matnr,
         item22 TYPE matnr,
         item23 TYPE matnr,
         item24 TYPE matnr,
         item25 TYPE matnr,
       END OF ty_items.
DATA: lt_items TYPE TABLE OF ty_items,
      wa_items LIKE LINE OF lt_items.
TYPES: BEGIN OF ty_base,
         vbeln TYPE vbeln,
         matnr TYPE matnr,
       END OF ty_base.
DATA: member  TYPE ty_base,
      members TYPE STANDARD TABLE OF ty_base WITH EMPTY KEY,
      position TYPE i,
      xout    TYPE string,
```

```
       iout     TYPE TABLE OF string,
       l_string TYPE string,
       t_csv    TYPE truxs_t_text_data,
       c_csv    TYPE truxs_t_text_data,
       h_csv    LIKE LINE OF t_csv.
FIELD-SYMBOLS: <fs_str> TYPE ty_items.
 **********************************************************************
*Selections                   (ˆ•ᴥ•ˆ)*·˚｡
 **********************************************************************
SELECT-OPTIONS: s_auart FOR vbak-auart, "Sales Order Type
                s_erdat FOR vbak-erdat, "Sales Order Create Date
                s_pstyv FOR vbap-pstyv. "Sales Order Line Item Category
PARAMETERS: p_lnam TYPE char75 DEFAULT 'C:\temp\'. "Directory to save to
 **********************************************************************
*Start-of-Selection           (ˆ•ᴥ•ˆ)*·˚｡
 **********************************************************************
 PERFORM get_data.
 PERFORM write_file.
 **********************************************************************
* ROUTINES                     (ˆ•ᴥ•ˆ)*·˚｡
 **********************************************************************
FORM get_data.
* Select all order numbers and materials from VBAK and VBAP
* based on the selection criteria on the first screen.
  SELECT vbak~vbeln, vbap~matnr
      INTO TABLE @DATA(lt_base)
      FROM vbak JOIN vbap ON vbak~vbeln = vbap~vbeln
      ##DB_FEATURE_MODE[TABLE_LEN_MAX1]
          WHERE vbak~auart IN @s_auart
            AND vbak~erdat IN @s_erdat
            AND vbap~pstyv IN @s_pstyv
            GROUP BY vbak~vbeln, vbap~matnr.

*Assign the work area structure to a field-symbol
  ASSIGN wa_items TO <fs_str>.

*LOOP at the list of orders and materials and group this by order number
  LOOP AT lt_base INTO DATA(wa) GROUP BY wa-vbeln.
    CLEAR members.

*LOOP at the group (single order number) and put it into the members
*table.
    LOOP AT GROUP wa INTO member.
      members = VALUE #( BASE members ( member ) ).
    ENDLOOP.

*How big is the members table? If it is not greater than
*one line then skip it. There is no association for one line orders.
    DESCRIBE TABLE members LINES DATA(i).
    IF i > 1.
      CLEAR: position, <fs_str>.
      LOOP AT members ASSIGNING FIELD-SYMBOL(<member>).
```

```
*We don't want to go over 25 lines on an order.
      IF position = 25.
        EXIT.
      ENDIF.
      position = position + 1.

*Create a variable for the item from item1 to item25.
      DATA(item_position) = `ITEM` && position.

*Assign the item (let's say ITEM1) to the field-symbol.
*This is like a pointer and if it is successful we can
*move the value into our work area.
      ASSIGN COMPONENT item_position OF STRUCTURE <fs_str>
          TO FIELD-SYMBOL(<fs>).
      IF <fs> IS ASSIGNED.
        <fs> = <member>-matnr.
      ENDIF.
    ENDLOOP.

*Append the work area to our table of items.
      APPEND <fs_str> TO lt_items.
    ENDIF.
  ENDLOOP.
ENDFORM.
************************************************************************
FORM write_file.

*Create a header. This is not truly necessary, but it doesn't hurt
  h_csv = 'item1' && `,` && 'item2' && `,` && 'item3' && `,` && 'item4' &&
  `,` && 'item5' && `,` && 'item6' && `,` && 'item7' && `,` && 'item8' &&
  `,` && 'item9' && `,` && 'item10' && `,` && 'item11' && `,` && 'item12' &&
   `,` && 'item13' && `,` && 'item14' && `,` && 'item15' && `,` && 'item16' &&
 `,` && 'item17' && `,` && 'item18' && `,` && 'item19' && `,` && 'item20' &&
  `,` && 'item21' && `,` && 'item22' && `,` && 'item23' && `,` && 'item24' &&
    `,` && 'item25'.

*Loop at the table of items and write it to a work area separated by commas
  LOOP AT lt_items INTO DATA(items).
    CLEAR xout.
    DO.
      ASSIGN COMPONENT sy-index OF STRUCTURE items TO FIELD-SYMBOL(<csv>).
      IF sy-subrc <> 0.
        EXIT.
      ENDIF.
      IF sy-index = 1.
        xout = <csv>.
      ELSE.
        l_string = <csv>.
        xout = xout && `,` && l_string.
      ENDIF.
    ENDDO.
```

```
        APPEND xout TO iout.
    ENDLOOP.

 *First append our header to the final csv output table
 *then append all the lines of the csv.
    APPEND h_csv TO t_csv.
    APPEND LINES OF iout TO t_csv.

 *Use SAPs standard download method to create a file and download it locally
    CALL METHOD cl_gui_frontend_services=>gui_download
      EXPORTING
        filename = p_lnam && `sales_wide_` &&
                   sy-datum && sy-uzeit+0(4) && '.csv '
      CHANGING
        data_tab = t_csv.
ENDFORM.
```

Cleaning the Data

We always need to do some cleaning of our data from SAP. However, because we wrote our own small custom program to extract the data, we took care to do it in such a way that the data would be pristine. It is important to not make assumptions about how well we did the extract program, so we'll read the CSV file into R Studio and take a look at it (the results are shown in Figure 8-4):

```
investigate <- read.csv("D:/DataScience/Data/mat.csv")
library(DT)
datatable(head(investigate))
```

	X	item1	item2	item3	item4	item5	item6	item7	item8	item9	item10	
1	1	4614559	4614573	4614321	4614335	4614348						
2	2	4614559	4614374	4614388	4614467	4614480						
3	3	4614599	4614520									
4	4	4614533	4614546	4614559	4614573	4614586	4614599	4614612	4614626			
5	5	9257192	9257205	9257219	9257232	8599265						
6	6	9257219	6544346									

Show 10 ▼ entries

Figure 8-4. Investigating the data from SAP for Sales Data Wide

Things look exactly as we would want them with the exception of the X column. However, this is something being added by our `read.csv` function. We could avoid this using the `row.names = NULL` parameter. When we load the data in a different way in our next step, we won't have this problem.

Analyzing the Data

Using the `arules` package (*http://bit.ly/2ltQ3iX*) allows us some amazing results very easily. Because we have nicely formatted our data using ABAP we can transform it into a `transaction` object (*http://bit.ly/2lvlPMm*) in R using the following code:

```
transactions <- read.transactions("D:/DataScience/Data/mat.csv",
                                   format = "basket",
                                   sep = ',',
                                   rm.duplicates=TRUE)
```

To create rules based on the transactions we loaded, use the following code. This is where the apriori algorithm (mentioned earlier) comes into play. We will set the support to be a minimum of .1% and our confidence to be 80%. The support is low because the dataset is huge and varied. We have over a half million rows of item sets. A support of .1% is still 500 occurrences. A confidence of .8 means that 80% of the time the rule is considered to be true.

 Data science is a combination of business logic, art, and actual machine learning knowhow. A certain degree of trial and error is needed to properly set the support and confidence values.

```
rules_transactions <- apriori(transactions,
                              parameter = list(supp = 0.001, conf = 0.8))
rules_transactions <- sort(rules_transactions,
                           by="confidence",
                           decreasing=TRUE)
```

We can see our results with confidence, lift, and support using the following command:

```
inspect(head(rules_transactions))
```

	lhs		rhs	support	confidence	lift	count
[1]	{4614440}	=>	{79353}	0.001040583	1	2.426768	2
[2]	{4360037}	=>	{79353}	0.001040583	1	2.426768	2
[3]	{8996481}	=>	{79353}	0.001040583	1	2.426768	2
[4]	{8709402}	=>	{79353}	0.001040583	1	2.426768	2
[5]	{8135285}	=>	{79353}	0.001040583	1	2.426768	2
[6]	{2911738}	=>	{79353}	0.001040583	1	2.426768	2

Lhs stands for *lefthand side*; rhs stands for *righthand side*. Items on the right were frequently purchased with items on the left with the listed support, confidence, and lift. While our support values are not very high, the amount of data we have is enough to provide good confidence and lift among our top values. For instance, line 1 above indicates that when item 4614440 is purchased there is a 100% confidence that item

79353 is also purchased. Furthermore, there is a lift of 2.4267 for this relationship. (Remember, a lift value near 1 indicates there is no effect of one item on the other.)

We have created our association rules; now we will save them as a *transaction* object to be used in our operationalization later:

```
save(rules_transactions,
     file = "D:/DataScience/Oreily/association_rules.RData")
```

 We are going to operationalize this at a local level first and move to a more universal level later.

Before we operationalize, we want to test what would happen if we analyze a simple result. Create a simple vector from a dataframe with the top result in it:

```
dataset <- as.vector(t(c("8135285")))
```

Now match the rules created with the results of our vector:

```
matchRules <- subset(rules_transactions, lhs %ain% dataset)
```

Inspect those rules like we did earlier with the `inspect` function. We see that it returns the same values that we had earlier when inspecting the rules manually:

```
inspect(matchRules)
        lhs          rhs     support    confidence lift     count
  [1] {8135285} => {79353} 0.001040583 1          2.426768 2
```

Now to create a simple API we need to first create a function from the following code with the *dataset* set as an input variable:

```
subset(rules_transactions, lhs %ain% <input_vector>)
```

You can create a very quick and simple web API in R Studio using the `plumber` library (*https://www.rplumber.io/*). You need to be on version > 1.2 of R Studio to use some of the features we will outline here. The first step to creating a web API is to open a new plumber file using the menu path File → New File → Plumber API, as shown in Figure 8-5.

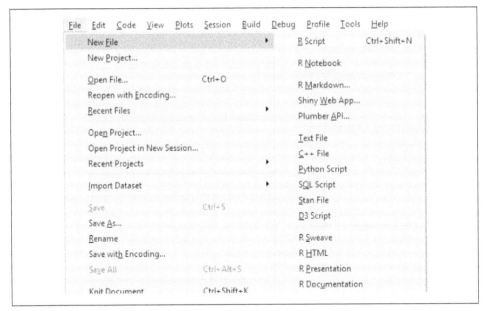

Figure 8-5. Creating your first Plumber API

This will give you a base file for `plumber` with a few examples in it. We will discard those examples and use the following code:

```
library(plumber)
#Load the association rules created in the load program
load(file = "D:/DataScience/Oreily/association_rules.RData")
#* Send back the confidence and lift
#* @param input Material Number
#* @get /arm
function(input) {
  #Convert the input value(s) into a vector.
  dset <- as.vector(t(c(input)))
  #Create a subset of rules matching the input
  match_rules <- subset(rules_transactions, lhs %ain% dset)
  #Display/Return those values (by default JSON)
  inspect(match_rules)
}
```

What this code says in human-speak is, "Take the input received and make it a vector so we can search with it. Create a new object that is a subset of our association rules that matched our input with the lhs (lefthand side). Return that result using the `inspect()` function."

The preceding code will render our association rules results in a JSON format when queried from a browser. The Plumber API is easy to use from R Studio; simply click on the Run API button in the upper-right corner of the window.

A window will appear that will allow the API to be reviewed and tested. It is shown in Figure 8-6.

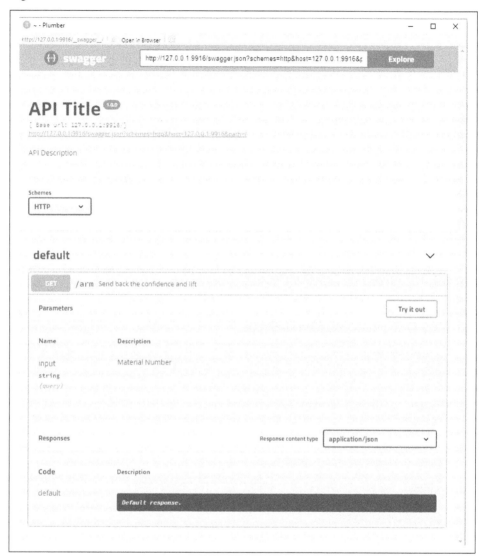

Figure 8-6. Swagger and the Plumber API

Click on the "Try it out" button and enter a material number. When finished click on the Execute button, as shown in Figure 8-7.

Figure 8-7. Testing the Plumber API with a material number

The results of the web API are displayed in the response section, as shown in Figure 8-8.

Order Items

Products			Edit
Product	Quantity	Weight	Price
15" Notebook Computer 8135285	10 PC	4.2 KG	956.00 USD

Add Product   Complete Order

Figure 8-8. Results of the Plumber API call

The results of the API show the following in JSON format:

- LHS (antecedent)
- RHS (consequent)
- Support
- Confidence
- Lift

This is all data that can be used in an application providing sales recommendations. We've successfully created a web API, but it is restricted to our local computer. There are many ways to host and publish APIs. This is largely governed by your company's environment. Does your company use Azure, Amazon Web Services, Digital Ocean, or something else? Perhaps there is no cloud environment at all and an on-premises server is deployed. The options are too varied to be covered in this little book.[2]

Remember: we're not building an entire mobile app here. This scenario assumes that Big Bonanza has an existing SAPUI5-based Fiori application, and that Greg, Paul, and Duane are just sprinkling in some extra logic. All of the changes suggested here are contrived examples, and while they require knowledge of HTML, JavaScript, and XML they do not require knowledge of developing full-functioning iOS or Android apps in their native programming languages.

Fiori

We have an operational, web-accessible point of reference to get at our Plumber API. As discussed at the beginning of the chapter, Big Bonanza uses an SAPUI5-based Fiori[3] application to allow field sales personnel to enter sales orders via smartphone. Before getting heavily into fun data science scenarios, Duane from the SAP team had a hand in designing the sales order entry application. He did a great job simplifying what can be very complex in the normal desktop SAP GUI down to a couple of screens on mobile.

---

2 We will be providing a follow-up blog on using Digital Ocean as a platform for a public API with R and plumber.

3 Also recall that SAPUI5 is a web application development framework. SAP's user experience capabilities have evolved a great deal in the last four to five years, and SAPUI5 is the leader of those changes.

To get the field salespeople really pushing those cookie-holder extras, let's map out a small enhancement to Duane's order entry app. We'll add a screen that pops up after the sales staff confirms a new order, which will list out the additional materials that are often purchased together with the order's items. The salesperson can then choose to add one or more of those items to the order by suggesting them to the customer on the spot.

 Visit *https://open.sap.com/* and search "SAPUI5" to learn more about building SAPUI5 applications for the Fiori experience.

SAPUI5 applications follow a common model-view-controller[4] structure. "View" files define the layout of the elements on the screen. "Controller" files define the behavior and logic. Woven through both are references to "models" that define how the data is stored on the client device for application use. For our use case, we will modify view files to create a little pop-up screen that holds the suggested new items. We will create a new model to hold information about the suggested products. Finally, we will modify controller files to ensure that the pop-up screen appears at the right time.

Big Bonanza has a very stripped-down UI like Figure 8-9. Just add items to the last screen after selecting a customer to submit to SAP to create the order.

We're going to put our recommendation flow into the process where the salesperson would tap Complete Order. Let's start with the view files that govern our buttons.

In the main view file (*Table.view.xml*, which governs this screen), the SAPUI5 developer has already defined the buttons in the footer. We can quickly check on that to see where we can hook up our extra logic:

```
<!-- SNIP! Lots of other application view code -->
 <footer>
     <OverflowToolbar>
         <ToolbarSpacer/>
         <Button text="Add Product"/>
        <Button text="Complete Order" press="onOrderPress" type="Accept"/>
        </OverflowToolbar>
 </footer>
 <!-- SNIP! Lots of other application view code -->
```

---

4 The model-view-controller structure (*https://en.wikipedia.org/wiki/Model–view–controller*) is one of the oldest, most-used architectures in software development with graphical user interfaces.

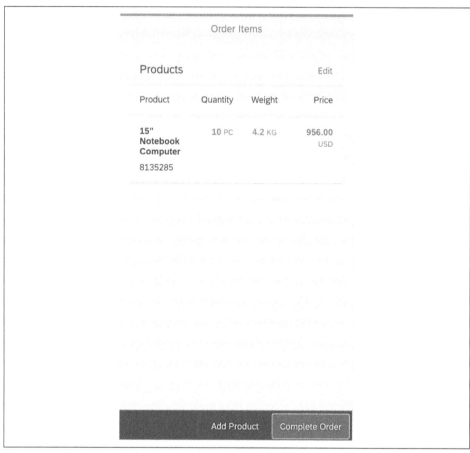

Figure 8-9. Simplified order entry with ability to add another product or to complete the order

The press attribute of the Complete Order button tells us what function (onOrder Press) will be executed when the user taps that button. So let's jump into that code, in the *Table.controller.js* file:

```
// SNIP! Lots of other application controller code
onOrderPress: function (oEvent) {
    // If the dialog box has never been opened, we initiate it
    if (!this._oDialog) {
        var oSuggestionsModel = new JSONModel();
        this.getView().setModel(oSuggestionsModel, "suggestions");
        this._oDialog = sap.ui.xmlfragment("Table.RecommendDialog", this);
        this._oDialog.setModel(oSuggestionsModel, "suggestions");
    }

    // Retrieve the product already entered on the screen,
    // build a query URL to the Big Bonanza ARM endpoint,
```

```
// then load that data into an intermediate placeholder, ARMModel.
var oModel = this.getView().getModel();
var product = oModel.getProperty("/ProductCollection/0/ProductId");
var bigBonanzaInternalUrl = "[FILL_IN_YOURS]";
var oARMModel = new JSONModel();
var endpoint = bigBonanzaInternalUrl + "/arm?input=" + product;
oARMModel.loadData(endpoint, {}, false);

// Based on results from the ARM retrieval, create a filter to retrieve
// the full product information for the recommended products.
var armData = oARMModel.getData();
var aFilters = [];

// The "Filter" object sets up the OData filter for SAPUI5
for (var i = 0; i < armData.length; i++) {
    aFilters.push(new Filter("ProductId", "EQ", armData[i].rhs);
    var finalFilters = new Filter({
        filters: aFilters,
        and: false
    });
}

// The base OData model is the OData API that is serving out the rest
// of the data points of this app. This is the API that houses the
// "ProductCollection" endpoint, where we can retrieve more details
// about the recommended data.
var baseODataModel = this.getView().getModel();
var that = this;
baseODataModel.read("/ProductCollection", {
    filters: finalFilters,
    success: function (oData) {
        // In here, we assign the suggestions to that model and open
        // the dialog box. See the "Table.RecommendDialog" listing.
        var oSuggestionsModel = that.getView().getModel("suggestions");
        oSuggestionsModel.setData(oData.results);
        that._oDialog.open();
    }
});
}
// SNIP! Lots of other application controller code.
```

There's one more piece to this puzzle. Near the top of the onOrderPress function, we call out to an XML fragment. This fragment defines the look and feel of the pop-up dialog that appears (Figure 8-10) after pressing Complete Order.

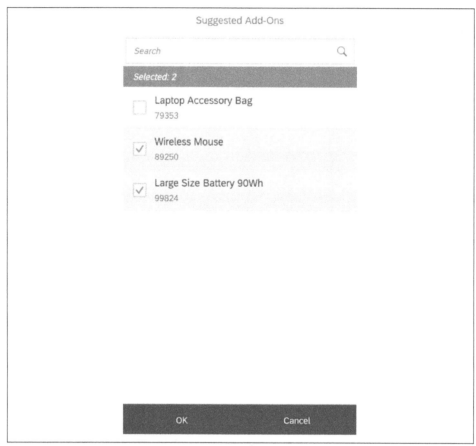

Figure 8-10. On mobile phone, the suggestions list shows over the top of the existing order items list, and allows for selecting one or multiple items to add to the sales order.

To set up the suggestion list dialog, create a file called *RecommendDialog.fragment.xml* in your SAPUI5 project, and add the following XML:

```
<core:FragmentDefinition
    xmlns="sap.m"
    xmlns:core="sap.ui.core">
    <SelectDialog
        noDataText="No Products Found"
        title="Suggested Add-Ons"
        confirm="handleClose"
        cancel="handleClose"
        multiSelect="true"
        items="{
            path: 'suggestions>/'
        }" >
        <StandardListItem
```

```
            title="{suggestions>Description}"
            description="{suggestions>ProductId}"
            type="Active" />
    </SelectDialog>
</core:FragmentDefinition>
```

Summary

With a mid-process prompt for selling associated items, Duane has given Amir the VP of Sales a powerful tool to prod his sales team to upsell on the spot. We used sales data gathered from SAP tables in an ABAP program that packed things nicely into a CSV file. Using R, we analyzed this data looking for three key factors in association rule mining: support, confidence, and lift.

The arules package gave us a quick way to analyze the raw data for those three factors. We layered a function on top of it, so as to quickly allow an input of a product number and an output of 1 to *n* products that have strong associations. Using the plumber library in R, we quickly turned that function into a web-callable API.

Given that sales team members in the field use SAP Fiori apps on their mobile phones to enter sales orders from customers, we looked at how to quickly adapt the SAPUI5 codebase of the Fiori application to present a "suggested items" prompt to users. This gives them one last upsell tool before submitting the order. Not every customer chooses to add the upsell items—but enough of them do that it has positively impacted Amir's sales numbers.

Association rule mining has been around in one way or another for a long time. Putting it in the hands of SAP users is a fresh take on a mature approach; the information is right there for the taking!

## CHAPTER 9

Natural Language Processing with the Google Cloud Natural Language API

"How often do consumers cut companies loose because of terrible service? All the time."
—Harvard Business Review, "Stop Trying to Delight Your Customers" (*http://bit.ly/ 2k4jYhh*)

Jeana is the Sr. Director of Customer Service at Big Bonanza Warehouse. According to the CEO the job is simply: "turn angry customers into happy customers." Angry customers have lots of power to hurt companies, since they can not only stop doing business but also multiply their effects by voicing their complaints via social media. Big Bonanza (along with every other company in the world!) is hyper-sensitive about what customers are saying about them online.

Customers register their complaints through the consumer-facing web storefront in a contact form designed to gather descriptions of their issues. Big Bonanza hooks up this contact form directly to SAP Customer Relationship Management (CRM) to capture these notes and create trackable complaint documents. After the CRM complaint is created, Jeana's team steps in. Her team deals with hundreds of complaints every day. They make their best effort to react quickly and provide quality service, but Jeana knows that in the daily pile of complaints are customers who will churn away if they do not get high-quality service, fast.

Duane, the SAP business analyst, also has deep knowledge of CRM. Jeana pitched him an interesting idea: "I have budget available to give small gifts or offers to customers who complain. It's not a huge budget, so I have to be careful how I spread out the love. I want to identify the most unhappy customers as quickly as possible, so I can apply this budget to them." Her hypothesis was that acting early in the process could prevent customer churn and bad social media messaging, but to engage that hypothesis she needed to find potential churners fast.

Duane knew from talking to Greg and Paul that data science has continued to make remarkable advances in natural language processing (NLP). He asked, "If I can extract those text complaints out of CRM, can we use NLP to quickly identify customers who may churn?" Greg and Paul showed Duane the possibilities afforded by using publicly available cloud APIs to efficiently examine the complaints for sentiment, shortcutting the modeling and training they'd had to use in other Big Bonanza SAP projects.

In this chapter, our goal is to establish a fast time-to-analysis pipeline of extracting sentiment from customer complaints, in order to help Duane recommend the best candidates for special support attention from Jeana's team. To do this we'll use ABAP to extract customer complaint notes from SAP CRM, and then use Google Cloud APIs to discover the positive or negative human emotion in each complaint.

 This may be the most practical of all of this book's chapters. That is intentional! We want you to understand that sometimes the modeling has been done already, and you can use preexisting tools to stay focused on the business scenario. One of the best ways to do that is to use the cloud AI toolkits offered from Amazon Web Services, Microsoft Azure, Google Cloud, and others. To keep things focused on the scenario we had to choose one toolkit, so we chose Google. No disrespect intended to the others.

Understanding Natural Language Processing

Natural language processing is a subfield of AI that focuses on enabling computers to understand human language. Two of the most common areas of NLP are sentiment analysis and translation.

Sentiment Analysis

Often referred to as opinion mining, sentiment analysis attempts to identify opinions from text. There are two basic approaches to sentiment analysis: the rule-based approach and the machine learning approach. Sometimes there is a hybrid of the two. The rule-based approach uses a set of manually crafted rules. Think of a list of positive words such as *awesome, incredible, neat,* and *good* put into one list labeled **positive sentiment.** Another list labeled **negative sentiment** has words such as *terrible, awful, sad,* and *depressing.* In a nutshell, the rule-based approach counts the occurrence of these words in a sentence, paragraph, or tome and decides if the overall sentiment is **positive** or **negative**. The machine learning approach is more modern and sophisticated. There are mature libraries in both R and Python such as topicmodels (*http://bit.ly/2m1rgTz*) and NLTK (*https://www.nltk.org/*) to make sentiment analysis simpler.

Both of these approaches use techniques such as removing stop words, tokenization, stemming, and lemmatization to format the human words into something a little easier to analyze.

Removing stop words simply eliminates words that have little or no value in opinions or sentiment—words such as *and, but, or,* and *the.*

Tokenization is the act of taking a sequence of words and breaking it up into pieces, or tokens. Along the way it often discards pesky things like punctuation. Figure 9-1 is an example of a sentence that has the stop words removed and has been tokenized.

The air was so soft, the stars so fine the promise of every cobbled alley so great, that I thought I was in a dream						
air	soft	stars	fine	promise	every	cobbled
alley	great	I	thought	I	in	dream

Figure 9-1. Removing stop words and tokenizing a sentence

Stemming and lemmatization are processes of removing the variance in word formation. Stemming simply removes the end of words to end up with the "stem" of a word while lemmatization uses a more sophisticated approach to find a word's true base. These are simple processes, but difficult to explain without examples. Figure 9-2 shows how a list of words would be stemmed based on standard rules, and Figure 9-3 is how a set of words would be lemmatized.[1]

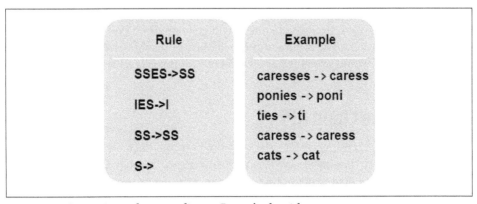

Figure 9-2. Stemming rules according to Porter's algorithm

---

1 Examples taken from Porter's algorithm: *http://snowball.tartarus.org/algorithms/porter/stemmer.html.*

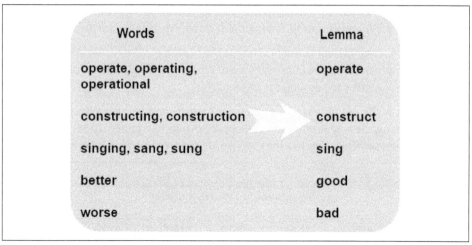

Words	Lemma
operate, operating, operational	operate
constructing, construction	construct
singing, sang, sung	sing
better	good
worse	bad

Figure 9-3. Lemmatization of words

This is the basics of sentiment analysis. However, in this chapter we are not building our own sentiment analyzer. Rather, we are going to use publicly available Google Cloud APIs that do the analysis for us.

Translation

In *The Hitchhiker's Guide to the Galaxy* Douglas Adams presents the reader with the "oddest thing in the universe": a Babel Fish. This little creature fed on brain waves and when put in your ear would translate any language. With machine learning for translation, such a thing is foreseeable. Modern machine learning translation uses neural networks to learn to translate one language to another. (We introduced neural networks in Chapter 2.) The accuracy and reliability of machine learning translations is reaching (some would argue it has already met) human-level translation capabilities.

Preparing the Cloud API

With a basic understanding of NLP, let's get down to the business of helping Duane and Jeana get what they need. We'll run this example through Google Cloud, but readers should note that comparable offerings exist from Amazon Web Services (AWS) and Microsoft Azure.

In a world full of publicly available artificial intelligence services, we love the way Google has established their toolset. Their libraries are high quality, simple, and flexible. Most importantly, their decades of machine learning research are at your fingertips. It's easy—almost shamefully so—to get started using Google Cloud APIs. Let's get started by setting up Google Cloud Platform to process the scenario.

To use Google's cloud services, you'll need a Google account. If you have a Gmail account or if your company uses Google for Work or GSuite, you're already all set. Otherwise, head to *https://accounts.google.com/signup* to sign up for an account. This is the same thing as signing up for a Gmail account; you'll have a new email address at the end of the process.

With that Google account, you're ready to gain access to the APIs. Head over to *https://console.cloud.google.com/* to start setting up the correct access. Depending on what type of account you have, you may need to set up a billing account. Don't worry: the free tier of service for our example in this chapter will be more than enough to get us learning and moving. Billing only applies when you start using these services for thousands of API requests, and at that point we hope you'll be providing so much value to your business that it won't matter.

In the Google Cloud Platform Console you need to give yourself access to the API we'll use for Jeana's work. Start by navigating to the APIs & Services section as shown in Figure 9-4.

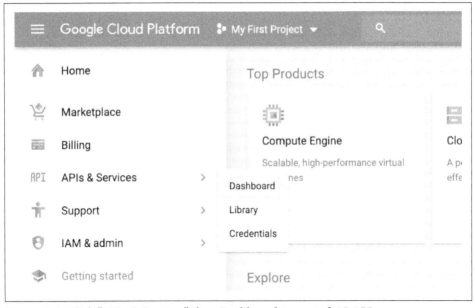

Figure 9-4. Click "APIs & Services" then Dashboard to control AI APIs

You'll be taken to a screen like Figure 9-5. Just click on "Enable APIs and Services" in the top portion of the screen.

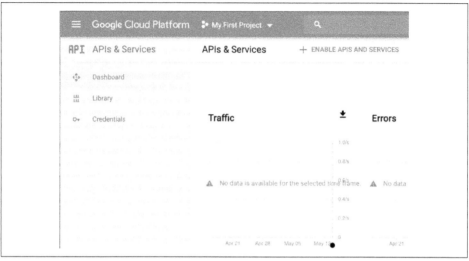

Figure 9-5. Click "Enable APIs and Services" to proceed to the search dashboard

You're then taken to the main screen to search among Google's hundreds of APIs. For Jeana's scenario, we'll enable just the Natural Language API. Start by searching for "language" in the search bar. You should see a result like Figure 9-6. Click on the "Natural Language API" result.

Figure 9-6. Search "language" in the API console search

Turn on your usage of the Cloud Natural Language API by clicking the Enable button in the detail screen, like Figure 9-7.

Figure 9-7. Enable the Cloud Natural Language API

Once you've clicked the Enable button, you're done with turning the API on. But there's one more step in our preparation. We need to get a service account that has the right credentials to make use of the APIs we just enabled. From the main Google Cloud Console screen (*https://console.cloud.google.com*), click on "IAM & Admin" then "Service accounts" as in Figure 9-8.

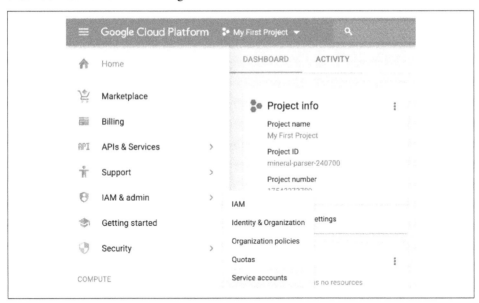

Figure 9-8. Service account navigation

In the service accounts screen, click Create Service Account at the top to go to the service account creation wizard. In the first screen of the wizard, fill out details similar to Figure 9-9. Be sure to write a good description so that when you come back to this project in two years, you'll have written documentation of which users perform what roles (believe us, you'll likely need a refresher!).

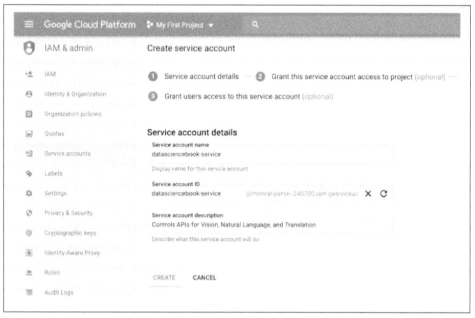

Figure 9-9. Service account details

Click Create at the bottom and move to the second step. You will want this service account to have full ownership of the project we're working with, so grant full project ownership to the accounts as seen in Figure 9-10.

Finally, on the last page of the wizard, create a JSON private key Figure 9-11. This is a file that will allow your computer to make service requests right from the Python command line, using the same credentials as the service user we've just created. Make sure you save that file in the same place where you'll be creating your Python scripts.

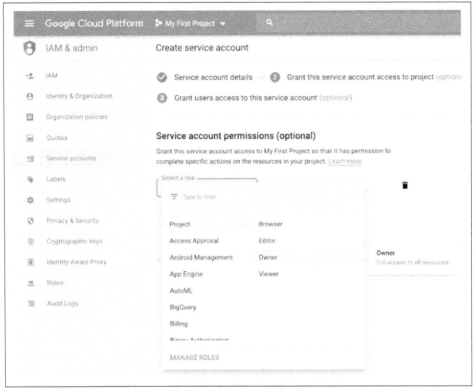

Figure 9-10. Granting full project owner rights to the service account

Figure 9-11. Creating a JSON key file

In one quick command, let's get the Google Python client set up and ready to go. In your favorite Python environment, run this pip command:

```
$ pip install --upgrade google-cloud-language
```

That's it! You're set up and ready to use the Google Cloud APIs to solve problems just like Jeana is facing at Big Bonanza.

Collecting the Data

Just like in Chapter 8, the simplest path is to output the complaint documents with their associated customer notes in CSV format. We have created the ABAP program shown here to meet this need:

```
REPORT zcomplaint_csv.

"We kept the variable declarations at the top to
"increase readability of comments
"with code below.
DATA csv_line TYPE string.
DATA csv_table TYPE TABLE OF string.
DATA full_note TYPE string.
DATA core TYPE REF TO cl_crm_bol_core.
DATA header TYPE crmst_adminh_btil.
DATA entity_up TYPE REF TO cl_crm_bol_entity.
DATA query TYPE REF TO cl_crm_bol_dquery_service.
DATA valid_from TYPE string.
DATA valid_to TYPE string.
DATA result TYPE REF TO if_bol_entity_col.
DATA entity TYPE REF TO cl_crm_bol_entity.
DATA entity_header TYPE REF TO cl_crm_bol_entity.
DATA entity_textid TYPE REF TO cl_crm_bol_entity.
DATA textid_col TYPE REF TO if_bol_entity_col.
DATA bt_textid TYPE crmst_textid_btil.

  "PARAMETERS sets up the SAP GUI screen to accept input,
  PARAMETERS: p_from TYPE dats,
              p_to   TYPE dats.

  "CRM uses the Business Object Library to provide
  "query services to access its data.
  core = cl_crm_bol_core=>get_instance( ).
  core->load_component_set( 'BTBP' ).

  "Use t-code GENIL_BOL_BROWSER to find the right query,
  query = cl_crm_bol_dquery_service=>get_instance(
    iv_query_name = 'BTQCompl' ).

  "Here and in the next block we limit the query to the two
  "dates entered on the input screen.
  valid_from = p_from.
  query->add_selection_param(
    EXPORTING
      iv_attr_name = 'VALID_FROM'
      iv_sign      = 'I'
      iv_option    = 'EQ'
```

```
    iv_low        = valid_from ).

valid_to = p_to.
query->add_selection_param(
  EXPORTING
    iv_attr_name = 'VALID_TO'
    iv_sign      = 'I'
    iv_option    = 'EQ'
    iv_low       = valid_to ).

"get_query_result( ) invokes the query.
result = query->get_query_result( ).

"This WHILE loop moves through each query result
"one at a time.
entity ?= result->get_first( ).
WHILE entity IS BOUND.
  "To get the text data from the complaint, we have to
  "move through several BOL relations. Again see GENIL_BOL_BROWSER.
  entity_up = entity->get_related_entity(
    iv_relation_name = 'BTADVSCompl' ).
  entity_header = entity_up->get_related_entity(
    iv_relation_name = 'BTOrderHeader' ).
  entity_textid = entity_header->get_related_entity(
    iv_relation_name = 'BTHeaderTextIdSet' ).
  textid_col = entity_textid->get_related_entities(
    iv_relation_name = 'BTTextIdHAll' ).

  "Retrieve header information to get the object ID - the
  "number of the complaint document.
  entity_header->if_bol_bo_property_access~get_properties(
    IMPORTING
      es_attributes = header ).

  csv_line = header-object_id && ','.

  "This WHILE block goes line by line through the text
  "lines in the complaint to build one long string of text.
  CLEAR full_note.
  entity_textid ?= textid_col->get_first( ).
  WHILE entity_textid IS BOUND.
    entity_textid->if_bol_bo_property_access~get_properties(
      IMPORTING
        es_attributes = bt_textid ).

    IF bt_textid-conc_lines IS NOT INITIAL.
      CONCATENATE full_note bt_textid-conc_lines
        INTO full_note RESPECTING BLANKS.
    ENDIF.

    entity_textid ?= textid_col->get_next( ).
  ENDWHILE.
```

```
"Safety check - if there were no actual texts added
"don't send this to the .csv
IF full_note IS NOT INITIAL.
  csv_line = csv_line && full_note.
  APPEND csv_line TO csv_table.
ENDIF.


  entity ?= result->get_next( ).
ENDWHILE.


"Document downloads to end user's computer.
cl_gui_frontend_services=>gui_download(
  EXPORTING
    filename = 'C:\Users\paul\Desktop\' &&
      sy-datum && sy-uzeit+0(4) && '_Complaints.csv'
  CHANGING
    data_tab = csv_table ).
```

This ABAP program stands out from other ABAP written in this book in that it does not retrieve data directly with SELECT statements. SAP CRM uses relational tables just like the ECC system in other chapters, but has been designed to be accessed through SAP's Business Object Layer (BOL) technology. The BOL defines relationships between business objects (for example, service orders' relationships to the parts they consume) and lets programmers use those relationships without having to know the underlying table structure.

Running this program in an SAP GUI screen produces a simple UI that asks for the two boundary dates in the PARAMETERS statement, as in Figure 9-12.

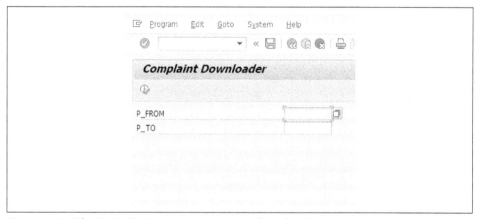

Figure 9-12. The SAP ABAP program screen to download the complaint data

---

This code produces a file filled with entries like below, a document ID and the text of the complaint:

```
5507234,"When the order was delivered, I could see the box was clearly mis-
handled. It is really up to you to make sure the product gets to me without
being destroyed...I want a full shipping refund!"
```

Analyzing the Data

Jeana and her customer service team want to act on this data frequently, so we will focus on an analysis that simply gives them an ordered list of priority customer complaints based on sentiment extracted from the text. We'll do that by using the program we just looked at to gather the day's complaints, store them in the CSV file, and then use Python to cycle through each complaint and ask Google's Natural Language API to analyze it for sentiment.

First, make sure that you're using the credentials you downloaded from "Preparing the Cloud API" on page 292:

```
$ export GOOGLE_APPLICATION_CREDENTIALS='[YOUR_PATH_TO_FILE]'
```

Next, we call the API to have a sentiment value extracted for each note. The sentiment analysis returns two values: sentiment and magnitude. The sentiment score ranges from -1.0 (fully and completely negative sentiment) to +1.0 (fully and completely positive). The magnitude score represents how strongly the text is weighted to that sentiment, and can range from 0 to infinity.

```python
# Get the right Google Cloud stuff imported.
from google.cloud import language
from google.cloud.language import enums
from google.cloud.language import types
import pandas as pd

comp = pd.read_csv('example.csv', names=['document', 'complaint'])

# A LanguageServiceClient handles the interchange
# between computer and Google services.
lsc = language.LanguageServiceClient()

# We are going to add the sentiment score and magnitude
# to the dataframe as we process them.
score = []
magnitude = []
for index, row in comp.iterrows():
    # Create a document for the request
    lsc_doc = types.Document(
        content=row['complaint'],
        type=enums.Document.Type.PLAIN_TEXT)

    # Send the document to be analyzed.
```

```
sentiment = lsc.analyze_sentiment(document=lsc_doc).document_sentiment

# Push the sentiment score and magnitude into lists for later.
score.append(round(sentiment.score, 2))
magnitude.append(round(sentiment.magnitude, 2))

# After we finish processing them all, add 'score' and
# 'magnitude' columns.
comp['score'] = score
comp['magnitude'] = magnitude
```

We're not quite done here. We have a sentiment score and magnitude for every document that has been queried, but let's ponder a bit before we give Jeana suggestions.

Consider this complaint raised on the Big Bonanza site: "Big Bonanza is the worst company ever." Google rates the sentiment of this statement at -0.9: extremely negative. But the magnitude is 0.9—and recall that the magnitude does not range from -1 to +1, it ranges from 0 to infinity! Jeana probably doesn't want to allocate any of her budget to give special attention to this complaint, as it is not specific. Giving this person a Starbucks gift card or some other form of reward is likely to be useless. They may not have even ordered any products. Clearly the magnitude affects the overall usefulness of the raw sentiment score.

Now consider this complaint: "I think this battery-powered coffee mug should be improved, because it doesn't heat my beverages properly. I'd like to return it." Google rates the sentiment as slightly negative at -0.2, and the magnitude is 0.5. In this case the reviewer does not appear to have high negative affectation, and the small magnitude suggests that the text has some positivity weighing in as well. Jeana probably doesn't want to allocate any of her budget for incentives to this complaint, as our reading and the scores indicate this person is not highly angry.

What about this one? "My mini-microwave stopped working almost as soon as I plugged it in. Somehow the door fell off the hinges after the first heating session, and then after repairing the hinge I could no longer power it on. This product is not good. I want a complete refund, including shipping!" Google rates it at a -0.5 sentiment and a 2.1 magnitude. Jeana probably should consider this person for a reward, as their sentiment is well into the negative range, and the magnitude has gone higher than the others. This person appears to be displeased, and has said a number of things supporting that.

Duane sets a couple of initial parameters to give Jeana data to act on. Given what he has observed in the data from these examples, he filters out complaints that do not fall below -2.5 in the raw score as well as complaints that do not have at least a 1.5 magnitude. He sorts the remaining complaints two ways—once to order by raw score and another to order by magnitude, and displays both for Jeana to review:

```
# Create a dataframe that filters out the higher scores and
# lower magnitudes.
```

```
filtered = comp.loc[(comp['score'] < -0.25) & (comp['magnitude'] > 1.5)]

# Create separate dataframes that order differently.
sort_score = filtered.sort_values(by='score')
sort_magnitude = filtered.sort_values(by='magnitude', ascending=False)

# Print them both out for director review.
print('Complaints weighing in as most heavily negative: ')
print(sort_score[['document', 'score', 'magnitude']].head())

print('Complaints with more total negative magnitude: ')
print(sort_magnitude[['document', 'score', 'magnitude']].head())
```

The results appear like this in the printout:

```
Complaints weighing in as most heavily negative:
   document score magnitude
10 7093024  -0.9      1.9
31 7065438  -0.8      2.1
16 7034597  -0.8      2.3
75 7084738  -0.7      2.0
22 7071324  -0.7      3.1

Complaints with more total negative magnitude:
   document score magnitude
52 7060923  -0.4      4.3
99 7092489  -0.5      4.1
77 7065486  -0.3      3.8
32 7098254  -0.5      3.6
44 7060766  -0.4      3.3
```

Summary

NLP enables computers to process human language in ways that were not possible only a few years ago. By training models on massive sets of human language data, cloud companies who offer NLP APIs have a unique advantage in generalized approaches to NLP. It's now possible to get high-quality textual sentiment analysis quickly and easily.

In this chapter we helped Jeana, a customer service director, apply NLP to suggest the most highly actionable customer complaints. We emphasized speed of delivery by using a pre-trained, cloud-enabled API from Google to analyze the individual complaints for human sentiment. By focusing in on the negatively scored complaints, Jeana can apply her limited budget of perks and make an effort to improve relations with customers who might otherwise churn away or even harm Big Bonanza in social media.

We deliberately chose a cloud API example to highlight to SAP analysts and data scientists alike: your job does not always have to be reinventing base, foundational algorithms. After listening to what Jeana needed, Duane, Greg, and Paul agreed that using a cloud API was the best approach here. Google Cloud Platform doesn't have a "Solve Big Bonanza Problems API," but when Big Bonanza employees apply creative thinking, SAP knowledge, and data science they can't be stopped!

## CHAPTER 10

Conclusion

With this chapter our journey comes to an end. We bid farewell and wish you the best in your continued travels with data science and SAP. As a conclusion, we'd like to revisit the original mission, recap what has been covered in the previous nine chapters, give you some tips and recommendations, and finally provide ways we can keep in touch.

Original Mission

We have been promised everything from self-driving cars (which, despite advancements, have not yet been widely manufactured) to AI we fall in love with (as depicted in the films *Ex Machina* and *Her*). We are also warned of a grim and desolate future in which we are replaced in the workforce by our own creations. These juxtaposing visions undermine the practical value of data science. The field of AI and data science has encountered a number of winters in its history. These were periods of marked hype followed by disappointment and a loss of interest. There is unfortunate speculation that we are entering, or even currently in, another downturn of interest. We hope to have shown in this book the immediate value simple machine learning methods can provide to enterprise data. When used with SAP data in particular, data science and AI aren't overhyped—they're underdelivered.

What we wanted most to do in this book was to build a bridge between business analysts and data scientists. Business analysts often have a clear understanding of their company's data and business processes. However, they lack a data science perspective. Data scientists have clear approaches to modeling and analyzing data. However, they often lack business process understanding. You've likely seen the popular data science use case example depicted in Figure 10-1). It is a scenario where machine learning or deep learning is asked to identify whether an image is of a Chihuahua or a blueberry muffin. With a scenario like this, it is no wonder business analysts have a hard time understanding how data science applies to enterprise data. We hoped to show that data science is more than just image recognition and Chihuahuas.

 There is a reason we have no examples of image recognition in this book. While it is probably the most cited example of data science and AI, it is rarely necessary in enterprise data.

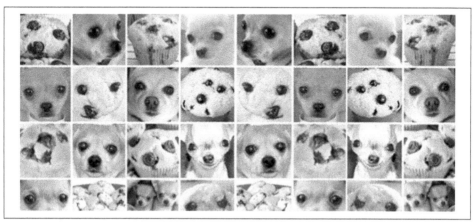

Figure 10-1. Is it a Chihuahua or blueberry muffin? How does this apply to business?

Recap

Chapter 1: Introduction

We introduced the concept of bridging the gap between enterprise data and data science. We also explained some of the fundamental concepts (and joy) of telling stories with data. In this chapter we first introduced data scientists to SAP concepts and SAP business analysts to data science concepts.

Chapter 2: Data Science for SAP Professionals

This chapter was for the SAP business analysts and introduced many data science terms. We explored concepts from machine learning and deep learning. The idea was to give a basis to the business analysts, a preview if you will, of what was to come.

Chapter 3: SAP for Data Scientists

Data scientists were the focus audience for this chapter. SAP has a wealth of data, but what is SAP, what kind of data lives there, and how can you get it? This chapter provided answers to those questions.

Chapter 4: Exploratory Data Analysis

The fundamental start to exploring data with data science is EDA. In this chapter, we introduced concepts for looking at SAP data from a data science perspective. In the end, we modeled our data and failed. This represents an important discovery—sometimes machine and deep learning models don't provide answers to our questions. The lesson in this chapter was to understand that our investment was minimal and move on to other data science ideas.

We deliberated on showing the failure of data science in a business scenario. However, we decided in the end, "This is real life," and left it as an example.

Chapter 5: Anomaly Detection with R and Python

This was a hefty chapter full of a lot of different concepts. We showed how to extract data using the NetWeaver Gateway, automate that function using Visual Studio, store the data in a SQL database, model the data using R and Python, and finally report on the findings using PowerBI. We showed how all these techniques used in concert can yield impressive first results when looking for anomalies.

Chapter 6: Prediction with R

The goal of this chapter was to make predictions on sales data. We created examples of prediction using both R and Python. We again used the NetWeaver Gateway to extract the data, but this time we augmented it. However, this was just the beginning and much more can be done.

Chapter 7: Clustering and Segmentation in R

Customers are an important but often neglected part of SAP data. This chapter sought to cluster and segment customers based on their buying habits. We showed how that can be done using a variety of machine learning techniques such as k-means, k-medoids, hierarchical clustering, and manual clustering. Telling a good story about results sometimes gets overlooked, so we showed how R Markdown can be used to deliver impressive reports.

Chapter 8: Association Rule Mining

In this chapter, we operationalized our data science investigation. Association rules are a common technique in finding customer buying patterns. We extracted SAP data using a simple program, created association rules in R, created an API of those rules, and then consumed the results in an SAP Fiori application. This illustrated how easy it is to use Fiori to deliver an operationalized model to the user. In this case, the operationalized model will likely lead to upsales when creating sales orders.

Chapter 9: Natural Language Processing with the Google Cloud Natural Language API

This chapter introduced publicly available Google Cloud APIs to the business user. We provided a scenario on sentiment analysis that required very little model programming. Publicly available APIs are so easy to use they almost seem like cheat codes. As avid developers, this was a hard chapter to write. We like to code, not just access APIs. However, from a business perspective, if an API fits the solution, often the economical choice is to use it.

Tips and Recommendations

If experience has taught us anything, it's these three principles: be creative, be practical, and enjoy the ride.

Be Creative

SAP and other forms of enterprise data are often easy to access and clean. This data is a goldmine. Business analysts who understand the basics of data science are in a great position to leverage this data. When receiving business requirements or project requests, think of the examples in this book and try and apply them to your situation. The business won't ask you for something to detect anomalies or to create association rules. You are the bridge. Innovative thinking about data and data science will lead you to rewarding solutions.

Be Practical

"If you build it...they will come." This is a common belief among data science consulting firms. In order to do data science you need a Hadoop cluster (perhaps a few), Spark, an ingestion engine, 17 R programmers, and a director with a doctorate in business analytics. We've seen companies spend millions on this thinking and end up with nothing. What do you need to plant a data science seed at your company? You need a computer, you need a programming language such as R or Python, you need to understand your data, and you need to be innovative. Data science is rewarding and fun. Don't let it get bogged down on its own infrastructure and buzzwords. You may need Hadoop later, you may want Spark or Cassandra later; cross that bridge when you get to it. For now, be practical and use tools that you already have.

Enjoy the Ride

Data science is challenging and rewarding beyond anything we've done in IT in our combined 40 years. Gravitate toward an aspect that you find appealing: association rule mining, anomaly detection, forecasting and prediction, or even deep neural network modeling. For us, nature-inspired algorithms are particularly appealing. We hope you have as much fun as we've had!

Stay in Touch

This is the beginning, not the end of our journey. We will follow up with blogs to augment this book...we've already begun. What kind of ideas do you have for your data? Has this book led you on a tangential journey you'd like to share? Is there something that is yet unclear or are you stuck? Well, you're on your own now. Good luck.

Just kidding. We are always available and truly look forward to hearing from you. You can reach us through any of the following means:

Greg
- Email: *gregfoss@bluedieseldata.com*
- Twitter: @bluedieseldata
- LinkedIn: *https://www.linkedin.com/in/greg-foss*

Paul
- Email: *paul@paulmodderman.com*
- Twitter: @PaulModderman
- LinkedIn: *https://www.linkedin.com/in/paulmodderman/*

Index

R

R, 194
  (see also exploratory data analysis (EDA))
  anomaly detection tools, 135
  data collection for sales prediction, 193
  data exploration for sales prediction, 194
  data identification for sales prediction, 193
  data modeling for sales prediction, 195-206
  importing data with, 104-107
  model evaluation for sales prediction,
      206-207
  package installation, 104-106
  PowerBI and, 174-183
  predicting sales in, 193-209
  recipes library, 124-126
R Markdown, 258-262
  code for, 261
  knitting findings with, 262
R Studio, 104, 276, 278-282
random forest, 17
recipes library, 124-126
recursive neural network (RNN), 38-38
reinforcement machine learning, 22-25
  hidden Markov models, 23
  Q-learning, 23-25
ReLU (Rectified Linear Unit) function, 32
response object, 234
RFM (recency, frequency and monetary value)
  clustering, 227
  dataframe for, 239
  manual RFM, 255-257
rgl library, 247
rsample library, 122

S

SAP
  ABAP Data Dictionary, 49-68
  as data source, 5, 8-11, 14
  basics for data scientists, 6-11, 45-91
  Core Data Services, 80-91
  data elements and domains, 54-56
  ECC system, 137-142
  getting started with, 46-49
  Netweaver Gateway, 142-152
  OData services, 68-79
  SE16 export, 68
  structures, 53
  tables, 49-68
  where-used analysis, 58-62

SAP Basis administrators, 46
SAP ECC system, 137-142
SAP Netweaver Gateway, 9, 69, 142-152
SAP professionals, data science basics for, 3-6,
      13-43
  (see also data science)
SAPUI5, 271, 282-283
scales library, 195
screen dumps, to Excel, 10
SE16 export, 68
seasonality, 207
segmentation
  clustering vs., 226
  defined, 225
semi-supervised machine learning, 21
sentiment analysis, 290-292
sigmoid function, 31
Silhouette clustering method, 242, 242
single layer perceptron, 34
slicer, 177-179
softmax function, 33
Split-Apply-Combine, 199, 237
SQL Express, 153
SQL Server, 153-174
SQL Server Integration Services (SSIS), 157-174
SQL Server Management Studio, 153
standardization, 119
stemming, 291
stop words, 291
stories, telling with data, 1-3
structures, SAP, 53
supervised machine learning, 15-17
  decision trees, 16
  linear regression, 15
  logistic regression, 16
  random forest, 17
support, in association rule mining, 269

T

tables
  ABAP QuickViewer and, 62-68
  SAP, 50-52
tanh function, 32
temporal convolutional networks (TCNs), 40
Tensor Processing Units (TPUs), 122
TensorFlow, 122, 126
Tidy Data, 199
Tidyverse, 104
time-series (defined), 191

About the Authors

Greg Foss fuses battle-tested deep SAP knowledge with a passion for all things data science. His SAP career spans all areas of the technology stack—server, database, security, back- and frontend development, and functional expertise. As an enterprise architect, he's been the steady guiding hand for years of managing, supporting, and enhancing SAP. As the founder of Blue Diesel Data Science, he focuses years of R, Python, machine learning algorithms, and analytics expertise on finding unique stories to tell from enterprise SAP data. Through Blue Diesel, Greg regularly contributes unique knowledge and insight into the data science blogging community, and is the principal developer and architect of VisionaryRX, an innovative pharmaceutical data dashboarding product.

Paul Modderman loves creating things and sharing them. His tech career has spanned web applications with technologies like .NET, Java, Python, and React to SAP soutions in ABAP, OData, and SAPUI5 to cloud technologies for Google Cloud Platform, Amazon Web Services, and Microsoft Azure. He was principal technical architect on Mindset's certified solutions CloudSimple and Analytics for BW. He's an SAP Developer Hero, honored in 2017. Paul is the author of two books: *Mindset Perspectives: SAP Development Tips, Tricks, and Projects* (Amazon Digital Services) and *SAPUI5 and SAP Fiori: The Psychology of UX Design* (SAP Press).

Colophon

The animal on the cover of *Practical Data Science with SAP* is the mouflon (*Ovis orientalis orientalis*). Scientists believe that the mouflon is the ancestor of all currently domesticated sheep breeds. The mouflon's range covers the mountains of modern Iran, Iraq, Armenia, and the Caucasus. Domestication began on Corsica, Cyprus, and other Mediterranean islands during the Neolithic period. It has also been introduced into Europe and the Americas, including Hawaii.

The mouflon ram has large horns that form an almost complete circle. Individual ewes may have small, curved horns, but most ewes are polled. Unlike many other sheep breeds, the mouflon doesn't grow long wool. Its coat is short and dark brown, with lighter patches on the animal's belly and sides. It stands about 3 feet at the shoulder and weighs up to 110 pounds.

Like similar endangered sheep breeds, the mouflon has been the subject of experimental cloning. Scientists in Italy first cloned a mouflon in 2001.

Many of the animals on O'Reilly covers are endangered; all of them are important to the world.

The cover illustration is by Karen Montgomery, based on a black and white engraving from *Lydekker's Royal Natural History*. The cover fonts are Gilroy Semibold and Guardian Sans. The text font is Adobe Minion Pro; the heading font is Adobe Myriad Condensed; and the code font is Dalton Maag's Ubuntu Mono.

O'REILLY®

There's much more
where this came from.

Experience books, videos, live online
training courses, and more from O'Reilly
and our 200+ partners—all in one place.

Learn more at oreilly.com/online-learning

Milton Keynes UK
Ingram Content Group UK Ltd.
UKHW050030091024
449443UK00007B/149